Securing Territory

Securing Territory

State Interests and Indigenous Land Titling in Latin America

GIORLENY ALTAMIRANO RAYO

OXFORD
UNIVERSITY PRESS

Oxford University Press is a department of the University of Oxford.
It furthers the University's objective of excellence in research, scholarship,
and education by publishing worldwide. Oxford is a registered trade mark of
Oxford University Press in the UK and in certain other countries.

Published in the United States of America by Oxford University Press
198 Madison Avenue, New York, NY 10016, United States of America.

© Oxford University Press 2025

All rights reserved. No part of this publication may be reproduced, stored
in a retrieval system, or transmitted, in any form or by any means, without the
prior permission in writing of Oxford University Press, or as expressly permitted
by law, by license or under terms agreed with the appropriate reprographics
rights organization. Inquiries concerning reproduction outside the scope of the
above should be sent to the Rights Department, Oxford University Press, at the
address above.

You must not circulate this work in any other form
and you must impose this same condition on any acquirer

Library of Congress Cataloging-in-Publication Data
Names: Altamirano Rayo, Giorleny. author.
Title: Securing territory : state interests and Indigenous land titling in
Latin America / Giorleny Altamirano Rayo.
Description: New York : Oxford University Press, [2025] |
Includes bibliographical references.
Identifiers: LCCN 2024021221 (print) | LCCN 2024021222 (ebook) |
ISBN 9780197770863 (hardback) | ISBN 9780197770887 (epub)
Subjects: LCSH: Indigenous peoples—Land tenure—Latin America. |
Land tenure—Law and legislation—Latin America. | Land titles—Latin
America. | Land reform—Latin America. | Privatization—Latin America. |
Environmentalism—Latin America—Citizen participation.
Classification: LCC GN449.3 .A48 2025 (print) | LCC GN449.3 (ebook) |
DDC 333.2—dc23/eng/20241004
LC record available at https://lccn.loc.gov/2024021221
LC ebook record available at https://lccn.loc.gov/2024021222

DOI: 10.1093/9780197770894.001.0001

Contents

List of Illustrations	ix
Preface and Acknowledgments	xiii

PART I. THEORETICAL FRAMING

1. Introduction: The Research Question, Rival Explanations, and Cases	3
Research Questions	9
Prevailing Explanations	10
The Argument in Brief	13
Broader Appeal of the Study	15
Research Design and Cases	20
Evidence	23
Qualitative Analysis	24
Definition of Key Concepts	27
Plan of the Book	30
2. Communal Property Rights of Indigenous Peoples and Ethnic Groups: Their Country-Specific Shape	34
3. The Argument: The Crucial Role of State Interests	37
Explaining Indigenous Land Titling: Predominant Approaches	40
Transnational Constructivism: External Pressures Drive Titling	40
Social Movement Theory: Local Social Pressures Motivate Titling	45
Economic Structuralism: Economic Interests Hinder Titling	47
Administrative Theory: Titling as a Function of Bureaucratic Capacity	49
A New Explanation: State Interests Shape Titling	53
The Centrality of State Interests in Titling Indigenous Lands	54
State Interests Mediate Internal Threats and External Pressures	58
Triggers of State Interests: Internal Threats or External Pressure	59
Internal Threats	59
External Pressures	61
Temporal and Spatial Patterns of Titling	63
Conclusion	67

PART II. THE POLITICS OF INDIGENOUS LAND TITLING IN THE AMERICAS

4. Nicaragua: Once Bitten, Twice Shy: Titling for Internal Order — 71
   - Limitations of Extant Approaches — 75
   - Legal Origins: Formal Institutions as Anti-Insurgent Strategy — 78
   - Titling Lands for Internal Order — 84
   - State Interests and the Timing and Rate of Titling — 85
   - State Interests for the Spatial Pattern of Titling — 94
   - The North Caribbean Autonomous Region — 96
     - The Making of New Communal Property Regimes — 97
   - Madriz — 99
   - Conclusion — 101

5. Honduras: Mine Not Yours: Indigenous Land Titling to Recover the Eastern Territory — 104
   - Limitations of Extant Approaches — 109
   - Titling Indigenous Lands to Recover the East — 112
   - The Centrality of State Interests in Titling — 113
   - State Interests and the Spatial Pattern of Titling — 122
   - The Eastern Province — 124
   - The Western Provinces — 127
   - Conclusion — 129

6. Brazil: On My Terms: Creating Indigenous Lands to Control the Borderlands — 133
   - Limitations of Extant Approaches — 137
   - Transnational Constructivism — 138
   - Economic Structuralism — 145
   - Administrative Theories — 147
   - The New Titling Model: Extending the State's Reach in the Borderlands Effectively — 148
   - State Interests as a Crucial Condition for Creating Indigenous Lands: Qualitative Evidence — 156
   - The BCV Frontier Zone — 159
   - Designating Indigenous Lands to Extend the State's Reach in the Borderlands — 159
   - The Heart of Amazonia — 167
   - The Xingu Cluster — 168
   - Conclusion — 171

PART III. CONCLUSION

7. New Ethnic Communal Property Regimes: The Devil is in the Details: Legal Implementation, International Norms, and State-Building in the Americas — 175
   Central Findings — 175
   Comparative Perspective — 180
   Variation in Indigenous Land Titling in Africa and Southeast Asia — 181
   Kenya: Titling for Internal Order — 182
   Indonesia: Titling to Extend the State's Reach — 185
   Broader Theoretical Contributions — 189

Appendices — 195
Appendix A: Quantitative Test, Indigenous Land Titling in Brazil — 197
Appendix B: Administrative Procedure to Title Indigenous Lands — 203
Appendix C: Coding and Operationalization of Indigenous Land Titling — 209
Appendix D: Survey on Indigenous Land Titling — 211
Appendix E: Sources of the Brazilian Indigenous Land Titling Database — 215
Appendix F: Interviews — 217
Notes — 219
Bibliography — 225
Index — 249

Illustrations

Figures

1.1. Timing and Rate of Indigenous Land Titling for Honduras, Nicaragua, and Brazil, 1982–2016	8
3.1. Transnational Constructivism	42
3.2. Social Movement Theory	46
3.3. Economic Structuralism	48
3.4. Administrative Theory	51
3.5. Mediation of Indigenous Land Titling by State Interests	58
4.1. Indigenous Land Titling in the Eastern Territory, 1987–2016	72
4.2. Total Number of Communal Titles Issued (Annually) and the Land Area Covered (Hectares) in Eastern Nicaragua	76
4.3. Levels of Government in the Eastern Territory	98
5.1. Indigenous Land Titling in Honduras since 1982	106
5.2. Suspected Drug Flights Detected Landing in the East and Cocaine Movements, 2008–2013	117
5.3. Homicide Rate in Honduras (per 100,000), 2005–2018	118
5.4. New Hierarchical Governing Structure (in Bold Text)	126
5.5. Lenca Lands in the West, per Province	130
6.1. Count of Indigenous Lands in Brazil by State, 1989–2015	141
6.2. Rate of Indigenous Land Titling in Brazil by year, 1989–2015	143
6.3. Top Ten Indigenous Lands with Highest Number of News Coverage, per Location	144
B.1. Titling Proceedings, Nicaragua	204
B.2. Titling Proceedings, Honduras	205
B.3. Titling Proceedings, Brazil	206

Maps

1.1.	Yanomami Indigenous Land, Brazil	4
4.1.	Status of Indigenous Land Claims, Nicaragua	73
4.2.	Miskito Territorial Claims in 1981, Nicaragua	83
5.1.	Titled Indigenous Lands, Honduras	107
6.1.	Spatial Clustering of Titled Indigenous Lands, Brazil	139
6.2.	Clusters of Titled Indigenous Lands in Amazonia, per Municipality	140
6.3.	Indigenous Lands and Indigenous Peoples, Brazil	141
6.4.	Indigenous Lands and Indigenous Peoples, Amazonia	142
6.5.	Size of Indigenous Lands as Percentage of Total, Brazil	146
6.6.	A–D Mineral and Hydrocarbons Inside or Around Indigenous Lands, per Subnational Region	158

Tables

1.1.	Indigenous Land Titling in Latin America	7
2.1.	Formally Recognized Communal Property Rights of Indigenous Peoples and Ethnic Groups in Central America and Brazil	35
3.1.	Levels of Internal Threat	61
3.2.	Levels of External Pressure	63
3.3.	The Centrality of State Interests	65
4.1.	Views of Rural Populations in the East about National Identity, Communal Property Rights, and Discrimination, 2004	88
4.2.	Views of Politicians in National Legislature about Indigenous Land Titling, Opposition Block, 2015	90
4.3.	Indigenous Lands in the East, 2007–2013	93
4.4.	Socioeconomic Conditions, Indigenous Land Claims, and Outcomes by Province	95
4.5.	Contextual Similarities and Differences in the Provinces, per Indigenous Group	96
4.6.	Chorotega Land Claims in Madriz	101
5.1.	Views of Active Mid-Ranking Military Officers in Training at the National Defense University about Indigenous Land Titling, 2015	121

5.2. Socioeconomic Conditions, Indigenous Land Claims, and Outcomes by Province   123

5.3. Contextual Similarities and Differences between Regions, per Indigenous Group   124

6.1. Location, Land Value, Indigenous Land Claims, and Outcomes by Region   157

6.2. Views of National Legislators about Indigenous Land Titling, per Chamber, March 2015   166

Preface and Acknowledgments

Why and how do some states title Indigenous lands in some places and at certain times but not others? What accounts for the selective implementation of Indigenous peoples' collective rights to land and natural resources? Conventional accounts hold that transnational activism and bottom-up social movements drive Indigenous land titling. Other commonly held views are that economic interests and state weakness are obstacles to these efforts. In contrast, I highlight an alternative, underemphasized motivation for titling Indigenous lands. State elites allocate land to Indigenous peoples, and in the process install new communal property regimes rather than recognize existing Indigenous territories, to ensure internal order and reinforce the state's territorial power in remote regions.

The state's territorial interests shape Indigenous land titling in fundamental ways. Two factors activate state interests: internal threats or external pressure. When state elites perceive high levels of internal threats, they act quickly and systematically to reinforce state power in vulnerable localities. In this situation, state elites act proactively to guarantee internal order and reinforce territorial control. Under conditions of heightened external pressure, the weaker stimulus, state elites react slowly and prioritize titling effectively stateless areas to build state capacity over time. Faced with these pressures, state elites guarantee sovereignty concerns first. State interests serve as a crucial conditioning factor that molds the property institutions installed in territory that Indigenous peoples claim as their ancestral homeland. State interests are a central component of the explanation: they shape the way titling is carried out on the ground.

I develop the argument through comparative case studies of Indigenous land titling in three Latin American countries since the 1980s. I draw on in-depth elite interviews—including interviews with former and sitting presidents, military generals, and top political advisers—original elite opinion surveys, administrative records, newspaper archives, and secondary literature. These sources of information corroborate the importance of state interests in the implementation of Indigenous land and natural resource rights.

This study adds to existing knowledge by showing how state elites reshape historical land claims of Indigenous peoples and transform pre-existing property institutions into a governing mechanism akin to indirect rule. By titling Indigenous lands, the state creates new institutional arrangements in property that allows for the subordination, monitoring, and management of Indigenous society. The broad implication is that state elites subject people that self-identify as Indigenous to a new hierarchical system that perpetuates their political dependency and socioeconomic marginalization.

Many people have helped me with this project. This book grew out of my doctoral dissertation at the University of Texas at Austin. I am deeply indebted to the members of my committee for their guidance during the many years that it took me to complete this project. I am grateful for the generous support of Kurt Weyland, who provided detailed, in-depth, and lightning-fast feedback. Daniel Brinks deserves special recognition for consistently providing me with perceptive advice and helping me move beyond strict legal reasoning. His insights and questions helped me think like a political scientist. Zachary Elkins saw the bigger picture of this project and pressed me to think about the policy implication of my work. Raúl Madrid's eye for detail and identification of soft spots during the defense made this study much stronger. Daniel Power's clear introduction to event history analysis, and continued supervision, allowed me to carry out the statistical component of the Brazil case study. I also want to thank Catherine Boone for helping me along the way. Although not part of my committee, she was exceedingly generous with her time and supported my research idea with great enthusiasm from the very start. Her own work on land tenure regimes provided the inspiration for my thinking about land rights in the Americas. Her extensive comments on my dissertation proposal helped me formulate my project in a coherent fashion.

Many others gave me invaluable support, while I was at the University of Texas at Austin. I am thankful to Wendy Hunter, Jason Brownlee, Henry Dietz, Michael Findley, John Gerring, Charles Hale, Stephanie Holmsten, Juliet Hooker, Nathan Jensen, Tse-Min Lin, Xiaobo Lü, Trish Roberts-Miller, H. W. Perry Jr., Christopher Wlezien, Mounira M. Charrad, and Yu Chen. In addition, I owe much to Miguel Pavón at the LBJ School of Public Affairs for teaching me GIS. I am particularly grateful to Roberto Armijo Keller, Cathy Wu, and Barea Sinno for their friendship and genuine interests in my project. I am also grateful to the staff of the University's Perry-Castañeda Library.

For particularly useful and stimulating comments at different stages of this project I thank Jonathan Bendor, David Collier, Carew Boulding, Thad Dunning, Jake Bowers, Matt Amengual, Robert Franzese, James Mahoney, Rose McDermott, Scott Moser, Elizabeth Maggie Penn, Beth Simmons, Theda Skocpol, James Robinson, and Dan Slater. I also thank the participants of the 2013 Institute for Qualitative and Multi-Method Research, the 2014 ICPSR Summer Program, the 2016 and 2017 APSA panels, the 2017 Behavioral Models of Politics Conference, the 2017 Transnational Criminal Law in the Americas Conference, the 2017 Southwest Workshop on Multi-Method Research at University of California at Riverside, and the Comparative Politics Reading Group at the University of Pittsburgh for having offered exceptionally useful suggestions on papers related this book. I also received helpful comments from participants at a book workshop generously hosted by the Institute for Politics and Strategy at Carnegie Mellon University. I am thankful to Kiron Skinner for her unwavering support. I am also grateful to Aníbal Pérez-Liñán, Moisés Arce, Kashwan Prakash, Scott Morgenstern, and Ilia Murtazashvili for their incisive feedback on earlier versions of the book.

During fieldwork, numerous scholars, civil servants, and activists facilitated my research. For offering institutional support, I thank Prof. Rebecca Neaera Abers at the University of Brasília, Prof. Alfredo Wagner Berno de Almeida at the Federal University of Amazonas, Julio Raudales at the Universidad Nacional Autónoma de Honduras, and Jessica Moreno at the former Central American University in Nicaragua. Conversations with Margarita Antonio, Terri Aquino, Galio Gurdián, David Kaimowitz, João Pacheco de Oliveira, Fany and Beto Ricardo, and Betty Rigby deepened my understanding of Indigenous politics.

In Brazil, Maia Sprandel's support was indispensable to secure interviews with senators and representatives in the National Congress. The staff at the National Indigenous Agency (FUNAI) in Brasília helped me collect crucial historical data. I am especially grateful to Jailson Araújo, who, for months, patiently searched and gave me access to hundreds of Indigenous Land regularization files. Cedeli Lima at the Ministry of Defense made possible the unforgettable trip to the Brazilian northern frontier zone. Ilka and Georgina Fagundes helped me navigate the Palácio do Planalto. At the Instituto Socioambiental, I am thankful to Tatiane Klein for generously sharing the data on legislative acts. In Honduras, I thank Ana Carolina Pineda Mejia at the National Agrarian Institute, Carlos Mejía Rodriguez at the World Bank,

Francisco Molinero at MOPAWI, and Rachelly Merrifield at the Ministry of Tourism for sharing their experiences and inviting me to tag along on inspections trips and meetings. In Nicaragua, Mathelly Casco Batres, Ana Patricia Elvir, Glenda Ramírez, and Anexa Alfred Cunninghan were indispensable to access data and secure interviews.

From Austin to São Paulo, I was fortunate to make many new friends that contributed to my project. For their generosity, I thank Celio Grandes, Laura García, Fernanda Frade, Ana Sampaio, Zirma Rosales Blandón, and Verónica Ríos. I am also grateful to María del Rocío Medina, Gregorio Hernández Zamora, Pedro Torres, Marianela Muñoz, and Marcelo Lima for pulling me out of my work and always sharing the best food in town. Finally, Juan Guillermo Rivera and Kevin Stotz deserve special thanks for giving me a crash course on Python and helping me complete the Brazil ECPR Database. All translations to English and errors are my own. The views expressed in this work are also my own and do not necessarily represent those of my employer.

This project would not have been possible without the generous financial support of the University of Texas at Austin's Teresa Lozano Long Institute of Latin American Studies, Graduate School, and Government Department. A dissertation improvement grant (1419866) from the National Science Foundation supported much of the data collection.

I owe the greatest gratitude to my family. I am especially grateful to Vera Kutzinski for encouraging me to pursue my academic interests with fearlessness. My dad, Haroldo Altamirano, gave me emotional support and ensured that I had enough coffee to keep going. Finally, I thank Santiago Sevilla, my husband, for agreeing to come along with me on this adventure and for supporting my crazy decisions without hesitation, even those that took me to the heart of the Amazon.

This book is dedicated to Guillermina Rayo, my grandmother, and Dr. Daysi Rayo, my mother, for inspiring me to live an authentic life.

PART I
THEORETICAL FRAMING

1

Introduction

The Research Question, Rival Explanations, and Cases

> Indigenous Lands are not a problem to national security as long as there are no restrictions to the interests of the state.
>
> Retired General Rubens Bayma Denys, March 20, 2015,
> Rio de Janeiro, Brazil

Brigadier Roberto de Medeiros Dantas visited a military frontier post located at Surucucu, in the remote northwestern jungles of the state of Roraima, Brazil, in October 2015. Dantas, director of the Calha Norte Program, an initiative of the Ministry of Defense that dated to the mid-1980s, was conducting a routine inspection of military installations in the Amazon. Most of the posts that the program helps maintain are located inside Indigenous lands—areas that the state delimits and allocates to Indigenous communities.[1] The garrison at Surucucu is located in the heart of the Yanomami Indigenous Land, a mineral-rich area created in 1992 that extends over more than 9 million hectares. The Yanomami reservation is located inside the frontier zone, a 93 mile-wide strip of land where the armed forces have unlimited jurisdiction. The reservation also houses two other military frontier units and an office of the National Indigenous Agency (FUNAI), the federal agency responsible for managing native affairs and Indigenous lands.

The case of the Yanomami Indigenous Land is similar to that of other areas claimed by Indigenous peoples as ancestral homelands. In Latin America, Indigenous peoples demand from the state the implementation of communal rights to land and the natural resources the land contains. These rights are formalized in international treaties and national constitutions. Indigenous peoples claim property rights over vast, sparsely populated, and resource-rich land. They demand the concrete application of these rights to maintain and strengthen their way of life, identity, and spiritual relationship with their traditionally occupied territories; to exercise their self-determination rights. In some countries, the state has implemented these formal institutions by identifying, delimiting, classifying, and titling specific areas to communities as Indigenous land. Indigenous land titling can have high technical, economic, and political costs. Nevertheless, central governments have issued titles—thereby defining the rights of land use and tenure—to marginalized Indigenous groups and ethnic collectivities that may have little to no primary loyalties to the state. The Yanomami case serves as a prime example. From 1991 to 1992, Brazil identified and delimited over 9 million hectares rich in gold, diamonds, niobium, and uranium as Indigenous land (see Map 1.1). In about fifteen months, the government made that political decision—which had been under consideration since the end of the 1960s—despite forceful resistance from powerful economic groups interested in mining. By classifying an area as Indigenous, the Brazilian state clarifies the property rights for one or more Indigenous groups claiming user rights and excludes ethnic outsiders from legally using the land and extracting its resources, including

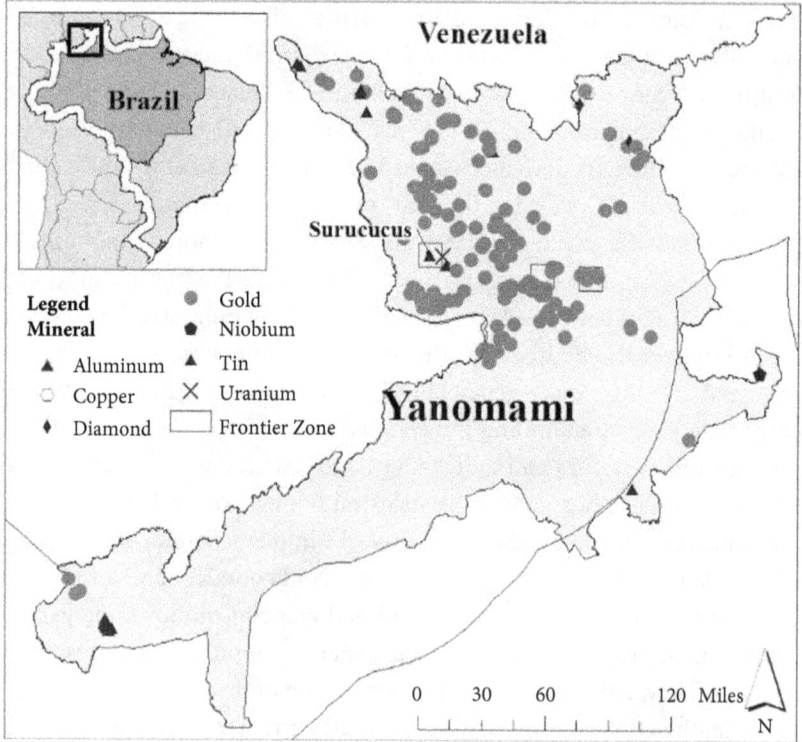

Map 1.1 Yanomami Indigenous Land, Brazil
Source: National Indigenous Agency (FUNAI), 2016; Brazil SGB/CPRM, 2016.

minerals. At first glance, the resulting winners appear to be the claimants; the losers, local ethnic outsiders, poor and marginalized themselves, and wealthy nationals and transnational companies that compete to use or extract resources from the land.

The phenomenon of Indigenous land titling is not confined to the Amazon. In Nicaragua, the central government has titled a whopping one-third of the country's territory as Indigenous land. In this case, officials from the state's central bureaucracy have worked closely with regional officeholders to diligently resolve more than three hundred communal land claims from Indigenous peoples and other ethnic collectivities. In less than a decade, from 2007 to 2016, the government has identified, delimited, and issued twenty-three communal land titles to Indigenous and ethnic groups. The titled communal lands form a continuous block that is roughly twice the size of neighboring El Salvador. By granting a communal land title, the Nicaraguan state clarifies property rights for Indigenous and afro-descendent groups claiming land and natural resource rights and excludes others from using, leasing, or extracting resources from the land. Local farmers in the area who are ethnic outsiders, and transnational companies that vie to extract timber from the region unencumbered, view titling as acting against their interests.

Not all Indigenous or ethnic groups that demand a communal land title receive it. The state may recognize the right of Indigenous peoples to land and natural resources in formal institutions—or written rules—either through constitutional, international, or subnational legislation (RRI 2014; Lucero 2013, 19–20; ILO 2013; van Cott 2006). Nevertheless, the actual application of these laws is uncertain precisely because Indigenous and ethnic collectivities, often poor and marginalized minorities, claim exclusive property rights over land and resources coveted by outsiders, both nationals and transnational companies (Stavenhagen 2013; Sawyer and Gomez 2014; Faundez 2010).

In the Americas, and many other parts of the world, promises enshrined in constitutions are routinely ignored or broken (Levitsky and Murillo 2009, 118, 2013). The uneven application of formal laws is a widespread phenomenon in a variety of issue areas, such as the selective judicial responses to police killings (Brinks 2008), discretionary implementation of laws against street vending and urban squatting (Holland 2015), and uneven enforcement of labor and environmental regulations (Amengual 2016). The gap between formal rules and practices is especially wide when rules are designed to favor the poor and politically marginalized (O'Donnell, Méndez, and Pinheiro 1999). In other words, it is common to find formal institutions that exist only on paper and have little to no substantial impact, while other, informal rules structure actual societal interactions. What is uncommon are instances when the state puts these formal laws into effect and ensures that they have actual bite (Huntington 1968, 2). Especially surprising are examples of the implementation of human rights that carry with them high economic and political costs for the benefit of historically marginalized people, as is the case with Indigenous land and resource rights (Stocks 2005).

Despite the gap between formal rules and actual practice, governments sometimes implement formal rules that the poor and marginalized demand. In fact, the extent to which governments title Indigenous lands at the local level varies dramatically, across countries and through time, as well as within countries. To illustrate, a few states are generous and have titled nearly a third of the national territory as Indigenous lands. Nicaragua and Colombia are cases in point. By contrast, Costa Rica has titled only 6 percent, a small fraction of its territory. On average, Latin American countries classify around 11 percent of their territory as communal property for Indigenous peoples. Table 1.1 illustrates the dramatic variation in Indigenous land titling across Latin America.

The rate and timing of Indigenous land titling across states is highly uneven. In some countries, constitutional provisions lie dormant for decades and are suddenly implemented. That was the case for Nicaragua and Honduras. Two decades after the adoption of communal property rights for Indigenous peoples and ethnic groups in its 1987 Constitution, Nicaragua quickly and systematically made these rights effective in 2007. In the case of Honduras, the state began formalizing extensive areas as Indigenous lands in 2012, three decades after adopting land rights for Indigenous peoples and ethnic groups in its Constitution and seventeen years after ratifying the International Labour Organization's Convention No. 169 on Indigenous and Tribal Peoples (ILO Convention No. 169). To be sure, the Honduran government had titled small plots as communal lands. However, until 2012, there were few, if any, initiatives to either classify vast areas as Indigenous land or title a grid of adjacent land blocks as communal property for Indigenous and ethnic groups. Efforts to make effective Indigenous land rights over vast territories began in 2012. In one year, the state had titled 42 percent of a pre-approved Indigenous territory, an area that represents 7 percent of the national territory; by the first quarter of 2016, the state had completed

Table 1.1 Indigenous Land Titling in Latin America

Country	Country Area (Mha)*	Titled Area (Mha)	Titled Area (% Country Area)	Claimed Area (% Country Area)	Sources
Argentina	273.67	8.03	3%	5.48%	National Institute of Indigenous Affairs 2012
Belize	2.28	0	0%	N/D	LandMark 2017
Bolivia	108.33	21.21	20%	N/D	LandMark 2017; National Institute of Agrarian Reform has 38.92 titled mha (2012)
Brazil	835.81	116.65	13%	Over 14%	National Indigenous Agency (FUNAI) 2016
Chile	74.35	2.31	0.22%	Over 3%	RRI 2014; LandMark 2017
Colombia	110.95	37.58	34%	Over 34.42%	RRI 2014; IEMP 2015; LandMark 2017
Costa Rica	5.10	0.33	6%	N/D	Gómez Meléndez 2014; RRI 2015; LandMark 2017
Ecuador	24.83	3.8	15%	19.33%	Riascos de la Peña et al. 2008
El Salvador⁺	2.07	0	0%	N/D	LandMark 2017
Guatemala	10.71	0.0015	0.0001%	Over 0.8%	Presidency Guatemala 2015; RIC 2011
Guyana	19.68	3.32	17%	N/D	Guyana Forestry Commission 2015; LandMark has 3.22 mha as titled (2017)
Honduras	11.19	1.41	12%	Over 15%	National Agrarian Institute Honduras 2016; ICF 2016
Mexico	194.39	21.08	11%	N/D	Boege Schmidt 2008; LandMark has 1.97 mha as titled (2017)
Nicaragua	12.03	3.91	33%	Over 33%	Attorney General's Office 2016
Panama	7.43	1.65	22%	31.61%	Herrer and Edouard 2013; LandMark 2017
Paraguay	39.73	0	0%	N/D	LandMark 2017
Peru	128	5.5	4%	10-12.27%	IBC 2014; LandMark 2017
Suriname⁺	15.6	0	0%	30.58%	RRI 2014; LandMark 2017
Venezuela	88.20	2.84	3%	33.67%	Ponte Iglesias 2013; LandMark 2017

Source: *The World Bank, Land Area, available at http://data.worldbank.org (accessed, May 1, 2017).

Note: ⁺These countries do not recognize formal Indigenous land and natural resource rights (Edouard 2010; IACHR 2007).

the titling program in the east. As a result, Honduras has designated about 10 percent of its territory as Indigenous land.

In contrast to the Central American experience, Brazil is a more typical case of sluggish rule implementation. The state has set aside roughly 13 percent of its territory as Indigenous lands. To date, however, only 65 percent of these lands have received that classification, well below the performance of Nicaragua and Honduras. Brazil has openly disregarded a constitutional deadline mandating the demarcation and titling of all Indigenous Lands by 1993. After over three decades, the government is nowhere near completing the job. Figure 1.1 shows the timing and rate of Indigenous land titling in Nicaragua, Honduras, and Brazil. Based on systematic review of official government data, I illustrate how titling has evolved in each country through time, since the formal adoption of property rights in the constitution in the 1980s until 2016.

In addition to cross-country and temporal differences in titling, there is also geographical unevenness within countries. In Nicaragua and Honduras, titling agencies have resolved claims in the east but have neglected the west. Similar to the Central American experience, Brazil has concentrated efforts in the Amazonian northern frontier zone despite Indigenous land claims being spread throughout the heart of the Amazon region. For instance, in the frontier zone north of the Solimões and Amazon rivers, Indigenous

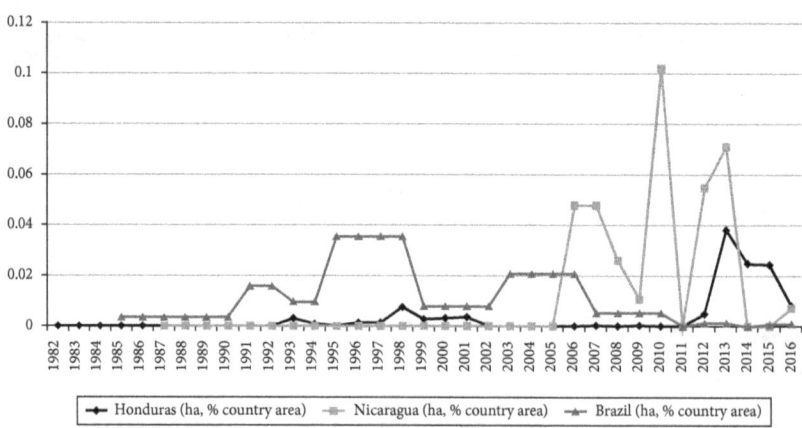

Figure 1.1 Timing and Rate of Indigenous Land Titling for Honduras, Nicaragua, and Brazil, 1982–2016

Sources: Honduras: IP (2016), ICF (2016); Nicaragua: Attorney General's Office (2016); Brazil: FUNAI (2016)

Lands have a 95 percent titling rate. The blocks in the northwestern frontier zone bordering Colombia and Venezuela have an even higher titling level at 98 percent. In stark contrast, the parcels located in the heart of the Amazon, 100 miles from Manaus, the capital of the state of Amazonas, have a titling rate of 65 percent.

Research Questions

As the discussion above highlights, the state titles Indigenous lands despite considerable economic, political, and administrative costs. Importantly, titling is neither systematic throughout the state's territory nor completely random. There are clear temporal and spatial patterns of Indigenous land titling across and within countries that vary greatly. What explains this difference? States make effective Indigenous land and resource rights in remote places while geographically closer claims remain unresolved. Why would states, especially poor and weak ones like Nicaragua and Honduras, suddenly apply dormant constitutional provisions in remote localities? Equally, and arguably more perplexing, is the titling of areas that contain energy-producing resources such as oil and gas, as well as other coveted non-renewable and renewable resources such as uranium, gold, diamonds, and timber. Under what conditions do central governments title Indigenous lands in resource-rich zones? In short, what motivates the titling of Indigenous land at the local level and the creating of obstacles for elites that are considered ethnic outsiders?

In this book, I examine closely why and how central governments implement formal property rights by issuing a communal land title to Indigenous peoples and other ethnic groups. In answering questions about the implementation of a specific property institution by focusing on Indigenous land titling, I also speak to broader scholarly debates about the functioning of formal institutions in developing countries. I examine the implementation question closely to understand the way formal institutions work. I am especially interested in cases for which making rules effective may carry substantial economic and political costs. Temporal and spatial variation of titling practices tells us about the selective effects of formal institutions, as well as why informal institutions become formalized and how the process of institutional change occurs, or does not (Levitsky and Murillo 2013, 99–103, Weyland 2006, 2009; Mahoney and Thelen 2010, 10–18; Capoccia 2015,

174). Thus, my research speaks to the following broader question: Why and how are formal institutions that marginalized groups demand activated?

Prevailing Explanations

There are four general approaches that seek to explain the variation in Indigenous land titling, which I label transnational constructivism, social movement theory, economic structuralism, and administrative theory. These general frameworks differ substantially in their views. First, transnational constructivist scholars focus on external factors, while social movement theory, structural economic analysis, and administrative capacity arguments mostly emphasize intra-country dynamics. Second, transnational constructivist, social movement theory, and economic structural scholars share the understanding that the interests and actions of societal groups provide the impulses or constraints that shape the patterns of institutional implementation. In contrast, administrative theories have a state-centric perspective and highlight the role that the state apparatus plays in determining outcomes. Scholars working with administrative theories often assume that political elites are lagging behind, but unwillingly. That is, they want to but cannot implement formal laws,[2] especially regarding the human rights of Indigenous peoples. Therefore, states that have cohesive, technically skilled, and politically insulated bureaucracies are expected to outperform those that have lower levels of administrative capacity. I briefly discuss each of these approaches in the following paragraphs.

The transnational constructivist account is the canonical explanation for Indigenous land titling. Scholars often point to the strategies that transnational advocacy networks employ to pressure high-ranking government officials to implement international human rights (Keck and Sikkink 1998; Brysk 2000, 2009; Risse, Ropp, and Sikkink 1999, 2013; Tarrow 2005). Using the Brazilian experience as a prime example, Margaret Keck and Kathryn Sikkink argue that an active global civil society pressures political elites to observe specific constitutional and international norms and rules (1998; Risse, Ropp, and Sikkink 1999, 2013). A crucial implication of this account is that the underlying logic of titling can be understood from the interests and actions of transnational groups that launch implementation campaigns. From this perspective, transnational activists push state elites, and these elites respond by titling Indigenous lands in areas claimed as ancestral homelands.

State elites would then focus their attention on a particular region or section of the country that may hold natural resources. After years of accountability campaigns, Indigenous land titling should be concentrated in subnational areas that are targeted by transnational advocates.

The empirical record partially supports the theoretical expectations of the transnational constructivist approach. Not simply reacting to external pressure, the state has also titled Indigenous lands proactively. For instance, in Nicaragua, the state has titled huge swaths of Indigenous lands without responding to transnational activist campaigns (Chapter 4). In this case, the state made Indigenous land and resource rights effective to appease interethnic tensions, not to quell international criticism. In the Honduran case, new drug-trafficking threats motivated the state to title Indigenous lands to project institutional power into vulnerable localities (Chapter 5). Political elites used international resources to title Indigenous lands in areas controlled by drug lords, while simultaneously increasing the military presence to reinforce the state's coercive power. Even when responding to external pressure, the central government does so selectively and only after safeguarding military interests. The Brazilian case is a good example of this dynamic. In Brazil, external pressure provided the initial stimulus to title extensive areas as Indigenous land but was not, in and of itself, enough to accomplish this (Chapter 6). The central government first ensured military interests inside Indigenous lands and then used titling to extend the state's reach into de facto stateless areas and to incorporate Indigenous peoples into the nation-state.

The second approach, social movement theory, is complementary to transnational constructivist theory, and highlights the role of bottom-up social activism as a main factor in rule implementation. Scholars often point to mass, peaceful demonstrations and marches that civil society and nongovernmental organizations (NGOs) organize to pressure state actors into titling Indigenous territories (Anderson 2009; Brondo 2013, Ch. 5; Mollett 2013). Under this approach, the interests and strategy of local civil society explains outcomes. State agencies should be more responsive to those groups that are better organized and have the expertise and mobilization resources to exert political pressure for rule observance. While local mobilization is an important source of pressure, the empirical record does not wholly support the expectations of this approach. In the Honduran case, for example, the central government has applied communal land titling practices that highly fragment the territorial claims of strong Indigenous organizations and has failed to protect grassroots leaders from repression (Chapter 5). Rather than implement a policy that would have bolstered local self-determination, as social movements had hoped, Honduras has applied a divide-and-rule logic in resolving the ancestral land claims of the strongest Indigenous organizations in the country.

The economic-structural approach typically contends that the state titles communal land mostly in peripheral regions that lack economic value (Hale 2011). Since the titling of Indigenous lands can hinder the extraction of rich natural resources, political elites ignore claims if the economic costs are too high or when competing economic interest groups resist (Brinks and Botero 2014; Sullivan 2013; Pacheco 2009, 325–54; Griffiths 2004, 55; Carvalho 2000, 462–64; van Cott 2000, 97–98). Under this framework, the state would title lands in areas reserved for environmental conservation purposes but not in resource-rich zones or economically productive areas. This theoretical expectation cannot account for many implementation practices, including those from Brazil, Nicaragua, and Honduras described above. In these cases, the central government has titled large extensions of Indigenous land although these areas are rich in economically valuable resources and are therefore coveted by powerful economic groups.

In the case of Brazil, the three largest Indigenous lands in terms of territorial extension—Yanomami, Alto Rio Negro, and Vale do Javari—contain huge deposits of gold, uranium, niobium, diamonds, and many other economically profitable resources like gas and oil. The state knew about the existence of these resources before designating and classifying the areas as Indigenous lands. To illustrate, the Alto Rio Negro Indigenous Land, located in the northwestern Amazon region known as Cabeça do Cachorro, holds the largest deposits of easily extractable niobium in the world (Klinger 2015, 15). The Brazilian government identified, explored, and mapped these deposits in 1972 and 1975, long before 1985, when the administrative process to classify the area as Indigenous land began. Despite the existence of niobium, and other valuable substances like gold, the President of Brazil confirmed Alto Rio Negro as an Indigenous land in 1998. Arguments that emphasize the power of competing economic interest groups also underestimate the extent of Indigenous land titling in Honduras and Nicaragua, where large extensions of agricultural and timber producing zones are now Indigenous lands. Thus, such arguments leave unexplained the titling of over 1.6 million hectares of Nicaragua's territory, and 1 million hectares of Honduras' territory.

Administrative theories assume that the state is willing to title Indigenous lands but does not have the bureaucratic capacity to extend its reach into remote regions (Faundez 2010; Risse 2011; Börzel and Risse 2013; Yashar 2005; Bunker 1985). Lack of capacity to make rules effective, and not lack of will, would prevent the state from titling Indigenous lands consistently and thoroughly across the national territory. Accordingly, the quality of the state apparatus, measured by the degree of meritocracy, technical capability, and coherence, crucially shapes outcomes. More firmly institutionalized agencies should perform better when enforcing laws. Lower-middle income countries like Nicaragua and Honduras, as well as upper-middle income countries like Brazil, lack the national-level implementation agencies with high degrees of internal coherence and institutionalization. Thus, under this framework, remote lands in countries with difficult geographies are unlikely to be titled.

The empirical record shows that Indigenous land titling can advance quickly in a country although the state's administrative capacity remains constant. For instance, after decades of ignoring constitutionally recognized communal property rights, Nicaragua suddenly began titling Indigenous lands in 2007. The same is true for Honduras, where implementation progressed quickly after 2012. Moreover, this can happen at a surprisingly high rate in remote localities in countries with difficult geographies. Brazil provides a good example for this type of pattern: the central government has a high titling rate in the nearly inaccessible northwestern jungles of the Amazon region but ignores land claims originating from places where the state has more presence (Chapter 6). Honduras and Nicaragua also grant land titles in remote, hard-to-reach places, where the state has little or no institutional presence. The administrative capacity argument is hard pressed to explain the temporal and spatial patterns of titling in weak states and in places that are far removed from the centers of power.

The Argument in Brief

Based on my research in Nicaragua, Honduras, and Brazil, I contend that existing theories only partially account for the timing, regional concentration, and manner in which the state titles Indigenous lands. The power and territorial interest of state elites is a key but often overlooked part of the explanation. My argument is that the interest of the central government in securing the territory and governing remote areas of the nation-state is a crucial mediating factor that shapes the way Indigenous land titling actually occurs and is designed to function. State elites use Indigenous land titling to ensure internal order and reinforce territorial control. Central government officials design titling programs to align with military interests and to engineer the institutional presence of the state for posterity inside Indigenous peoples' homelands. Indigenous peoples become restricted to the geographical extension designated as communal land, regardless of what had traditionally been their ancestral territory. The central government designs the institutions to exert influence on the internal organization and political arrangement of the communities. The outcome of tilting processes is the fragmentation of Indigenous peoples' ancestral territory and the institutionalization of relations of domination.

Security challenges motivate state elites to consider titling as the best way to meet their goals and resolve internal threats and external pressure, the former being a more powerful stimulus than the latter. When strong internal threats jeopardize the state's power, the central government titles Indigenous lands quickly and systematically in a way that reinforces state control over vulnerable regions. In this first situation, state elites seek to guarantee internal order. The central government reacts to external pressure by safeguarding sovereignty concerns first and then gradually titling Indigenous lands to build the state's infrastructural capacity over time. In this second situation, state elites seek to reinforce territorial control. In both cases, state interests are a central component of the explanation.

My argument underscores the strategic nature of the political decision to design and formalize communal property institutions. In a context of internal or external pressure, state elites title Indigenous lands to safeguard, consolidate, and reinforce the political dominance and control of the nation-state over Indigenous communities located in remote localities. In doing so, the central government superimposes an institutional structure that enhances the power and extends the reach of the state in these distant territories. In that sense, Indigenous land titling does not imply that the state is applying policies that enhance local autonomy, respect self-government, and uphold the rights to self-determination that Indigenous peoples have secured as a human right in international law. On the contrary, the state establishes communal property regimes, overwriting pre-established land tenure systems and limiting customary local political practices.

State elites mediate societal demands in fundamental ways. In the process, the central government titles Indigenous lands in a way that thwarts potential Indigenous resistance and enhances the state's institutional power. By redesigning customary property institutions that link the central apparatus of the government with remote rural areas, state elites are using a strategy that allows them to consolidate power, while fragmenting the integrity of Indigenous territory and the cohesion of customary political organization. Clearly, my proposed model suggests that Indigenous land titling is more an instrument with which state elites try to secure order and extend power over Indigenous territory than an unobstructed road toward Indigenous self-determination. In the process of building the modern state, government officials create a diverse institutional landscape that shapes the political paths, including economic trajectories, of Indigenous societies.

Broader Appeal of the Study

Focusing on the implementation patterns of legal provisions underscores a political factor that shapes the transformation of informal institutions that are practiced at the local level into formal ones, with state encouragement. Theoretically, implementation questions touch upon scholarly debates about the underlying reasons for the origin and evolution of institutions (North 1990; Ostrom 2005; Levitsky and Murillo 2014, Ch. 9). Entitlements to land and land-based resources on the basis of Indigenous culture or ethnicity are written in constitutional provisions that become activated (or deactivated) at certain specific moments in particular regions. The reasons behind the activation, I contend, lie in the government elites' interests in building and reproducing the state's institutional authority by using differentiated property institutions and systems.

In this book, I show that perceived security challenges, in the form of internal threats and external pressures, motivate the central government to activate formal communal property rights. These factors interfere with, or potentially block, the state's direct control over territory and people. If the state's interest in controlling territory differs, depending on the existence of these factors, then government elites activate written laws to reinforce state power. State elites act when and where they need it most, and only in a state-serving manner. State elites will not develop the institutional apparatus that societal actors demand. Instead, they will design a property regime in land that can be coopted and manipulated from the center. Where the state has a strong grip on territory and people, these differentiated property institutions may remain on the books indefinitely.

State elites' interests and power help explain why and how communal land institutions become activated or remain dormant. Thus, a focus on Indigenous land titling allows not just for an understanding of a major evolutionary transition of formal institutions but also elucidates the political origin of differentiated institutions of domination that operate at the grassroots level. While Indigenous land claimants seek to resist centralized power and to make effective the rights to self-determination through local self-government, the relationships of power that the state institutionalizes through land titling arguably have the opposite effect. The resulting communal property regime allows the state to assimilate Indigenous peoples and ethnic communities as differentiated subjects and to reinforce asymmetrical power relationships. The state imposes its own vision and engineers the institutional framework for Indigenous political order, rather than allow Indigenous peoples to govern themselves according to their own pre-existing institutions.

This way of looking at land institutions as mechanisms to secure state rule comes from an extensive literature in political science and comparative sociology, which supports the idea that the state designs, and redesigns, land tenure regimes to reinforce its rule (Anderson 1979; Scott 2009). From a historical and comparative perspective, the argument I present here is not surprising: central government officials have allocated land to guarantee security objectives in disparate contexts, including North America, Africa, and Asia (Mamdani 1996; Boone 2003, 2014; Engerman and Metzer 2004; Davidson and Henley 2007; Harris 2002; St. Germain 2001). Yet arguments about Indigenous land titling as a means to secure state rule have not resonated in the Latin American literature. Most of the work on Latin America regards Indigenous land titling as a way to uphold indigenous autonomy, rather than as a strategy that reinforces state power. In that sense, I propose a new perspective here for the Latin American cases using new evidence.

This book speaks to human rights scholarship about Indigenous self-determination. Indigenous land rights are at the heart of Indigenous self-determination struggles and form the basis of the international Indigenous rights regime (Anaya 2004; Xanthaki 2007; Kuokkanen 2019, 40–41). The United Nations Declaration on the Rights of Indigenous Peoples (UNDRIP) not only recognizes that "Indigenous peoples have the right to self-determination" (Art. 3) but further adds that they have the right to exercise it through autonomy and self-government arrangements (Art. 4).³ The declaration has an important caveat: Indigenous self-determination should not impair the territorial integrity of the nation-state (Art. 46). As Rauna Kuokkanen correctly notes, the declaration reasserts member states' sovereignty interests and excludes alternative Indigenous interpretations of self-determination (2019, 30–34). Despite its limitation, the declaration enshrines Indigenous people's collective right to lands, territories, and resources by reason of traditional use and confers an obligation on states to legally recognize traditionally occupied lands (Art. 26). The legal recognition of communal land is intended to prevent forceful removal of communities and to protect Indigenous values and culture linked to these lands. Land is intertwined with cultural survival and self-government, which includes respect for Indigenous land tenure systems and dispute settlement mechanisms on land matters. As Kuokkanen explains, "[t]he collective integrity of Indigenous peoples hinges on the integrity of the land. Regardless of region, Indigenous people commonly describe self-determination as a relation with the land" (2019, 40). Without secure property rights to lands and natural resources, Indigenous peoples' subsistence, through cultural and also economic means, is permanently threatened. The challenge is to make these formal institutions a reality in practice.

While indigenous land titling is a first step toward securing Indigenous property rights, it is not sufficient to guarantee Indigenous self-government and further self-determination. As the case studies in this book show, the state does not simply recognize existing Indigenous institutions, land tenure systems, and traditional land boundaries as Indigenous peoples demand. In the Central American cases, the state redraws land boundaries and creates new land governing institutions to manage land relations. Seen as less costly than repression and more legitimate to external stakeholders, these new institutions are nevertheless prone to cooptation. In the Nicaraguan case in particular, state elites perceived Indigenous peoples' claims to ancestral land as an existential threat, rather than as an opportunity to strengthen democracy and the state itself. In their unfounded mistrust, Nicaraguan state elites engineered an institutional mechanism to co-opt Indigenous leaders and limit communities' abilities to govern themselves without the central government's interference. In the Brazilian case, the state not only redraws territorial boundaries but also ensures a military presence in Indigenous territory and bolsters its ability to determine the acceptable forms of land and natural resource management inside Indigenous lands. Even when

Indigenous peoples per se are not perceived as a security threat, such as in Honduras and Brazil, the state has the compulsion to fortify state power over Indigenous territory to face actual or perceived security challenges. In other words, the state has enormous discretionary power to limit Indigenous self-government in practice while titling Indigenous lands. In that regard, my study shows that an overreliance on legalistic approaches is not sufficient to ensure local self-government and make Indigenous self-determination effective. By highlighting the state's mechanisms for dominating Indigenous society while implementing international Indigenous land rights, this book joins scholarship that points to the limits of the international Indigenous rights framework—which excludes broader Indigenous conceptions of self-determination (Kuokkanen 2019, 12, 37–38)—to restructure Indigenous-state relations in practice.

My work also speaks to debates regarding the extent to which international political factors matter for domestic political phenomena. Understanding implementation dynamics is fundamental to examining whether, and to what extent, international institutions and external factors have a real effect on the ground (Victor, Raustiala, and Skolnikoff 1998; Lutz and Sikkink 2000; Schwarz 2004; Cardenas 2007; Hill 2010; Posner 2014). Because the adoption of formal rules may be a façade built to redirect pressure from transnational activists that push for norm observance (Hafner-Burton and Tsutsui, 2005), I look beyond the passing of formal laws in countries that have both adopted constitutional provisions and ratified international laws that recognize Indigenous land and resource rights, such as UNDRIP and ILO Convention No. 169. I examine the real impact that international human rights institutions have at the subnational level after considering the strong, persistent push by societal groups for human rights adherence after treaty ratification (Simmons 2009). In that respect, the analysis conducted in this book contributes to the recurrent debates in political science about the relative importance of international factors and institutions in initiating, magnifying, or shaping domestic political phenomena (Weyland 2014; Trejo 2012; Levitsky and Way 2010; Keck and Sikkink 1998).

In addition, Indigenous land titling can have tremendous implications in Latin America and beyond. Scholars working within the commons literature have linked government-recognized local communal property rights and clear boundaries as characteristics conducive to the sustainable management of natural resources. Elinor Ostrom (1990, Ch. 3, Ch. 5, 2005, 260–69) has found that robust socio-ecological systems share two attributes:

(a) clearly delimited physical boundaries, and (b) the central government's official recognition of local resource management rules. Indigenous land titling—by identifying and delimiting the physical boundaries and officially defining communal land and resource rights locally—may lead to the long-term sustainability of natural resources (Sarukhán and Larson 2001, 45). My work links to this discussion by homing in on the conditions under which governments officially delimit and recognize common property rules over land and resources, a precondition for stable and sustainable use of communal natural resources (Ostrom 1990, Ch. 3, Ch. 5, 2005, 260–69). My study includes the examination of the central government's titling practices over areas located in the Amazon River Basin, which contains the largest tropical rainforest in the world, and lands that overlap with areas designated for conservation purposes in the Mesoamerican Biological Corridor of Central America (Finley-Brook 2014). Communal lands completely overlap with the Bosawás Biosphere Reserve and with 90 percent of the Río San Juan Biosphere Reserve in Nicaragua. In Honduras, communal lands overlap with 35 percent of the area of the Río Plátano Biosphere Reserve.

Indigenous land titling may also be consequential for the economic growth trajectories of underdeveloped countries. Currently, academics, policy analysts, and financial institutions alike have emphasized the importance of secure private property as a necessary condition for economic development. Economists have continued to argue that the transition of common property regimes to private property institutions is necessary for the development and growth of modern, Western societies (North and Thomas 1976) and the alleviation of widespread poverty (Meinzen-Dick 2011). Donors and international financial institutions—like the World Bank and the Inter-American Development Bank—advise developing countries to clearly define and secure private property rights to alleviate poverty in agriculture and industry and further economic development. Private property and communal property seem to be at odds when it comes to known forms of economic development that made the contemporary world. Despite the perceived incompatibility, analysts prescribe the securing of communal land rights based on ethnicity by governments (Plant and Hvalkov 2001, 74–75, Deininger et al. 2010). For instance, Klaus Deininger of the World Bank's Research Department, suggests transferring property rights to autochthonous communities and historically disadvantaged groups "even if they do not imply an immediate increase in economic efficiency" (2003, xxvii–xlv). My book joins the work of scholars that examines in detail when and why government elites prioritize titling Indigenous lands to ethnic groups (Kashwan 2017). Under conditions of internal threats and external pressure, political elites choose to deprioritize economic interests in exchange for political order and control over rural populations. In these situations, political elites disregard private property institutions that they perceive to be necessary for economic development. The type of property institutions that are enforced are, consequently, especially important for the development trajectory of poor countries such as Nicaragua and Honduras, as well as for middle-income countries, like Brazil. Since the debate about the causes and consequences of communal land regimes are not confined to Latin America, my findings should also be of interest to scholars working on land regimes in the Global South, such as in sub-Saharan Africa (Boone 2014; Mamdami 1996; Moyo 2005) and in Asia (Baird 2013; Majumder 2010; McCarthy 2000).

Research Design and Cases

The main focus of this book is Latin America, a region where most of the world's contemporary Indigenous land titling activity has taken place (RRI 2014). In principle, I could draw empirical material from any country in Latin America that has recognized communal property rights of Indigenous and other ethnic groups as formal institutions, either by signing UNDRIP, by ratifying ILO Convention No. 169, or through constitutional recognition, and has applied these laws locally to develop and propose arguments about implementation. To test rival hypotheses and generate alternative theoretical propositions, I choose a subset of three countries in the Americas: Brazil, Nicaragua, and Honduras. I couple these comparisons with in-depth study of a total of six subnational regions. The units of analysis are subnational territories within the countries, jurisdictional units the state's central authority has categorized as areas to be delimited and titled as Indigenous lands. That is, the objects of analysis are the specific subnational areas that the state has promised to title as Indigenous lands. I begin the study in the 1980s, after the adoption of the latest constitutional provision formally recognizing, and thereby making legally applicable, Indigenous land and resource rights in the country.

The cases of Brazil, Nicaragua, and Honduras are particularly well suited to analyze variation in implementation practices. These countries are representative of the state of affairs of most countries in the Americas where Indigenous peoples are a minority of the population (van Cott 2010, 400; Hall and Patrinos 2012; Gerring 2007, 91–97; Yashar 2005, 19–21).[4] All country cases simultaneously experienced two fundamental changes in the 1980s: democratization and the explicit recognition of Indigenous land and resource rights in the constitution (Hoekema, van der Haar, and Assies 2000). Nevertheless, countries differ in the extent to which central governments have applied these institutions locally over time. These three countries vary along the main explanatory factors under both my explanation and the alternative approaches mentioned above. The cases span a country with a long history of Indigenous and environmental activism, Brazil, and others with comparatively weaker social movements, Nicaragua and Honduras. The provenance and strength of internal threats to the state's authority also varies across and within the countries under study, allowing me to trace the spatial effect of different degrees of internal threats on implementation outcomes. Furthermore, countries vary in their relative levels of administrative capacity. Brazil, an urban upper-middle-income country, has a more capable bureaucracy than Nicaragua and Honduras, two lower-middle-income agrarian countries. Differences in the magnitude of economic competition over land and land-based resources provide additional leverage for evaluating the explanatory power of my hypothesis and that of alternative approaches.

In many ways, Brazil is a fortuitous case to study the effects of transnational activism on implementation. The Brazilian Amazon has been the focus of intense international attention from human rights and environmental activists pressuring the central government to implement Indigenous land rights since the 1980s (Keck and Sikkink 1998; Barbosa 2015, Ch. 2). Brazil enshrined Indigenous land and resource rights in the constitution, ratified ILO Convention No. 169, and signed UNDRIP. The persistence of external pressure on a specific policy issue allows for an assessment of the extent to which, and under what conditions, global activism can truly push for rule observance. Because of striking spatial patterns in Indigenous land titling within Amazonia, as well as the availability and reliability of fine-grained geocoded data, Brazil also provides a remarkable opportunity to assess the explanatory power of my propositions in comparison to alternative theories, including those approaches that emphasize administrative capacity or economic interests as factors that matter for implementation.

The book details how the institutional interests of political elites in the central government motivate the design, redesign, and categorization of communal property regimes at specific moments in time and in certain localities, but not in others. A cross-national and subnational approach is particularly well suited to study uneven titling practices in one policy area as it allows for detecting spatial-temporal variations that may be overlooked or underemphasized in more macro-level studies. I employ a comparative within-case study method to closely observe the causal mechanisms at play inside countries over time, while keeping the cross-country comparisons in mind to assess the explanatory power of other frameworks (transnational constructivism, social movement theory, economic structuralism, and administrative theory). Therefore, I focus on a subset of six sub-national regions drawn from the larger pool of observations within countries (van Evera 1997, 24–25; Gerring 2007). I chose subnational cases to take full advantage of the different values of key factors, while controlling for demographic factors typically associated with demands for land, such as the size of the rural, Indigenous, and ethnic population.

In Nicaragua, I chose observations located in the Autonomous Region of the North Caribbean that borders Honduras in the northeast, paired with Indigenous land claims originating from the Madriz province located in the west. These regions are home to the two largest Indigenous groups in the country: the Miskitos in the east and the Chorotegas in the west. Roughly 30 percent of the population identifies as Miskito in the northeast and around 20 percent identifies as Chorotega in Madriz (INIDE 2005). These regions are very similar in other key factors, such as level of economic development and percentage of the rural population (INIDE 2005; UNDP 2005). Indigenous peoples in both regions have claimed rights over agricultural and forest lands (Attorney General's Office 2009, 51–53). External pressures to title Indigenous lands are present, but weak, in both regions. Despite the many similarities between regions, there are widely different titling outcomes. In the northeast, the central government systematically delimited and titled Indigenous lands after 2007. In Madriz, by contrast, demands for titles have long been ignored. I compare both cases across time to explain the stark variation in outcomes.

In Honduras, I compare Indigenous land titling practices in the eastern province Gracias a Dios, home to the majority (90 percent) of the people that identify as Miskito, with the communal land titling practices in the western provinces of Lempira, Intibucá, and La Paz, where a majority (80 percent) of the Lenca people live. The Lenca form the largest and most organized ethnic group in the country; the Miskito are the second largest (INE 2013).

In Gracias a Dios, a poor, sparsely populated, remote, and timber-rich province, local Indigenous leaders have claimed ancestral land rights over vast areas since the 1980s. The central government ignored these claims for nearly three decades, until suddenly, in 2012, the president decided to grant communal property titles over fifteen enormous land blocks to the Miskito. Following that decision, by early 2016, the state had classified around 10 percent of the territory as Indigenous land. The titled lands in the Gracias a Dios province represent around 80 percent of all Indigenous lands in the country. In the west, by contrast, the state has titled small communal land plots to Lenca villagers, who live in remote mountainous areas. The state recognized Lenca land, itself divided into three hundred communal titles, comprises about 1 percent of the country's territory. I conduct a longitudinal analysis of the central government's titling behavior in the Gracias a Dios province, in contrast to practices in the west, to explain the divergent outcomes.

Finally, in Brazil I chose subnational regions in the Amazon River Basin with the goal of maximizing the variation in the factors under study. I compare cases within Amazonia that differ in relation to their proximity from the northern frontier zone—a military buffer area along the international border. The case selection allows a comparison of Indigenous lands located inside and outside of the frontier zone—a priority for the state—while controlling for external pressure from global environmental and Indigenous human rights activists. Observations also differ in the existence (or lack) of mineral deposits, oil, and gas inside Indigenous lands, as well as overlapping federally protected environmental areas. Whereas the claims originating in the frontier zone have a higher titling rate, those located in the heart of the Amazon have a much lower rate. To document the causal mechanism at play, I analyze state elite decision-making in the Yanomami Indigenous Land case, which resulted in a titling model that safeguarded military interests and ensured the unhindered reproduction of the state's institutions in Indigenous peoples' ancestral territories. The within-region comparison and detailed case study demonstrates that state elites respond to external pressure selectively to gradually extend the state's institutional apparatus in otherwise stateless regions.

Evidence

I am particularly interested in assessing broad causal associations, as well as in explaining specific historical events (Mahoney and Thelen 2015;

Lieberman 2005). I rely on qualitative sources of evidence to support the main theoretical propositions, and to account for implementation across and within countries (Collier and Elman 2009). I use various sources and types of evidence to assess the strength of the hypothesized causal associations. Because my aim is to further theory building, I present a systematic, fine-grained, and persuasive analysis of the reasons behind the observed patterns of Indigenous land titling in three specific countries of the Americas.

The data used in the analysis were collected on-site during twelve months of uninterrupted, original field research during the 2014–2015 academic year divided as follows: Brazil (7 months), Honduras (3 months), and Nicaragua (2 months). I also collected evidence during exploratory research trips to Nicaragua in the summer of 2012 and Brazil in the summer of 2013. For the Brazil case study, I collected different types of data—interviews, primary documents, and reliable, updated, and publicly available geo-referenced statistical data—and both employ qualitative analysis and use quantitative data to support my argument. The Appendix A contains a statistical analysis of longitudinal and geospatial data for hypothesis testing.[5] For Nicaragua and Honduras, where systematic and reliable data only exists about titling outcomes, I analyze qualitative sources of evidence, such as in-depth interviews with political elites and experts, government reports and policy documents gathered onsite, and administrative proceedings regarding Indigenous land claims and outcomes. Data from an original survey that measures political elites' attitudes toward Indigenous land titling complements my analysis for all country-cases.

Qualitative Analysis

I support my main causal propositions and assess the validity of competing explanations with fine-gained qualitative evidence. Recreating the chain of sequential events that lead to Indigenous land titling, which allows me to include historical narratives and a temporal dimension in the study, is fundamental to making strong causal arguments about the patterns of the outcome in each country (Brady and Collier 2010; Hall 2006). As explained above, I conduct in-depth case studies on a small number of key cases in each country, presenting them as within-case comparisons. The cases were chosen on the basis of geographic titling patterns under the logic of the comparative case study method (Snyder 2001, 96–97; van Evera 1997, 24–25). I compare regions with similar values on a multitude of key factors of interest but that vary on their location (e.g. inside or outside of the northern frontier zone in Brazil). My goal is to assess how differently situated Indigenous groups with similar characteristics might experience different treatment from the state regarding their land claims. In other words, I seek to assess nearly identical Indigenous land claims and whether one crucial difference accounts for the different experiences in outcomes.

My sources of data are more than 110 structured and semi-structured interviews with former and current presidents, Indigenous leaders, and other decision makers; copies of technical and administrative proceedings; ministerial and legal reports about Indigenous land titling; reports of externally funded land administration projects; and extensive field notes. I conducted in-depth interviews with state and Indigenous political elites and dozens of experts in all three countries. I interviewed those presidents that made the decision to title Indigenous lands in each country, as well as the Indigenous leaders and seasoned activists that were at the forefront of titling struggles. I also interviewed former and current military strategists and high-ranking military decision makers, senior political advisors (from the central government and from the Indigenous communities), high-ranking and middle-ranking government bureaucrats, national-level legislators, and subject matter experts (mainly scholars and policy analysts). These interviews provide firsthand accounts and insights into the motivations (or reservations) of political elites to title Indigenous lands, as well as political insiders' views regarding the factors that matter most when considering the decision to classify vast extensions of resource-rich territories as Indigenous lands. The themes and patterns I identified in these interviews allow me to go beyond assessing the conditions under which politicians title Indigenous lands and to specify exactly why state elites title in some places, and at certain times, but not in others. The Appendix F contains a list of interviews cited in this study.

Furthermore, I also draw on particular sources of qualitative evidence for specific country cases. In Brazil, I use documentation stored at the Ministry of Justice's National Archive and the Ministry of Defense's Documentation Center containing information about internal exchanges between government officers about the Yanomami Indigenous Land case in the 1985–1992 period. This information contains key pieces of evidence regarding the motivation of political elites to redesign and revamp the Yanomami territory, an important precedent used to create Indigenous lands in later years. The analysis of the sequential evolution of historical events allows me to show the significance of the interaction between state interests and external pressure in the decision to title Indigenous lands at moments of high external pressure. The trail of evidence also permits me to recreate the beliefs and expectations of political elites that led to changing the institution of Indigenous lands.

I conducted interviews with Indigenous leaders claiming land rights in the three country-cases to better understand the process from the perspective of Indigenous peoples. I also attended four conferences organized by civil society organizations and funded by NGOs that were held to pressure the government into titling Indigenous lands. In Brazil, I attended a meeting of Indigenous leaders from the northwestern Amazon that gathered in Santa Isabel do Rio Negro, Amazonas, in the spring of 2015. In Nicaragua, government representatives and local Indigenous leaders met in Bilwi, in the summers of 2012 and 2015. In Honduras, Indigenous leaders met with high- and mid-ranking government representatives in Catacamas, Olancho, in the summer of 2015. Detailed records about the motivations of Indigenous peoples to demand land rights inform my thinking. The Appendix B contains details about the administrative process that Indigenous peoples have to embark on to title Indigenous lands in each country.

I complement my findings with results from an original survey designed to measure political elites' attitudes on Indigenous land titling. I administered the survey to national-level legislators in all three countries and show the results for Nicaragua and Brazil. The results of the survey allow for replicable evidence of some of the main assertions about elite motivation that I make here. For Honduras, I provide supplementary evidence with results from the same survey instrument administered to middle- and high-ranking military officers enrolled in post-graduate level courses at the National Defense University.[6]

As mentioned before, Appendix A contains observational quantitative data to illustrate broad titling patterns, as well as to assess the plausibility of my argument and the persuasiveness of alternative explanations. The temporal and spatial statistical analysis I carry out in this book is based on a quantitative database that I constructed for Brazil. The database enables me to analyze the temporal evolution and spatial titling patterns in Brazil from 1988 until 2016. It allows me to examine the significance of state interests in titling, assessed by whether an Indigenous land is located inside the northern frontier zone or not. In addition, I can ascertain associations between external pressures, operationalized as the extent of news exposure of each Indigenous land claim, with the titling status. I control for other key explanations, such as demographic factors and the presence of wealth-generating resources.

Definition of Key Concepts

In this section, I clarify and delimit the boundaries of the core concepts used throughout the book. I draw a conceptual distinction between implementation and compliance. Although scholars sometimes use these concepts interchangeably, I delineate the contours of implementation narrowly to enhance clarity and contribute to scholarly understanding of the phenomena (Sartori 1970; Ostrom 2005).

I seek to explain the variance in the implementation of communal property rights recognized to Indigenous and other ethnic groups between states and within countries. These property rights are formal institutions that govern the access, use, management, and tenure of land and land-based natural resources that apply to members of state-recognized Indigenous peoples and ethnic groups. The formal recognition of rights (de jure rights) happens when the state adopts rules establishing them in its constitution or enacts legislation integrating international rules into the domestic legal apparatus.

Formal property rights are not self-enforcing. The central government needs to implement these formal laws that exist only on paper and turn them into active institutions (Carey 2000; Levitsky and Murillo 2009). Indigenous and ethnic communities may exercise de facto property rights, but the state may not support these informal institutions when challenged by outsiders (Ostrom 1990). For Indigenous peoples to hold clear, well-defined, and secure property rights in land, state authorities must first identify, delimit the physical boundaries of, and title communal lands. In fact, Indigenous peoples in the three countries under study demand secure property rights via the application of rights contained in the constitution and national laws, ILO Convention No. 169, and UNDRIP. For their implementation, the government must formalize communal land regimes in areas that Indigenous peoples claim as their ancestral homeland. Thus, implementation entails three interrelated political decisions that state elites must make: (1) whether to incorporate Indigenous peoples and ethnic groups into the modern state; (2) whether to do so by titling private property in land (freehold) or titling communal property based on customary use in the targeted area; and (3) whether to formally recognize customary land regimes at the village or inter-village level.[7]

Therefore, implementation happens when the government titles Indigenous land by issuing an official political document, such as a collective property title or a presidential decree approving the administrative proceeding that identifies and classifies an area as Indigenous land.[8] By backing a particular land claim, the central government officially cedes to Indigenous peoples or ethnic groups either user's rights or exclusive decision-making power over the land and natural resources in that land in perpetuity. Through that political action, the state also delegates power over individuals, assigns valuable resources, and devolves local administrative functions to local leaders. Put differently, the central government transfers a substantial amount of power to local groups and relinquishes direct control over people and territory at the lowest level of the political administrative structure of the state. Implementation entails the public recognition of customary land tenure through the award of a communal land title.

The territorial extension of the area officially classified as communal property is a core attribute of the political decision to title Indigenous lands. The state can either title at the village level, creating micro-territories, or at the inter-village level, creating macro-territories. In the first case, the state breaks Indigenous territories apart and allocates small communal lands at the village level to pre-authorized local political organizations. Alternatively, the state can amalgamate separate villages together and allocate a large continuous area with its surrounding environment to a pre-authorized political organization. Consequently, local elites have decision-making authority over large tracts of land and land-based natural resources. Although I mention titling of micro-territories, my analysis explains titling macro-territories. It is one thing to classify 49 hectares as Indigenous land, and quite another to title 9 million hectares as such.

By my definition, implementation is separate from rule compliance. Implementation entails a political act at a distinct moment in time. Compliance more broadly refers to the general accordance to formal institutions, be they constitutional or supranational, by the state across time (Risse, Ropp, and Sikkink 2013; Huneeus 2011; Simmons 1998, 2009). Compliance includes cases of relatively high degrees of voluntary conformity to rules without much need for periodic enforcement (Ostrom 2005, 167–70, 265–67; Levi 1989). The concept of compliance includes cases of rule-abiding behavior rooted in habit, reciprocity, or ethical reasons (Amengual 2016, 30–31; Levitsky and Murillo 2009). Compliance requires self-initiated and routinized behavior on the part of the state; it happens when political elites internalize rules and abide by them with a high degree of self-commitment. Instances of self-enforcing formal institutions are rare and unexpected in asymmetrical political relations, particularly when compliance with formal institutions leads to a substantial redistribution of power and resources from well-connected and wealthy groups to the poor and marginalized.

I focus on the politics of implementation, rather than the politics of compliance, because Indigenous land titling is the necessary *first* step that the state must take before investing in incentivizing compliance with land tenure institutions (Ostrom 1990). In other words, aside from the difficulties of accurately measuring compliant behavior, Indigenous land titling is necessary for the initial clarification and specific delineation of property rights on the ground. Once property rights are clearly defined at the local level, questions of compliance with these property rights by ethnic insiders and outsiders arise. In sum, implementation leads to clear or well-defined property rights, which is a necessary, although insufficient, condition for compliance.

Finally, each of the behaviors that involve implementation and continued compliance are highly contested among groups and exceedingly complex in practice. Precisely because I recognize these complexities, I focus on the single task of titling, which in itself is a conceptual category that can encompass different actions and stages. To document titling empirically, I distill the sequential political steps the central government needs to take to achieve full implementation into conceptual categories that are meaningful and applicable across countries. The challenge is to quantify pending and approved Indigenous land claims. In some countries, like Brazil, the task is relatively uncomplicated: FUNAI publishes and updates a list of all recognized Indigenous land claims, specifying their status in the administrative proceeding that leads to titling. Therefore, the number of land claims "under study" is readily quantifiable in Brazil.

In Honduras and Nicaragua, the quantification is not straightforward. A single Indigenous community may claim customary rights over a substantial portion of the country's territory, a claim that the government may not recognize as legitimate or politically feasible. A case in point is the Miskito land claim in eastern Honduras. Since the 1980s, the Miskito group has claimed land rights over La Mosquitia, a historical territory that spans about 2 million hectares (equivalent to about 18 percent of the country's territory), situated in the present-day provinces of Colón, Olancho, and Gracias a Dios (Bryan and Wood 2015, Ch. 6; Chapin and Threlkeld 2001). The government, however, decides where and how much land to title for the Miskito and does not necessarily take into account the entire extension of the historic Miskito claim. In this case, I take a predetermined land area in the Gracias a

Dios province only as the baseline for measuring progress. In the Nicaraguan case, Indigenous communities in the west claim land rights based on historic communal property titles, known as colonial titles, some of which date back to Spanish colonial times. In the east, although some Indigenous groups claim rights based on property titles from the early twentieth century, most substantiate their claims on ancestral possession without having any legal documents.[9] I take the old colonial titles from the west and the government's decision to classify blocks of land as Indigenous in the east as the baseline for my analysis. By doing so, I can include much of what Indigenous peoples claim in practice, along with the government's decisions and directives. That is, I can separate cases when the government is ignoring claims altogether from instances of feet dragging in claims processing. In that way, I minimize as much as possible measurement errors when ascertaining much of what the government does.

Based on this analysis, I develop a strategy for operationalizing and measuring implementation, conceptualized as a dichotomous variable. No implementation occurs when the government ignores land claims or colonial titles registered in the land cadaster without titling in modern times (after the 1990s). Implementation happens when the state has demarcated the physical boundaries and concluded the technical proceedings by issuing a communal land title. That is, implementation refers to the act of issuing an official paper title or presidential decree that approves the classification process. This final political act provides formal land tenure security to a state-recognized Indigenous or ethnic group and officially formalizes the application of a differentiated land regime in the designated area. Along with a description of the titling proceedings in each country, the Appendix C contains a simple scale and a full explanation about my operationalization strategy, the number of observations in each category per country, and the sources of information.

Plan of the Book

This book proceeds in three parts: Theoretical Framing (Part I), The Politics of Indigenous Land Titling in the Americas (Part II), and Conclusion (Part III). Following this introduction in Part I comes Chapter 2, which provides a brief overview of Indigenous land and resource rights in each country under study. In Chapter 3, I proceed to fully develop a model of Indigenous land titling and outline a series of hypotheses about the location, timing, and rate of titling. I contrast my explanation with that of leading frameworks. The analytical focus is the spatial and temporal patterns of Indigenous land titling within countries and across states. I explain why state elites title vast territories to some Indigenous communities, but not others.

Part II is the empirical backbone of the book. Chapters 4, 5, and 6 present evidence supporting my titling model from Nicaragua, Honduras, and Brazil, respectively. Each chapter begins with the portrayal of wider patterns of Indigenous land titling in each country. The cases exhibit a variety of political and economic conditions, including levels of economic development and administrative capacity, relative strengths of interest groups pushing against titling, and strength of transnational advocacy campaigns pushing for titling. I show that although all countries have formalized communal property regimes locally, titling has varied according to the priorities established by institutionally motivated political elites, not by the relative strength of local or global activists, competing interest groups, or administrative weakness. First, contrary to predominant explanations that emphasize social activism as the main driver of the phenomenon under study, titling neither requires nor directly corresponds to grassroots or external pressure. Second, unlike arguments that emphasize administrative capacity, titling occurs in poor countries with flawed bureaucracies following state impulses to reach remote areas. Finally, it occurs despite the resistance of strong and powerful economic groups that compete for the right to possess or extract wealth-producing, land-based resources.

Drawing from qualitative and quantitative data, in Chapter 4, I present a case study of Nicaragua, where the central government has titled vast areas as communal lands. I analyze a matched comparison of two provinces that experience different titling outcomes, while controlling for the existence of external pressure, as well as variables typically associated with land demands and governmental implementation practices such as demographic, economic, and environmental factors. In the within-country comparisons, I isolated the effect that differences in location and the legacy of Indigenous resistance had on the formalization (or not) of communal property regimes. Through detailed process tracing, I conclude that the dramatic regional differences in titling practices stem from political elites' motivation to thwart massive Indigenous defiance of state power. Indigenous land demands originating from the east, where there was an intense war in the 1980s, were quickly resolved after the leader of the revolutionary government in the 1980s regained power in 2007. Indigenous land claims originating from the west, where there was no Indigenous resistance, are ignored. The central government's preemptive actions against Indigenous resistance drives titling patterns. In sum, the Nicaraguan case shows that Indigenous land titling can be motivated by state interests to maintain internal order.

Based on national-level quantitative evidence, Chapter 5 illustrates how the Honduran state regularized about 10 percent of the national territory as Indigenous lands from 2012 to early 2015. The central government titled extensive communal lands in timber-rich zones of the remote Gracias a Dios province. I conduct a controlled paired comparison of the state's titling practices in the east with those in the west. Although land claims from the east and the west are otherwise similar, the central government designs, delimits, and titles communal property very differently. The Miskito from the east, I argue, obtain title to enormous territories because the state has weak control of that remote province, which is a popular trans-shipment point for drugs en route from South America to the United States (DoS 2014, UNODC 2013). Political elites identify and title extensive forest lands, driven by the need to reinforce state power over vulnerable territory. Contemporary drug trafficking activities weaken the power and control of the state over the Gracias a Dios province. Where the power of the state is threatened by drug lords, political elites title Indigenous lands to extend its reach. The Honduran case shows that medium to high levels of internal threats are sufficient to trigger state elites to title Indigenous lands.

In Chapter 6, I analyze titling patterns in Brazil, with a special focus on the Amazon region. For the Brazil case study, I combine a unique set of observational data to propose and assess arguments about the motivation of political elites to allocate vast resource-rich lands to Indigenous groups. Based on an analysis of the Yanomami case, which served as a precedent for resolving later Indigenous land claims in the Amazon, I am able to isolate the causal impact of the state's security concerns on the demarcation of lands for Indigenous peoples. In situations with high external pressure, land titling takes place only after political elites guarantee fundamental military interests. I support my claim that the need to safeguard military interests takes precedence over external pressure by examining in detail the sequence of historical events that led to the decision to redesign the Yanomami land and by exploring the motivations that underlie Indigenous land titling in vast, mineral-rich areas on the Amazonian frontier. To better understand the importance of state interests, I conduct a controlled paired comparison of two sub-regions of the Amazon River Basin: the frontier zone that experiences high titling rates and the heart of the Amazon that has drastically lower titling rates. The Brazil case shows that state interest heavily mediates transnational activism.

In Part III, I conclude by probing the explanatory power of my state-centric theory to explain the titling of vast extensions of Indigenous lands in other regions of the Global South: Africa and Southeast Asia. In Chapter 7, I explore how my explanation travels outside of Latin America through case studies of countries with analogous formal institutional features in Kenya and Indonesia. Then, I return to the problem of weak institutions and articulate the consequences of Indigenous land titling for contemporary state-building practices and the effective realization of Indigenous peoples' self-determination rights.

2
Communal Property Rights of Indigenous Peoples and Ethnic Groups

Their Country-Specific Shape

I begin the analysis of Indigenous land titling by specifying the type of property regime that Nicaragua, Honduras, and Brazil recognize to Indigenous peoples and ethnic collectivities in law. While property regimes can arise from the state or from society (Murtazshvili and Murtazshvili 2017), this study focuses exclusively on the role of the government in allocating rights over land and resources, that is, property rights that come from the state.

As explained by Ostrom, "property rights define actions that individuals can take in relation to other individuals regarding some 'thing'" (2003, 249). The government can bestow property rights to the state itself, private individuals or corporations, and communal groups based (or not) on ethnicity.[1] In formal institutions, governments specify the set of rights that allow recipients to take an action and others the duty to respect that action. Usually, there are five types of property rights to land bestowed to Indigenous peoples and ethnic groups in Latin America, the right to access the land; to withdraw or obtain resources from the land; to manage the physical area of, or resources produced by, the land; to determine who can access and enjoy the land and its products; and the right of alienation, that is, the right to sell, lease, gift, or in other form transfer the mentioned rights (Ostrom 2003, 251).

Much of the literature about Indigenous land rights equates property rights to the four-pronged set of rights of access, withdrawal, management, and exclusion of others from the land granted to a group or community, without the right of alienation. The right of alienation would turn the land regime into private property because property-rights holders are full owners that can trade their interests in the land for money or other goods (Ostrom 2003, 250). In other words, private property is frequently defined with the right of alienation.

The "bundle" of property rights that states formally grant varies across countries (Roldán Ortega 2002). In turn, differences in property rights translate to differences in degrees of self-government. On the one hand, central governments can provide a greater degree of collective control over land and natural resources. On the other hand, national legislators can give the rights of access and use but very limited or nonexistent managerial rights (Ostrom and Hess 2007, Agrawal and Ostrom 2001, 491). Table 2.1 summarizes country variations in recognized property rights.

Nicaragua recognizes a bundle of four property rights as listed above—access, use, management, and exclusion—per the Constitution (1987), the Autonomy Law (1987), and the Communal Property Regime Law (2003). Similarly, Indigenous peoples and ethnic groups in Honduras have the right of access, use, management, and exclusion per the Constitution (1982), the Agrarian Modernization Law (1992), and the Property Law (2004). In these two countries, the state recognizes property rights to all groups that self-identify as Indigenous or Afro-descendant people and that make ancestral or customary claims to communal territory (Hooker 2010).

By contrast, property rights for Indigenous peoples are weaker in Brazil: all areas classified as Indigenous Land are federal property where the state retains management and exclusion rights for itself per the Constitution (1988) and the Indian Statute (1973). In Brazil, Indigenous peoples are not owners of the land but authorized users. They have rights to enter and to harvest some, but not all, products from the land's surface. An important legal limitation for Indigenous peoples is that property rights over the land's surface do not extend to the subsoil and to energy-producing resources.

Additionally, the subjects of communal property rights also vary across states. Although Indigenous peoples and human rights experts have argued

Table 2.1 Formally Recognized Communal Property Rights of Indigenous Peoples and Ethnic Groups in Central America and Brazil

Property Right	Nicaragua	Honduras	Brazil
Access	X	X	X
Use	X	X	X
Management	X	X	Retained by the state
Exclusion	X	X	Retained by the state
Alienation	Not granted	Not granted	Not granted

that Indigenous peoples should not be conflated with ethnic groups,[2] states in Central America make no legal or practical distinction between communal land claims arising from Indigenous peoples and those from ethnic groups. In stark contrast, Brazil recognizes a specific set of communal property rights to Indigenous peoples, which do not extend to Afro-descendant groups, who have a separate set of property rights by law (Leite 2015).

In all cases, the state recognizes to members of a clearly identified Indigenous or ethnic group the legal right to use land and land-based natural resources in perpetuity, plus the right to petition to the state the exclusion of nonmembers of that group from using and benefiting from the land. These groups do not have the right of alienation of land or land rights: the sale or transfer of land by donation or mortgage is illegal. The state restricts market forces and removes areas titled as communal land from the land market. Hence, neither individual members, nor the community, have full ownership rights.

Indigenous peoples and ethnic groups in Latin America have different sets of property rights. Indigenous and ethnic groups in Central America are proprietors that have a more comprehensive set of rights over land and resources. In Brazil, only Indigenous peoples are authorized users with much weaker property rights. Accordingly, the state retains a higher degree of control over Indigenous peoples in Brazil than in Central America.

3
The Argument
The Crucial Role of State Interests

> Titling communal lands prevents conflict and establishes new institutions that facilitate the governability of the region.
> Paul Oquist Kelley, August 6, 2015, Nicaragua

This chapter develops a model to explain the patterns of Indigenous land titling in Latin America. I set out to achieve three goals. First, I present the prevailing approaches that seek to explain Indigenous land titling and draw out their observable implications. Second, I identify evidence that reveals the limitations of these specific hypotheses and show that they do not fully account for the variance of outcomes observed in Nicaragua, Honduras, and Brazil. Third, I propose a new, complementary approach that centers on the preferences of state elites. My explanation highlights the role of state interests as a mediating factor that accounts for why and how Indigenous land titling happens.

Specifically, I show that transnational constructivism, social movement theory, economic structuralism, and administrative theory provide important insights but do not fully explain patterns of titling behavior within and across countries. These patterns are (a) the sudden outbursts of systematic Indigenous land titling in Nicaragua and Honduras in 2007 and 2012 respectively, (b) the slow and unsystematic titling in Brazil since the 1990s, and (c) a striking concentration of titled Indigenous lands in remote regions with little state presence.

Whereas the first two approaches stress external and bottom-up pressure as the motivating factors that drive titling behavior, the third emphasizes internal economic forces against titling. Accordingly, they anticipate that the outcomes largely depend on the underlying motivations of societal groups, be they external or internal to the polity, and their normative and material power and influence over political decision makers. Specifically, transnational constructivists and social movement theory predict Indigenous land titling to disperse in geographical localities targeted by global or local activists, not the clear regional differences in outcomes observed in the countries. By contrast, the third approach anticipates little titling because of competing economic interests, instead of the quick-fire and systematic action observed in eastern Nicaragua and Honduras. Finally, the fourth approach expects worse outcomes in the remote regions of countries with little institutional capacity, instead of the concentrated titling bursts observed in distant regions of weaker states.

To be more concrete, transnational constructivism and social movement theories anticipate that the sustained efforts of global and local activists pushing for Indigenous land titling will produce government action in countries and regions they target. Several factors should increase the interconnectedness and influence of global activists: the increasing density of global linkages; the proliferation of issue-specific conferences that link activists, donors, and government representatives; the salience and growing importance of environmental problems that require transnational action; and technological improvements that aid the flow and exchange of information. In turn, these global activists acquire more legitimacy and material support to pressure governments to implement Indigenous land and resource rights domestically.

Transnational constructivists expect political elites in targeted countries to cede to external material and normative pressure. As globalization intensifies and global activists gain influence and material leverage, scholars anticipate that political decision makers will be more responsive to external pressure and activists' strategies. For instance, in the Brazilian Amazon, the dense and well-funded activist network that works on environmental protection and Indigenous rights should have been able to systematically push their preferences about titling, which should have resulted in much more steady and homogenous action in that region. Likewise, pressure from transnational activists should have resulted in uniform levels of titling in vulnerable, aid-dependent, and peripheral countries, such as Nicaragua and Honduras, rather than the concentration of titled Indigenous lands in one region, and their absence in others. Similarly, social movement theorists expect political elites to respond to the mobilization tactics of organized civil society. Hence, titling is expected to correlate with the strength and interconnectedness of grassroots organizations.

Alternatively, economic structuralists focus on internal political dynamics. These scholars stress the counter-pressures that Indigenous peoples face to secure communal land titles. This resistance comes from powerful economic interests that vie for the land and land-based natural resources that Indigenous groups claim as their ancestral homeland. Because economic interest groups have substantial clout and prestige, they gain access to political elites and are able to shape political decision-making in their favor. Consequently, economic structuralist accounts predict very little Indigenous land titling, especially in countries with steep socioeconomic inequality and high levels of elite corruption. If this account were correct, these powerful and influential economic interest groups should have induced political decision makers to block titling efforts, especially when deciding over property claims concerning land rich in valuable commodities and wealth-producing resources. Accordingly, these economic counter-pressures should have typically resulted in much less Indigenous land titling within and across countries over time.

Finally, administrative theorists foresee faster and systematic Indigenous land titling in more advanced countries and in localities closer to the centers of power, but not in poor nations nor in the borderlands. These accounts do not directly examine the motivations for or resistance to implementing property rights. Instead, this approach contains an implicit assumption that the state wants to title Indigenous lands but cannot.[1]

As such, scholars stress the differential capacity of the state's central bureaucracy to penetrate the national territory. The state's power emanates from the center of the polity and expands to peripheral regions. Therefore, scholars expect that titling will be more faithful and faster in countries with higher institutional capacity and in localities proximate to the centers of power, while being spotty in weak and poor nations, especially in remote places. To illustrate, countries with higher bureaucratic capacity like Brazil should have engaged in more advanced titling than Nicaragua and Honduras, two countries with less capacity. In addition, Indigenous land claims that are closer to cities like Manaus, where the Brazilian state has greater institutional presence, should have had higher titling rates than claims that overlap with the northern frontier zone, where the state is barely present.

While these approaches have made important contributions to our understanding, there is still a remarkable variation in Indigenous land titling in Latin America that remains unexplained. Consequently, the third section of this chapter develops a new model that specifies the motivation of key actors to account for titling patterns. My framework stresses that the institutional interests of government officials provide a crucial, overlooked factor that shapes Indigenous land titling. State interests decisively affect when, where, and how titling happens. As explained in detail below, state elites title Indigenous lands to secure internal order and extend the state's territorial power in remote regions. Political elites title Indigenous lands in a manner that ensures the continuation of the state in these remote places.

Explaining Indigenous Land Titling: Predominant Approaches

Why do states title communal land to some Indigenous groups but not others? What explains the striking patterns of Indigenous land titling across countries, within them, and over time? Most existing studies propose one of four general accounts to explain titling outcomes. I label these approaches transnational constructivism, social movement theory, economic structuralism, and administrative theory. The first three approaches identify civil society as the main locus of causality and de-emphasize the role of the state. Conversely, the third approach focuses on the state and its bureaucracy and de-emphasizes societal factors and the motivations of actors within the state. The first framework depicts politics as a process by which government action, or inaction, is determined by unmediated demands rooted in international civil society (transnational constructivism) or in domestic interest groups (social movement theory and economic structuralism). In contrast, administrative theory emphasizes the capacity of government bureaucracies as a key factor shaping outcomes. These frameworks provide valuable insights about the politics of Indigenous land titling but leave unexplained the notable variations observed in the timing, rate, and geographic concentration of titled lands. I examine each account in turn to assess their strengths and shortcomings.

Transnational Constructivism: External Pressures Drive Titling

Perhaps the most influential argument today emphasizes the strength of transnational normative and material pressures in persuading state behavior. Transnational constructivists maintain that a vibrant global civil society drives Indigenous land titling by promoting the enactment and implementation of rights that Indigenous peoples demand. First, transnational activists can persuade states to incorporate new ideas into international institutions (Brysk 1996; Finnemore and Sikkink 2001, 398–400; Sikkink 2005; Graubart 2008, Ch. 2; Eisenstadt 2013, Ch. 1; Escárcega 2013; Gómez Isa 2016). Second, these activists invest resources to socialize state elites to internalize these new norms and enshrine them in domestic legal frameworks (Risse, Ropp, and Sikkink 2013, 5–22; Goodman and Jinks 2013, Ch. 2). Finally, a global network of NGOs employ moral and material pressure to push government officials to observe these new institutions and activist's preferences (Keck and Sikkink 1998; Tarrow 2005, 24–34, 2013, Ch. 5; Simmons 2009).

For instance, Alison Brysk highlights how Indigenous activists successfully changed an assimilationist paradigm in international discourse and introduced the right of Indigenous peoples to land and natural resources in international treaties (Brysk 2000; Morgan 2004). Scholars often stress that contemporary developments in international and constitutional law are responsive to and reflect the aspirations of Indigenous peoples to self-determination and its practical application, self-government (Yashar 2005, 1999; van Cott 2000; Anaya 2004; Sieder 2002, Ch. 7; Rodríguez-Piñero 2005; Rodríguez-Garavito and Arenas 2005, 241–50; Silva 2009; Åhrén 2016, Ch. 5–6, 8; Wheatley 2005; Barelli 2016, Ch. 5). In this view, regardless of the initial preferences of political elites, state actors adopt the new social norms as a prerequisite for good standing in the international community (Goodman and Jinks 2013; Risse, Ropp, and Sikkink 2013). Thus, formal institutions are more than mere cheap talk (Gleditsch et al. 2016).

Margaret Keck and Kathryn Sikkink argue that transnational activists drive the implementation of new progressive institutions, especially in image-conscious countries. Using Brazil as a case study, scholars argue that activist networks mount effective global campaigns that lead to Indigenous land titling by exchanging information, using material resources, and high-level lobbying (Keck and Sikkink 1998, 5–13, 23–29, 121–63, 202–209). Titled Indigenous lands result from the demands of an internationally linked civil society: political elites respond to social pressure and act under the logic of appropriateness, even when doing so goes against their long-held preferences and short-term interests. The source of transnational activists' power resides in their international prestige, use and management of information, and ability to frame contentious issues in ways that advance their preferred solutions or policy prescriptions (Keck and Sikkink 1998,

30; Tarrow and McAdam 2005, Ch. 6; Bennett 2005, Ch. 9; Della Porta and Tarrow 2005; Sikkink 2002, 303). That is, the influence of transnational networks stems from being better informed and interconnected, which allows them to take full advantage of the technological advances of globalization (Evans 2000; Harper 2001; Andolina, Laurie, and Radcliffe 2009; Wortham 2013).

Global activists also press international financial institutions to support their policy preferences, and, in turn these financial institutions effectively incentivize political elites to observe them (O'Brien et al. 2000; Riker 2002; Chiriboga Vega 2001; Hochstetler and Keck 2007, Ch. 4; Sieder 2010, Ch. 7). As Kathryn Sikkink puts it, "movements calling for norms that challenge powerful economic interests and political institutions will face great barriers, but ultimately, interests are not completely given, but are interpreted, and the norms structure is part of what helps states (and firms) interpret their interests" (2002, 303). In this way, transnational activists transform political elites' understandings of state interests and affect state behavior toward norm observance (Smith, Chatfield, and Pagnucco 1997, 59–77). Scholars argue that transnational activists can impose their ideational blueprints and preferences on states. Figure 3.1 illustrates this approach.

Transnational constructivists, therefore, expect political elites in peripheral countries to act in line with the advances of global activists. The rate, timing, and geographical concentration of titled Indigenous lands should depend on the material and moral pressures that transnational advocates exert on political elites (Keck and Sikkink 1998). As globalization advances, global civil society gathers more prestige, material resources, and persuasive strength. Therefore, in countries that global activists target, political elites should adopt the substantive content of external demands (Risse, Ropp, and Sikkink 2013, Ch. 1). In places with a long history of transnational advocacy campaigns that focus on a particular region, such as the Brazilian Amazon, there should be in-country variation that is a direct function of the geographic focus of external tactics and strategies. Above all, political elites should focus on titling lands in targeted geographies, at the country level or within regions in a country, to reproduce the substantive policy prescriptions of transnational activists.

Global Titling Demands ⟶ *Titling Outcomes*

Figure 3.1 Transnational Constructivism

The transnational constructivist approach is successful at explaining the ratification of international norms. Scholars are correct in highlighting the shift away from overt assimilationist ideas and the recognition of Indigenous peoples' land and resource rights in international fora, the cornerstone of Indigenous self-determination rights (Anaya 2004, Ch. 3; Xanthaki 2007, Ch. 6). For instance, the United Nations and the International Labour Organization have formally recognized the collective rights of Indigenous peoples to territory, self-determination (self-government), and cultural integrity (non-assimilation). Articulated as a precondition for cultural survival, the right to territory is a broad legal concept that encompasses the total environment of traditionally accessed, used, occupied, or owned land (UNDRIP Art. 26; ILO Convention No. 169, Art. 13.2).

But Indigenous land rights are not above the prerogatives of states, even in these progressive international instruments. In fact, countries have strengthened provisions that guarantee the state's territorial integrity (Jetschke and Liese 2013, 35–42; Zacher 2001). In addition, states have severely restricted the notion of Indigenous self-determination and inserted ambiguities in the language of treaties to enhance sovereign state powers and reduce Indigenous autonomy (Gilbert 2006, 201–208; Xanthaki 2007; Engle 2010, 6–9; Altamirano Jiménez 2013, Ch. 1; Kuokkanen 2019, 30–38). Despite advances, states ensure that international instruments guarantee their continuation as the preeminent actor in international politics.

Transnational advocacy networks are less successful at ensuring the effective implementation of international treaties with progressive ideas (Schwarz 2002). Since international human rights treaties are not self-enforcing (Simmons 2009), governments must make decisive action to implement them on the ground. It is unlikely that state elites will internalize Indigenous land and resource rights; after all, Indigenous land titling may entail the allocation of valuable economic assets to marginalized groups and devolution of substantial political power at the local level. To hold states accountable to international legal standards and induce governments to bridge the gap between promises made and actual practice, activists would have to consistently exert pressure. Accordingly, transnational advocates would have to invest enormous resources, normative capital, prestige, and material wealth to push states to title Indigenous lands.

Transnational activists cannot easily pay attention to the minutiae of policy implementation across and inside countries. Even when activist networks are numerous and densely connected, they lack the cognitive capacity to process the information necessary to push political elites toward implementation in all of the cases and at all times (c.f. Weyland 2014, 48–50, 57–59, 69). Activists simply do not have the ability, nor sufficient material resources, to pressure states to resolve hundreds, and potentially thousands, of specific communal land claims. Instead, they must strategize and focus the limited resources that they do possess on a few emblematic cases to rally widespread public support and push for implementation in concrete instances. Realistically, transnational activists can only be effective in titling a few high-profile land claims that catch worldwide attention and capture international headlines. They are not able to effectively encourage implementation all of the time, in all of the cases, especially in continent-size countries like Brazil, nor afford to invest limited resources in non-priority countries, like Nicaragua or Honduras.

Moreover, I have not observed the spatial and temporal patterns expected by transnational constructivists. My research does not find dispersed titling across targeted countries or regions, as this approach predicts, but rather stark regional differences in outcomes, especially in Central America. Similarly puzzling are the uneven titling patterns found in the Brazilian Amazon. The dense concentration of Indigenous land titles in one sub-region, but not others, suggests that external normative and material campaigns are not the cause behind the phenomenon. In addition, Indigenous land titling should have followed external titling campaigns. But in Nicaragua, the second poorest country in the Americas, transnational activists were not able to persuade or push the state to title Indigenous lands after democratization in the 1990s, when political elites were expected to be more receptive to external demands because of the transition from authoritarian rule to democracy. Instead, the opposite is true: the government began titling after 2007, when external pressures were low, and the regime changed from a democracy to an autocracy. In other words, the prestige and material resources of transnational activists were not necessary for the central government to begin titling.

Finally, observable evidence does not support transnational constructivists' predictions about the acceptance of external normative models in targeted countries. The way that central governments implemented Indigenous land and resource rights on the ground falls short of activists' expectations. Instead of enhancing Indigenous self-determination by allowing for greater Indigenous self-government, as transnational activists and Indigenous communities have demanded for decades (Hannum 2011), the Central American states have superimposed a communal property regime structure that diminishes local autonomy. The evidence suggests that the form of Indigenous land titling in practice does not fit the predictions of transnational constructivists.

To be sure, external pressure *is* an important factor for the implementation of Indigenous land and resource rights that I take into account in my model. However, this factor alone is not sufficient to explain titling outcomes. Brazil, a case that transnational constructivists use to support their social pressure theories, illustrates my point. Although external campaigns were important in beginning titling large Indigenous lands under Brazilian democracy, transnational constructivists' expectations of wholesale adoptions of external normative prescriptions have not been borne out. In this case, international pressures were especially high following the return of democracy after 1985 and in the early 1990s. Since then, Indigenous land and resource rights have gained traction in international forums and diplomatic discourse, globalization has intensified, and transnational activists' prestige has increased. Nevertheless, political decision makers have created administrative backlogs and have withheld the approval of technical titling proceedings, which indicates lack of political will to engage in Indigenous land titling.[2]

Moreover, political elites have not fully adopted the externally promoted models for Indigenous land titling. Instead, the government thwarted external pressures and insisted on securing the state's sovereignty interests *before* titling. The state modified the titling model preferred by external activists to further its own institutional objectives, namely to extend the state's apparatus inside Indigenous lands. In addition to external pressure, we need to pay closer attention to the state's sovereignty interests to understand fully why and how Indigenous land titling takes place. My own explanation complements transnational constructivism by showing that state interest mediates external pressures and substantively shapes outcomes.

Social Movement Theory: Local Social Pressures Motivate Titling

Social movement theorists argue that the rationale for Indigenous land titling can be broadly categorized as a response to demands by sub-national Indigenous and ethnic groups (Martí i Puig 2007; Reyes-García et al. 2014, 285–87). Observers have argued that central governments listened to

Indigenous peoples and their allies, who have demanded for decades the effective recognition of collective ownership of ancestral territories with their natural resources, as a way to protect their land from dispossession and outside encroachment. Kröger and Lalander (2016) particularly stressed that Indigenous land titles are the culmination of major political mobilizations by Indigenous communities against capitalist expansion, in particular, agribusiness and land grabbers. According to this perspective, the government responded to Indigenous peoples' demands to help mitigate inter-group land conflict (Kröger and Lalander 2016, 691–93).

Another mechanism that generates Indigenous land titles, according to this perspective, is the conciliatory lobbying strategies that Indigenous leaders employ to persuade bureaucrats of the cultural validity of their territorial claims and the environmental benefits it provides (Jung 2008; Stahler-Sholk, Kuecker, and Vanden 2008; Jackson and Warren 2003, 553–54). According to Gómez Suárez, convincing ethno-environmental arguments produce titles over extensive lands (2004, 317). More broadly, Warren and Jackson (2003, 8–11) argue that Indigenous leaders have been able to establish their legitimacy through the rhetoric of cultural continuity when advocating for local autonomy, which has allowed them to gain official recognition, protection, and access to large territories. Figure 3.2 illustrates the argument.

However, land conflicts are spread throughout countries like Honduras and Nicaragua and the government's response varies from neglect to repression. In fact, civil-society organizations that represent Lenca people in Honduras, the largest and most organized Indigenous group in the country, have been demanding territorial rights since the mid-1980s (Mollett 2013, 1231; Slack 2009, 117–21). Government officials have ignored their relentless mobilization. Moreover, although Indigenous and ethnic people organized in civil-society organizations have couched their territorial claims on environmental conservation and cultural continuity arguments, the Honduran government has mostly resisted these demands. For instance, the Organization for Ethnic Communal Development (ODECO) has established working relationships with government officials to defend the territory

Figure 3.2 Social Movement Theory

of Garifuna people with limited success (Anderson 2009, 56–57). The same applies to claims that Indigenous peoples make in the southern and eastern states of Brazil (IBGE 2012). In Brazil, the government criminalizes land claims made by Indigenous peoples outside of Amazonia despite decades of mobilization. In particular, the state vehemently rejects extensive territorial claims in Mato Grosso do Sul by the Guarani, the largest Indigenous group in the country (CIMI 2005–2017; IBGE 2011). Another case in point is Chile, where the government has heavily repressed the territorial claims of the Mapuche, the most numerous, vocal, and politically involved Indigenous group in the country (see, Meza 2009; Carruthers and Rodriguez 2009; Haughney 2012; Bauer 2016).

If social movement theory was correct, the state would respond positively to peaceful protest strategies of Indigenous peoples. That is, political elites would agree to title Indigenous lands to protect Indigenous cultural rights and reap the environmental benefits that communal property can provide. Instead, state elites disregard and sometimes even criminalize Indigenous groups that make territorial claims. In short, social movement theory has limitations in explaining the extent to which the state would repress, rather than legitimize, Indigenous land claims.

Economic Structuralism: Economic Interests Hinder Titling

Economic structuralists posit that powerful economic interest groups influence political decision makers and hinder the implementation of Indigenous land and resource rights (Carvalho 2000, 462–64; Brinks and Botero 2014, Ch. 10; Sandbrook 2014). Analysts who pursue this line of argumentation emphasize the clout of interest-based alliances led by sectors within business and agriculture, perhaps allied with politicians in power, which identify Indigenous land titling as a costly political decision that disproportionately hurts them. Scholars attribute political decision-making on land titling to behind-the-scenes economic influence, especially in highly unequal countries with endemic corruption in the top echelons of political office. Political elites drag their feet precisely because Indigenous groups claim exclusive property rights over vast areas rich in resources coveted by economic elites (Juris 2008; Postero 2007; Rice 2012). Under this approach, the power of economic interest groups is hegemonic in the politics of Indigenous land titling: they dissuade, halt, hinder, or altogether reverse outcomes.

In this view, the state will not title vast Indigenous lands when economic interest groups pressure political decision makers to halt the process, or when the government faces substantial economic costs from doing so (Pacheco 2009, 325–54; Weaver et al. 2012). In countries mired in corruption, economic interests have overwhelming influence over political elites' decisions. Scholars who stress economic influences in political decision-making expect land titling only in areas that have little economic value, such as barren lands or areas already designated for environmental conservation (Hale 2011, 200; Stocks 2005, 97; Martí i Puig 2007, 82–83; Brondo 2013). Under this logic, political elites ignore or deny claims in resource-rich areas that hold untapped economic potential, such as mineral-rich zones, agricultural land, or timber-producing areas (Assies 2008; Postero 2013, 25–50; Hall, Hirsch, and Li 2011; Doane 2012). Figure 3.3 illustrates the argument.

Yet contrary to the expectations of economic structural accounts, many areas that political elites have permanently assigned to Indigenous groups have enormous economic value. Political officials are very much aware that Indigenous peoples demand land rights over extensive territories with potential for economic exploitation. Examples abound in Brazil, especially in the northern frontier zone, where titled Indigenous lands have a plethora of untapped and easily extractable mineral resources. Famous, although somewhat exceptional examples are the Yanomami, Alto Rio Negro, and Vale do Javari areas (Chapter 6). These huge territorial units, which together add up to over 26 million hectares—an area larger than Ecuador, in South America—hold substantial deposits of uranium, niobium, diamonds, gold, and aluminum. Vale do Javari has verifiable oil and gas deposits.

The expectation of economic structuralists finds no evidentiary support in Nicaragua and Honduras. In Nicaragua, the central government quickly titled over 1.6 million hectares of timber-producing and agricultural land to Indigenous and ethnic groups; these areas do not overlap with environmental protection zones (Chapter 4). In Honduras, continuous titled areas

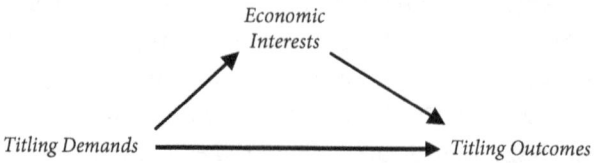

Figure 3.3 Economic Structuralism

that are economically suitable for timber production and agriculture extend to over a million hectares (Chapter 5). Therefore, even in Nicaragua and Honduras—two of the most corrupt countries in the Americas where economic elites seem to have a disproportionate advantage in the influencing of political decision makers—the state has quickly titled extensive and continuous swaths of economically profitable areas as Indigenous lands (Transparency International 2014; World Bank WGI 2015; Brondo 2013, Ch. 9).[3]

If the economic structural expectations were correct, the state would title only few such areas to Indigenous groups. That is, political elites would resist Indigenous land titling to privilege powerful economic actors that demand the right to exploit resources from these lands or even own them. Instead, central governments have used the power of the state to disregard powerful economic interests. By removing a substantial percentage of the national territory from the land market, state elites work against the basic interests of well-connected economic groups; after all, Indigenous land titling constrains market forces by making the sale, transfer, or mortgage of land illegal (Boone 2019, 390). In short, economic structuralism does not always explain the extent to which the state titles Indigenous lands, nor the type of lands that states classify as such.

Administrative Theory: Titling as a Function of Bureaucratic Capacity

Whereas transnational constructivism and economic structuralism emphasize societal forces that directly affect Indigenous land titling, administrative theory focuses on the bureaucratic apparatus of the state. This framework does not directly examine the motivations (or objections) that political elites might have to title Indigenous lands. Instead, scholars consider the question of motivations a moot point and assume that states want to implement the law. Even if political decision makers were willing to title quickly and systematically across the national territory, the argument goes, they would not be able to do so because Latin American states lack the required administrative capacity. Studies often point to the fact that developing countries fall far short of the postulates of a meritocratic and cohesive bureaucracy typified by Max Weber (Migdal 1988, 13–22). In particular, Latin American states are considered to be "paper leviathans" that have barely managed to assure their basic geographical shape and to hold nominal authority over a territory (Centeno and Ferraro 2013, 407–14).

If Latin American states lack the capacity to penetrate their territory, then this deficit limits their ability to implement policies and impart the political preferences of government officials in peripheral regions, especially in places with difficult geographies (Bunker 1985, 7–15, O'Donnell 1993, 1358–59, Brysk 2000, 107–11). As Guillermo O'Donnell puts it, "[s]tates are ostensibly unable to enact effective regulations of social life across their territories . . . In many emerging democracies, the effectiveness of a national order embodied in the law and the authority of the state fades off as soon as we leave the national urban centers" (1993, 1358). Specifically, scholars refer to the limited capacity of the state in developing countries to acquire and update technology, process information, and build organizational structures that are conducive to better policy outcomes (Centeno and Ferraro 2013, 10–12). Therefore, Indigenous land titling depends on the administrative quality of the state's bureaucratic apparatus, gauged by its meritocracy, coherence, and technical sophistication (Faundez 2010; Risse-Kappen 2011; Börzel and Risse 2013; Kiser and Schneider 1994; Rauch and Evans 2000).

A clear expectation of scholars drawing on administrative theory is that political elites in states with weak bureaucracies are largely unable to title Indigenous lands. Scholars hypothesize that states with agencies that are highly institutionalized and that have clear mandates, technical capacity, and internal cohesiveness should be more successful at titling lands than countries without such bureaucracies. Little titling should occur if the state's central bureaucracy lacks the administrative and technical ability to identify, demarcate, and regulate vast tracts of lands in remote areas with sparse population density. Consequently, scholars predict variation in the rate and extent of titling across states dependent upon differences in state capacity. Developing and middle-income countries that have institutions with low technical abilities and that routinely use un-meritocratic practices for hiring and promoting personnel should have little to no titling.

Another prediction is that variations in the speed and spread of Indigenous land titling within countries should be a function of the state's ability to extend its reach to the far corners of the territory. Low titling levels should exist for Indigenous peoples claiming lands that are located in remote localities, distant from the centers of administrative power. Countries with difficult geographies should not title Indigenous lands located in inaccessible

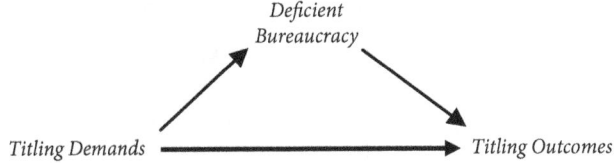

Figure 3.4 Administrative Theory

regions. The problem would be particularly acute for poor states that have little expertise, technical capacity, and limited material resources to invest in solving Indigenous land claims that originate in the peripheries. Figure 3.4 depicts this framework.

Arguments that emphasize the quality of the state's bureaucracy have difficulty accounting for the rate and extent of Indigenous land titling in poor countries with little administrative capacity. For one, progress has been swifter and more systematic in less capable states, such as Nicaragua and Honduras, than in relatively more institutionalized states, like Brazil. Another case in point is Colombia, where the government titled large extensions of Indigenous lands in areas contested by paramilitaries (Rueda-Saiz 2017). If administrative theories were correct, high titling rates in weak states are puzzling. As Chapter 4 will show in more detail, Nicaragua suddenly began titling Indigenous lands although the state's levels of administrative capacity remained low. Nicaragua finished the politically difficult and technically arduous task of identifying, delimiting, and titling all communal lands in a large, remote region in record time. In only six years, between 2007 and 2013, at 5 percent of the territory per year, the central government titled nearly a third of the country's territory as Indigenous land. By 2016, the central government had resolved all communal land claims in the east. If administrative capacity accounts were accurate, the state would not have been institutionally capable of completing such a feat, especially because the quality of its bureaucracy—in terms of meritocracy, cohesiveness, and technical sophistication—and the country's levels of economic development were low.

Similarly, in Honduras, a case explored in Chapter 5, the state quickly titled vast swaths of land without a prior increase in administrative capacity or income level. Despite high degrees of institutional fragmentation, interagency competition, and government change, the central government titled 10 percent of its territory as Indigenous land between 2012 and 2015. The titling rate in Honduras is 3 percent of the territory per year. In three years,

Honduras resolved 75 percent of communal land claims originating from the east, the most politically contentious and technically difficult claims.

Surprisingly, Brazil, a country with a far more capable bureaucratic apparatus and higher income level, has had less impressive results (Chapter 6). Brazil has taken over three decades to resolve 65 percent of Indigenous land claims (since 1988). Titled Indigenous lands cover just under 13 percent of the country's territory. The titling rate in Brazil is 0.47 percent of the territory per year. Given that Brazil had a constitutional mandate to finish titling by 1993, and that the state has better bureaucratic quality than the Central American countries, its sluggish rate is noteworthy. In fact, in light of the evidence from Brazil, the findings from Nicaragua and Honduras suggest that Indigenous land titling is mostly a matter of political will, not administrative capacity.

In addition, the expectations of administrative theories, which predict little titling in remote regions, have not come true. In fact, my research shows that the opposite is in fact the case: remote localities with difficult geographies have higher titling rates. Indigenous land claims that are closer to the centers of power have considerably lower titling levels. Brazil is a case in point (Chapter 6). In the Amazon region, the state has focused on titling the distant jungles of the northern borderlands, an area with very little state presence. Indigenous Lands that are located in the northwestern frontier zone—the Amazonian borderlands—are the most extensive and have the highest titling rates. The central government has titled 95 percent of Indigenous land claims there. Those land claims concentrated from the remote Venezuela-Colombia-Brazil frontier have a 98 percent titling rate. In stark contrast, for parcels located 150 miles from Manaus, the capital of the Amazonas state and a center for state power, the titling rate is 65 percent.

Examples that run against the predictions of administrative theories also abound in Nicaragua and Honduras, where the central government has concentrated efforts to title vast expanses of land in the peripheral regions. In Honduras, the state has titled continuous land blocks in the Gracias a Dios province exclusively, a neglected region to the east, where the state apparatus is barely present (Chapter 5). In Nicaragua, the central government has ignored Indigenous land claims that originate from the west, where the state has more institutional reach and presence (Chapter 4). Land claims that are closer to the centers of administrative power have fared a lot worse than those in the periphery. Simple, capacity-based administrative theories cannot account for the titling patterns found within countries.

A New Explanation: State Interests Shape Titling

The analytical perspectives assessed so far make important contributions and contextualize the issue of Indigenous land tiling in Latin America. However, these perspectives do not provide a complete explanation for the decisions of political elites to title Indigenous lands in some places, and at certain times, but not others. This book intends on building upon existing theoretical work. I offer a complementary political explanation that focuses on why political elites title Indigenous lands in contemporary times, as well as how and where they do it.

I draw from state-centered understandings of the interests of political elites in power to offer an account of the phenomena under study (Huntington 1968, 25–27; Skocpol 1979, 29–30; Weir and Skocpol 1985, 117–19; St. Germain 2001, 10–12; Grugel 2004, 38; Scott 1998, 2009; North, Wallis, Weingast 2009, 268–71; Slater 2010; Staniland 2012; Boone 2014, 2019; Slater and Kim 2015; Albertus 2015, 50–52; Krupa and Nugent 2015; Kuokkanen 2019, 78). As previewed in the Introduction, I focus on the institutional interests that are held by high-ranking government officials as a mediating factor that shapes titling outcomes. While informed by the perspectives of Indigenous elites and activists, I take a top-down approach and focus mainly on the state's motivation to title Indigenous lands—a deliberate choice given that executive decisions have an overwhelming impact on determining political outcomes in Latin America. I argue that state interests mediate societal pressures and tell us why and how titling takes place.

My central argument is that political elites' interests in guaranteeing the state's power and controlling people in remote localities are key factors behind the patterns of Indigenous land titling. The explanation that follows has four main parts. First, I highlight the centrality of state interests. Second, I complement existing theoretical work on formal rule implementation by identifying how state interests mediate two distinct conditions that incentivize titling action: internal threats and external pressures. I argue that internal threats are more powerful incentives for titling Indigenous lands than external pressure. While state elites act quickly to prevent the escalation of internal threats, they are slow and selective when reacting to external pressures. External pressures are insufficient to generate a wholehearted pro-titling response and to override the state's fundamental sovereignty concerns. Third, I specify how the interaction between state interests and these two triggering conditions leads to different spatial and temporal titling patterns. Finally,

I highlight how political elites mold titling in a way that serves their institutional interests. The titling model that results is designed to build an infrastructural apparatus that increases and reinforces state power over people and territory in remote regions. State elites weave new communal property structures to bind people and territories to the nation-state.

The Centrality of State Interests in Titling Indigenous Lands

States, in Max Weber's definition, are compulsory organizations with continuous operations that claim "the monopoly of the legitimate use of physical force in the enforcement of its order" (Weber 1978, 54).[4] While part of a web of socioeconomic relations, state organizations attempt to control a delimited territory and the population in it (Skocpol 1979, 31). States are composed of a set of administrative, policing, and military organizations that are coordinated by an executive office (such as the president in Latin American countries). To be sure, the state is not a monolithic entity (Migdal, Kohli, and Shue 1994). Specific bureaucracies and offices have different, even competing, mandates and perform a variety of functions that range from adjudicating Indigenous land claims to guaranteeing external defense. Yet high-ranking political elites within state organizations, especially the presidency, have roles and functions to pursue and secure the state's most basic concerns.

Political elites in government have distinct institutional or state interests. There are two core state interests: (a) to maintain the integrity of the national territory, which includes reinforcing power over people, and (b) to guarantee external defense. This book focuses mainly on territorial control. The interest to control territory and people is not reducible to the interests of any group in society (Skocpol 1979, 22–32), nor does it necessarily coincide with the short-term interests of individuals that work within state organizations (Huntington 1968, 25–27).

"Institutional interests differ from the interest of individuals who are in the institutions," Huntington observed. "Individual interests are necessarily short-run interests. Institutional interests, however, exist through time; the proponent of the institution has to look to its welfare through an indefinite future" (1968, 25). That is, there must be a strong and stable coalition of individuals within the state that prioritize institutional, long-term interests, rather than individual, short-term interests.[5] State rule includes the guarantee of internal order (and external defense) and the extraction of resources to sustain a centralized authority and administration (Tilly 1985, 170). Moreover, state rule also involves attempts to actively shape societal values and restructure social institutions (Giddens 2013, 19). Thus, political elites within the government actively pursue policies to incorporate people into the state's apparatus (Giddens 2013, 210; Scott 1998; Nugent 2010).

The state's administrative and coercive apparatus is the power base of political elites holding government office (Mann 1986, 123–25; Skocpol 1979, 29). They uphold and increase their own power by maintaining and building state power. Once elected officials and government bureaucrats take office, they tend to adopt and defend the state's basic institutional needs. State elites reproduce the power of the state by guaranteeing its territorial integrity and maintaining, or attempting to preserve, infrastructural control over the territory and the population (Mann 1993, 59). In so doing, state elites continuously attempt to direct social action within the state's territorial boundaries. By securing territorial unity, state elites can exercise exclusive jurisdiction within a defined territory and extract resources from the land and the population. In other words, political elites safeguard the prerogatives over resources that the state claims for the present moment and for future times. For example, the state can extract minerals from the subsoil and recruit members of the local Indigenous population to serve in the military. Even if the land itself has low population density and low market value, the territory of the state has high symbolic value (Johnson and Toft 2014, 8). Territorial dismemberment is associated with the loss of political and coercive power.

State elites can increase the logistical capacity of government institutions to implement political decisions and permeate social life in distant regions. Over time, the power of the state—and of state elites—increases. State institutions break the continuity of transnational Indigenous and ethnic groups and gradually increase the capacity of the state to manage local conflict and regulate social life.[6] For these reasons, the core interest of the state remains the same regardless of changes in government. High-ranking political office holders have overriding incentives to safeguard the state's sovereignty and territorial integrity.

The distinctiveness of political elites' institutional interests, which do not necessarily reflect societal preferences, carves a space for the state to be an agent of, and actor in, political processes and not just a conveyor belt of societal demands. In that respect, the state is an autonomous political force in its own right (Weir and Skocpol 1985). This feature is particularly conspicuous when state elites formulate policies in their continuous quest to reinforce their control over people in vast territories, as is the case of policies related to Indigenous peoples. Political elites transform societal demands and devise ways to implement policies that reinforce the state's power when and where they need it most. In other words, political elites look after institutional needs. In doing so, they mold societal demands and structure the character of policy outcomes.

Moreover, the state's sovereignty interests outweigh all other political concerns. Even if the preferences of some government officials align with the demands of Indigenous groups, the state's military apparatus restricts the ability of pro-Indigenous voices to formulate Indigenous policy in a way that might threaten national security. Political elites cannot act alone or be completely swayed by international or domestic societal demands when these go against the fundamental goals of the state to maintain territorial integrity and internal order. The state constrains and imposes conditions that limit concessions to Indigenous peoples demanding self-determination, that is, the autonomy necessary to govern relations with land and people according to their own values and preferences (Nasasra 2017, Ch. 1). In short, security interests systematically filter and fundamentally shape the interests of political elites holding government office.

Above all, the state continues to be the central actor in domestic and international politics even in the era of transnational activism (Finnemore and Goldstein 2013, 15–16). The state's core sovereignty interests take priority over international human rights norms. Political elites have insisted on reinforcing institutional guarantees of the state's territorial indivisibility and sovereignty despite decades of international normative advances attempting to shape state preferences to favor Indigenous self-determination and political autonomy over territories claimed as ancestral homelands (Zacher 2001; Johnson and Toft 2014; Cassese 1996, Ch. 5; Assies, Salman, Martí i Puig, van der Haa 2014, 163; IACHR 2019, 30; Kuokkanen 2019, Ch. 1). In fact, transnational normative pressure is mostly ineffective when state sovereignty is concerned (Cardenas 2007, Ch. 2). Governments are particularly insensitive to normative pressure in the context of a security threat, as even constructivists admit (Sikkink 2011, Ch. 7).

Moreover, governments can manage to sway public opinion on limiting human rights when issues of national security and territorial integrity are at stake. State elites can openly ignore or confront transnational activists that challenge the exclusive authority and sovereignty of the state (Jetschke 2011). For instance, states have been successful at blocking human rights efforts when advocates identify with self-determination movements in Turkey (Cizre 2001); and they fully repress such movements and disregard human rights norms in India and the Middle East (Kohli 1997, 341–44; Bengio 2014, 3–6). As Anja Jetschke and Andrea Liese put it "[s]overeignty with all its connotations of legitimate authority over territorially defined space . . . still poses a potent protection against challengers of state authority" (2013, 42). Despite significant transnational pressures, human rights norms do not override the institutional prerogatives of the state to maintain internal order and territorial integrity (Summers 2013, 229–49).

In what follows, I highlight two conditions that state elites perceive as security challenges and activating state interests: internal threats and external pressure. I theorize that internal threats are the stronger stimulant and are the product of two additive factors: (1) the state's low coercive and infrastructural power in remote localities and (2) rising instability caused by nonstate actors. I assume neither that the state's bureaucracy fits the image of an all-powerful Leviathan nor that the state in developing countries is failing. Instead, I hold that the state has varying levels of coercive and infrastructural capacity across its territory. Then, I hypothesize that medium to high levels of internal threat activate state interests, which in turn mediate titling outcomes. Contrary to administrative theory, I posit that low administrative capacity in remote places propels, rather than frustrates, Indigenous land titling.

In addition, I posit that external pressure, which combines normative and material pressure, is the weaker stimulant. I contend that external pressure is perceived as an attack on state sovereignty. In that sense, this book complements, rather than competes with, theoretical work by transnational constructivists—and legal scholars (Donnelly 2013)—that highlights the importance of external monetary and normative, but not military, factors as serious challenges to sovereign power. Observed evidence shows that external pressures alone cannot produce widespread Indigenous land titling. While external pressures can capture the attention of decision makers, state interests determine whether, and to what extent, government officials actually respond to these pressures at all (Hodgson 2011; Boone 2019).

State Interests Mediate Internal Threats and External Pressures

The institutional interests of state elites are decisive for explaining the observed patterns of Indigenous land titling. Internal threats and external pressures prompt state elites to attend to Indigenous demands for land and natural resources, the foundation of Indigenous self-determination rights (IACHR 2019, 30–34). *Internal threats* are destabilizing forces in remote regions that can increase the likelihood of internal instability or undermine the state's control over a particular territory. *External pressures* are challenges to state sovereignty by way of issue-specific campaigns tailored to generate titling action. These pressures challenge the state's unchecked control over the local population and limit its unrestrained power to access and rule over territory. These factors cause the central government to safeguard state interest and title Indigenous lands if state power is challenged. When state interests are not triggered, the central government is not highly motivated to title Indigenous Lands. In other words, internal threats and external pressure affect titling outcomes through state interests.

In the model illustrated in Figure 3.5, state interests specify *why* and *how* Indigenous land titling happens (Baron and Kenny 1986, 1174–76). Internal threats or external pressures are factors that activate state interests. In turn, state interests mediate these societal factors and shape titling outcomes.

State interests are necessary to explain titling patterns. On their own, pressure from external actors and threats from internal challenges are not sufficient to explain outcomes. Neither of these stimuli directly affect titling behavior. Political elites transform societal demands to further the state's own institutional and governability needs. In doing so, state elites reassert their authority rather than wait to respond to full-fledged security threats. Internal threats and external pressures are the initial triggers. Indigenous land titling depends on how political elites respond to these triggers in their attempt to safeguard and reinforce state power.

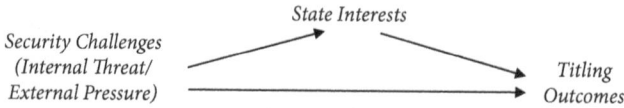

Figure 3.5 Mediation of Indigenous Land Titling by State Interests

Triggers of State Interests: Internal Threats or External Pressure

Indigenous land titling is costly to the state. The government forgoes direct control over land and people. The government also relinquishes its ability to establish a different system of property institutions in the area, to exploit natural resources unabated, and to implement nation-building policies that assimilate the local Indigenous population fully into the nation-state. Instead, the government sets up a system in which intermediaries serve as the link between Indigenous peoples and the central government. Although direct control might be the preferred mode of rule, in contemporary times the state elites turn to indirect rule in the face of internal threats and external pressures. That is, their preferred model, direct rule, becomes infeasible and they instead choose the second-best option, indirect rule.

Precisely because Indigenous land titling is a politically and economically costly measure, the government does not implement these formal institutions without a reason. It takes high levels of perceived threats, be they internal or external, to induce state elites to title Indigenous lands. Given considerations of internal and external legitimacy, and high costs of repression, state elites use Indigenous land titling as a way to curb further challenges to state power. In this respect, internal threats are more powerful triggers than external pressures. When facing internal threats, state elites act assertively to thwart these challenges in a rapid, thorough, and systematic manner. By contrast, political elites respond to external pressures selectively after safeguarding military interests.

Internal Threats

Internal threats are a crucial, overlooked factor that activates state interests among political elites and prompts the implementation of Indigenous land and resource rights at the local level. Risks to state power and its control over people and territory arise in remote localities where the state is scarcely present. In these areas of limited state reach, internal threats arise from the capacity of non-state actors to cause or facilitate internal turmoil and render the locality difficult or nearly impossible to govern. From the perspective of state elites, subnational authorities may flare up tensions, incite violent confrontations, and facilitate the formation of secessionist movements within the state's borders. In addition, non-state subnational actors may obstruct access to particular geographies, impede the enforcement of national laws and policies, and even fuel criminal activity. In other words, internal threats arise in subnational territories where the state has low coercive and infrastructural capacity.

Internal threats to the state's power differ in severity. A combination of response capacity and security challenges determines the nature or degree of internal threats that have the potential to undermine state control. As for response capacity, the state's coercive power and infrastructural reach are crucial components of internal threats. Low coercive and infrastructural power stems from the paucity of state institutions—such as the military and the police—in charge of maintaining internal order and enforcing public policies in remote sections of the state's territory. There is a latent threat where the state's apparatus is scarcely present. This threat stems from the state's inability to manage areas inhabited by antagonistic actors or groups that have potentially weak loyalties to the nation. For a time, scattered bureaucratic presence may be sufficient to keep control of remote regions. But internal threats can turn from latent to acute when security challenges are present.

As regards challenges, the worst threat arises when subnational non-state authorities violently resist state power. In this case, antagonistic groups have the motive and capacity to sustain war. For instance, an ongoing ethnic conflict with secessionist objectives poses the greatest threat. Somewhat less intense is the existence of latent resistance to state power. The legacy of ethnic defiance serves as a facilitating factor for violent collective action in places where the state exerts limited control. This factor only slowly diminishes through time. Thus, state officials anticipate an increase in internal threats when a change in government leadership flares up antagonistic sentiments. For instance, Nicaraguan state officials expected unrest in the east when the Sandinistas came back to power in late 2006 because they caused an ethnic war there in the 1980s. But in Panama, where the Kuna revolted against the state in 1925, state elites perceive levels of internal threat as low (Howe 1998; Assies 2014, 238).

At moments of medium levels of internal threat, local de facto authorities interdict access to specific localities but do not oppose state rule. In this case, the ability of the central government to enter and manage a portion of its territory is obstructed. The Gracias a Dios province in eastern Honduras is a good example of this type of threat. There, drug lords impede the access

Table 3.1 Levels of Internal Threat

Intensity	Contextual Conditions
5	Scant State Presence + Violent Resistance to State Authority
4	Scant State Presence + Latent Resistance to State Authority
3	Scant State Presence + Obstruction of State Authority
2	Scant State Presence + Contestation of State Authority
1	Scant State Presence in Remote Localities
0	No internal threat

Note: The intensity of internal threats is determined by the historical and geographical factors that jeopardize state control.

of the police and the military to their operating bases; their goal is to profit from illegal activities without the interference of the central government. Conversely, lower levels of internal threat exist where scattered groups do not acknowledge the legitimacy of state rule and instead identify along Indigenous or ethnic lines but may not have the capacity to frontally resist or obstruct state rule. This situation is found in the northern frontier zone of the Brazilian Amazon region. The source, nature, and strength of the perceived threat influences the government's response.

Table 3.1 shows a 5-point scale (0 = no threat; 5 = extreme threat) that is meant to capture the progressive increase in levels of internal threats in a country. The degree of internal threats rises in peripheral regions with weak state presence (1 = low threat) as minority groups begin to contest state authority (2 = low-medium threat). The obstruction of state access to peripheral regions exacerbates the threat (3 = medium-high threat). In remote localities with a collective memory of violent collective action, the intensity heightens when state authorities expect local defiance after a change in government (4 = high threat). Internal threats are highest (5 = extreme threat) during war over land.

External Pressures

External pressures are material and normative campaigns used by transnational interest groups to push states into titling Indigenous lands. These campaigns challenge the authority of the state to manage or control people inside its territory (della Porta and Reiter 2011, Ch. 5). In this sense, external demands limit the state's ability to conduct internal affairs without external interference and state elites perceive them as security challenges.

The intensity of external pressures varies across time. At moments of heightened international pressure, governments face heavy reputational and economic costs. International pressures take the form of social pressure campaigns designed to generate public support for a cause. For instance, activists mounted a global media campaign in the 1980s to push the Brazilian state to respect the Yanomami's rights to territory and self-determination. Donor countries and international financial institutions threatened to withhold funds until the government titled specific areas as Indigenous lands. During times of low external pressure, however, government actions vis-à-vis Indigenous peoples are below the radar. The media directs its attention elsewhere. Donors and international financial institutions may make funds for land titling projects available but will only rarely condition resources on the resolution of a particular land dispute.

To clarify, international campaigns utilize the language of human rights, such as the collective right to cultural survival, in order to demand Indigenous land titles from the state. External pressures emanate not only from transnational activist networks but also from international financial institutions that push to increase the definition and security of land tenure locally, such as the World Bank and the Inter-American Development Bank (Deininger 2003). External pressures, however, do not include the use or threat of military force by a foreign country.[7] In Latin America, ideological rivalries that elicited external military intervention in domestic affairs have been rare after the end of the Cold War. By far the most common types of external pressures endured in Latin America are economic and normative in nature, not military.

Furthermore, external pressures may coincide with the interests and goals of domestic civil society, but these internal actors alone are too weak to achieve their goals.[8] Indigenous peoples and ethnic collectivities lobby and attempt to garner material and political support from international courts, global activists, and donors. For instance, Indigenous peoples from Argentina, Brazil, Chile, Colombia, Ecuador, Nicaragua, Paraguay, Panama, and Suriname have sued their respective states before the Inter-American Court of Human Rights demanding land and natural resource rights (IA-Court 2016, 2018, 2019). Domestic NGOs and civil society groupings also compete and lobby for material support from foreign aid agencies and donor countries like Denmark, Norway, Spain, and Germany (OECD

Table 3.2 Levels of External Pressure

Intensity	Contextual Conditions
5	Great Power Intervention
4	International Financial Institution Conditions + Critical Intergovernmental Organization Reports + Global Media Outcry
3	Intergovernmental Organization Reports + Global Media Coverage
2	Issue-Specific International Nongovernmental Organization in Country
1	Issue-Specific Nongovernmental Organization in Country
0	No external pressure

Note: The intensity of external pressure is gauged from the capacity of international NGOs to influence third parties to pressure political elites in targeted countries.

2012; Dicklitch 2001, 182; Aguilar-Støen and Hirsch 2015, 186; personal correspondence with David Kaimowitz, Ford Foundation, May 14, 2016). In the absence of internal threats, state elites are more likely to be receptive to demands from external sources than from local groups alone. In other words, the extent to which domestic strategies work depends on the ability of Indigenous peoples and their allies to obtain and sustain outside support. After all, external pressures often come with offers of, or threats to withdraw, material support to induce political elites' behavior.

Table 3.2 presents a 5-point scale (0 = no pressure; 5 = extreme pressure) meant to capture the extent of external pressure in a country. The level of external pressure rises as issue-specific NGOs (1 = low pressure) connect with like-minded international NGOs (2 = low-medium pressure). The pressure rises when those NGOs become allies with intergovernmental organizations and attract the global media (3 = medium-high pressure). Finally, levels of external pressure heighten even further when international NGOs influence international financial institutions to condition fund allocations on government behavior, and intergovernmental organizations and the global media criticize government behavior (4 = high pressure). Intervention by a great power is an extreme form of external pressure (5 = extreme pressure).

Temporal and Spatial Patterns of Titling

State interests mediate internal threats and external pressures and help explain Indigenous land titling patterns. State interests can account for the remarkable episodic burst and the regional concentration of titled Indigenous lands in Central America, as well as the slow and uneven titling pattern in Brazil.

As described above, titling is contingent on factors that trigger state interests. These factors elicit state action while they persist. The nature, source, and intensity of triggering factors affect the way in which state elites perceive the need to title Indigenous lands. When internal threats and external pressures interact, state elites anticipate territorial fragmentation. In this case, the central government would grant greater concessions to Indigenous groups in a bid to prevent the dismemberment of the state. By themselves, however, internal threats are a more powerful stimulus than external pressure.

When facing high internal threats, the state has strong incentives to title Indigenous lands quickly and systematically. The central government takes proactive measures to prevent the escalation of societal challenges. If state elites perceive strong internal threats, the central government would focus on subnational localities where the threat originates. In this instance, Indigenous land titling is state driven and determined by political elites' objectives to thwart possible uprisings and reinforce control over territories that are hard to govern. By titling communal lands, state elites nip the internal threat in the bud.

By contrast, when facing external pressures, the central government reacts slowly and selectively. Political elites secure the state's sovereignty before titling Indigenous lands. The government resists external pressure and, instead, strengthens domestic institutions and upholds the primacy of military interests over other competing interests. Only after guaranteeing the state's core security concerns, state elites slowly title lands in strategic, remote localities. Their goal is to expand the reach of state institutions into frontier areas at their own pace. Under this condition, the government is not compelled to resolve outstanding claims. Instead, the government tends to title Indigenous lands gradually in a piecemeal manner by prioritizing vulnerable regions with low state presence and thus build the state's administrative capacity over time. Table 3.3 summarizes the posited relationship between state interests and outcome by trigger type.

In the absence of triggering factors, the state does not title Indigenous lands. Instead, political elites ignore or disregard Indigenous land claims. However, when internal threats and external pressures challenge the state's authority, titling Indigenous lands becomes a way that meets the security

Table 3.3 The Centrality of State Interests

Trigger	Level	Contextual Conditions	State Interest	Outcome
Internal Threats	3	Scant State Presence + Obstruction of State Authority	Guarantee internal order	Systematic titling where the threat originates
External Pressure	4	International Financial Institution Conditions + Critical Intergovernmental Organization Reports + Global Media Outcry	Guarantee territorial control	Selective titling in strategic, remote areas

needs of government officials and becomes the most effective mechanism to gain societal acquiescence while actually reinforcing state power and maintaining internal order. Under these conditions, the central government has strong incentives to design and classify vast areas as Indigenous land to establish its presence in remote regions. Indigenous land titling is useful to control localities that are hard to govern or that can become a problem spot for the central government. Put differently, Indigenous land titling is the smoothest way to mark state authority in remote, under-protected areas and establish the administrative apparatus to reinforce and reproduce state power over the local population.[9] By building a differentiated infrastructure that can rely on indirect rule to maintain internal order and governability, the state is able to increase its power to penetrate and centrally coordinate the social lives of Indigenous peoples.

Importantly, state elites title Indigenous lands when full blown nation-building is not feasible. While assimilation would be preferred by nationalists, they chose Indigenous land titling as a second-best option. Political elites embrace the "lesser evil" by formalizing communal property regimes: titling serves the interests of the state by increasing institutional presence in the periphery relative to the status quo and avoids territorial dismemberment or loss of territorial power. The government's strategy is to put in place an institutional framework that reinforces state authority and manages local conflict over land and land-based resources. Barring other options, the government can efficiently categorize and settle the local population into state-designed communal areas in a non-violent way.[10]

The institutions that state elites create and maintain by titling Indigenous lands are governing arrangements akin to indirect rule. These are institutions of cooptation and management that are designed to thwart political challenges to the state's power (Naseemullah and Staniland 2016; Slater and Kim 2014; Boone 2019). The resulting political order is rooted in the design and redesign of Indigenous lands and the restructuring of societal relations. As James Scott would put it, the identification, delimitation, and classification of Indigenous lands do not merely describe local society's system of land tenure, but make society legible for the official state observer (Scott 1998). State officials standardize and rationalize a bewildering complex land tenure system into one with a more convenient and simple administrative format that is easier to rule. State officials are effectively creating new institutional structures that simplify the task of governing people dispersed across vast, inaccessible, and remote territories (Krupa 2015, 99–125; Asher 2009). In addition, rather than enhancing Indigenous self-determination and local autonomy, these new institutional structures become the links to negotiate, manipulate, and control local social and political life in a top-down fashion. For state officials, Indigenous land titling is just another way to restructure land tenure customs to suit their governability goals. Under pressure, the government titles extensive Indigenous lands against all other competing claims, including those of powerful opposing economic interest groups. Thus, while perhaps not giving the state as much control as direct rule or the status quo, Indigenous land titling is the most effective option (Scott 1998, 2009) in certain well-defined situations. In other words, state elites choose Indigenous land titling not because it is their ideal solution, but because it is the best state-building strategy given the conditions.

In sum, state interests shape Indigenous land titling. The institutional interests of state elites inform their understanding of what Indigenous land and self-determination rights can be in practice. In turn, that influences the configuration and the structure of communal land regimes. Political elites respond to factors that triggers Indigenous land titling in ways that serve their security objectives and governability needs. The central government engineers the construction of differentiated institutions, based on carefully designed land regimes that ensure the continuation of state policies inside Indigenous ancestral territory. In this fashion, the state penetrates the political lives of Indigenous peoples in peripheral regions and ensures the continuation of state rule. Thus, the interests of the state shape the way in which the central government applies Indigenous land rights on the ground, while also affecting its rate and spatial reach.

Conclusion

The present chapter undertook three tasks to advance the analysis of the politics of Indigenous land titling in Latin America. First, I reviewed the main approaches that seek to explain the remarkable variation in titling across and within countries: (a) the striking titling burst in Nicaragua and Honduras in 2007 and 2012 respectively; (b) the sluggish movement toward titling in Brazil since the 1990s; and, (c) the notable concentration of titled Indigenous lands in the remote regions of all three countries.

I show that explanations that emphasize the influence of external pressures, the strategies of bottom-up social pressure groups, the power of rival economic interests, or the limited administrative capacity of state bureaucracies do not fully account for the observed titling patterns. Transnational constructivist, social movement, and economic structuralist accounts emphasize societal factors as the determinants of Indigenous land titling. Administrative theories highlight the deficiencies of state institutions to implement formal property rights successfully. These accounts either overestimate the power of societal pressure, as transnational activism and grassroots movements, or underestimate the advance of Indigenous land titling in Latin America, as economic structuralism and administrative theory do.

Specifically, transnational constructivists expect the even allocation of Indigenous land titles within targeted countries and regions, not the radically uneven spatial patterns observed. In addition, transnational pressure cannot explain the timing nor the dramatic advance of Indigenous land titling in cases that lacked targeted titling campaigns. Social movement theories, in turn, expect titling to correlate with the strength and mobilization power of grassroots organizations, rather than co-vary with areas where the state has an interest that it wishes or needs to control militarily. Arguments about the power and influence of economic interest groups predict very little, if any, titling, not the observed titling of vast tracts of land rich in coveted resources. Finally, administrative theories expect weaker states with limited bureaucratic capacity to advance more slowly than stronger states. Moreover, this approach predicts the incapacity of states to title Indigenous lands in unguarded localities and remote regions. The patterns found in this study go against these predictions.

Given these limitations, I developed a complementary account of Indigenous land titling. This approach highlights how state interests interact with societal stimuli to produce the observed patterns. I emphasize the power and interests of state elites to transform land titling models to fit the state's security and governability needs and affect the rate and extent of titling. The state—specifically, political decision makers within state organizations—has distinct institutional interests and wields considerable autonomy when anticipating or reacting to internal conditions and external societal demands. Therefore, what matters is not merely the existence of societal pressure to title Indigenous lands, but why and how state elites react to these pressures.

I highlight that state interests are an overlooked and powerful motivation for Indigenous land titling and delineate the way in which state interests interact with what they perceive as security challenges: internal threats or external pressures. State interests help explain the timing, rate, and striking spatial variation of Indigenous land titling across and within countries. When facing serious internal threats, the government responds to fears of domestic turmoil or loss of territorial control. Consequently, the state titles Indigenous lands proactively in vulnerable localities to prevent conflict, guarantee order, and reinforce power. When confronted with external pressure, the government defensively thwarts international demands by guaranteeing the primacy of military interests over Indigenous rights. Political elites respond to external pressure selectively, transforming demands in ways that extends the state's administrative apparatus in otherwise stateless localities. In both cases, state elites title Indigenous lands in line with their security interests: maintaining internal order and reinforcing state power in peripheral regions. In the absence of activated state interests, by contrast, the government does not have the incentive to title Indigenous land. Instead, the government maintains the status quo or disregards Indigenous rights to land and natural resources by implementing a different type of property regime in the area.

The following part, composed of Chapters 4–6, is the empirical backbone of the book. I undertake comparisons across and within Nicaragua, Honduras, and Brazil, taking care to note the form, as well as the temporal and spatial patterns, of Indigenous land titling in each country. These cases provide detailed evidence that allows me to assess the explanatory power of competing theories, as well as the data to propose state interests as a key factor in the politics of Indigenous land titling.

PART II
THE POLITICS OF INDIGENOUS LAND TITLING IN THE AMERICAS

4
Nicaragua

Once Bitten, Twice Shy: Titling for Internal Order

> Indigenous land titling "guarantee[s] national unity and prevent[s] ethnic war ... [The] political will [to title Indigenous lands] stems from an actual historical demand."
>
> (Lumberto Campbell, July 30, 2015, Nicaragua)

> Titling Indigenous lands "is a fundamental pillar for national unity, to prevent conflict; [it is] a way to govern the country ... based on the historical lesson that Nicaragua is hard to govern."
>
> (Paul Oquist Kelley, August 6, 2015, Nicaragua)

Nicaragua experienced one of the most surprising advances in Indigenous land titling in contemporary times. The central government shocked observers, activists, and local people by suddenly implementing constitutional provisions from the mid-1980s that recognize the right of Indigenous and ethnic groups to communal land and natural resources. In 2007, when Daniel Ortega—the leader of the revolutionary regime of the 1980s and the Sandinista National Liberation Front ("Sandinistas") today—returned to power, Indigenous land titling increased dramatically. At the time, state elites set, and accomplished, the ambitious goal of resolving all communal land claims in eastern Nicaragua—a huge and remote region that was the site of a devastating war over Indigenous self-determination between the Miskito people and the Sandinistas in the 1980s. In this chapter, I show that state elites perceived high levels of internal threat in the potential for violent Indigenous mobilizations, and this in turn shaped titling patterns.

The speed, breadth, and geographical scope of the Sandinista communal land titling program is remarkable. Nicaragua titled over 3.7 million hectares in only six years (2007–2013). By early 2016, the state had resolved all communal land claims in the east. Against all expectations, in only nine years, the central government delimited, titled, and officially recognized

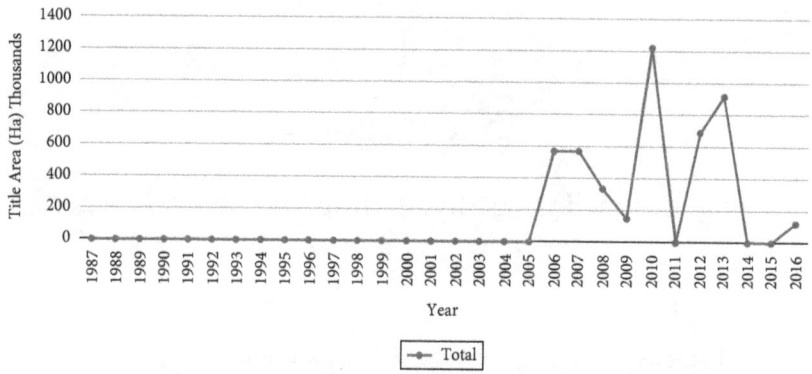

Figure 4.1 Indigenous Land Titling in the Eastern Territory, 1987–2016.
Sources: UNDP 2011; Attorney General's Office 2016; Álvarez 2016.

twenty-three adjoining land blocks as "Indigenous Territories." As a result, the state created new communal property regimes over an area that, in comparative terms, forms a continuous land mass that is roughly twice the size of El Salvador. Figure 4.1 shows the progression of Indigenous land titling in eastern Nicaragua after 1987—when the state codified property rights in the Constitution.

Importantly, there is a stark difference between Indigenous land titling practices in the eastern and western part of the country. The state focused exclusively in the remote regions of the east, despite Indigenous demands for secure property rights in the more proximate west (López and Sapón 2011, 72–77). Map 4.1 illustrates the location, number, and status of all the Indigenous land claims in Nicaragua.

In a country with weak formal institutions, mired in political corruption and high levels of socioeconomic inequality, the sudden change in fortunes toward widespread titling in favor of the politically and economically marginalized Indigenous population of the east is unquestionably striking. What caused the sudden outburst of Indigenous land titling in 2007? Why is there such a striking gap in titling outcomes between the east and the west? In short, what accounts for the Indigenous land titling patterns in Nicaragua?

As discussed in Chapter 3, standard arguments partially account for these titling patterns. Based on primary evidence collected during fieldwork, this chapter shows that the Nicaraguan behavior is a case of quick, systematic, and spatially concentrated Indigenous titling in a context of low levels of external pressure but high levels of internal threats. I demonstrate that political

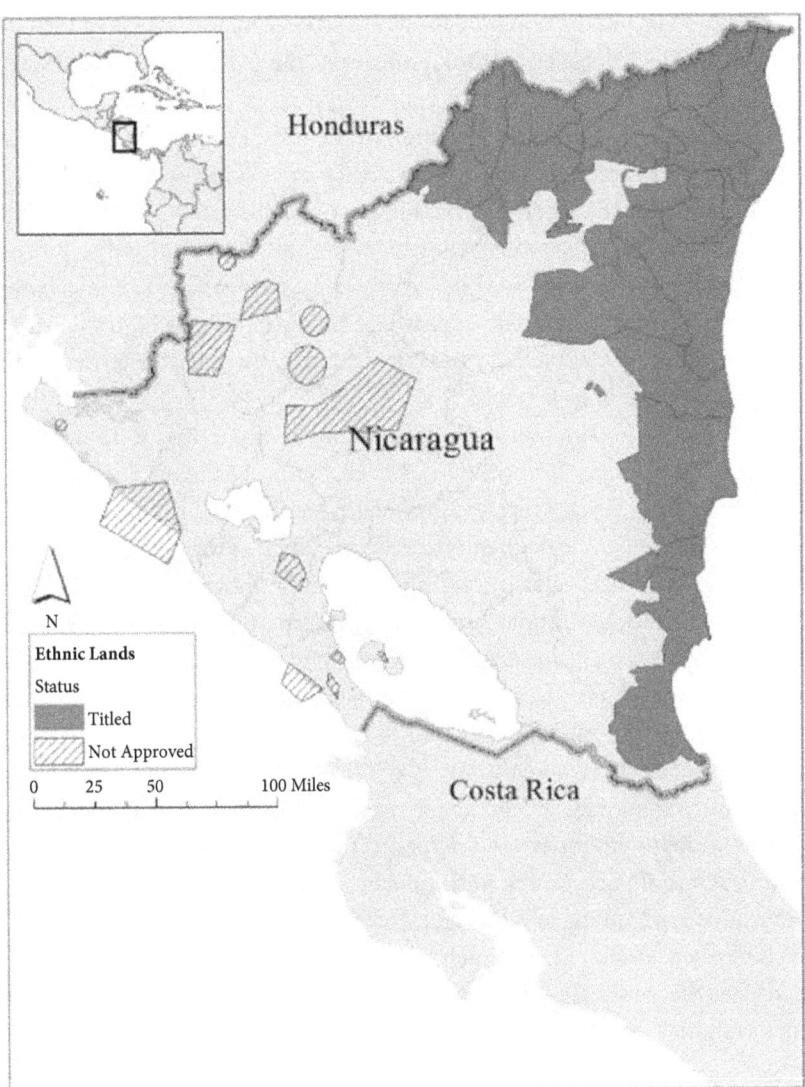

Map 4.1 Status of Indigenous Land Claims, Nicaragua
Sources: Attorney General's Office 2016; Olguín Martínez and ILO 2006; Álvarez 2016.

elites' institutional interests in guaranteeing internal order played a crucial role in shaping Indigenous land titling. The temporal and spatial patterns observed, I posit, reflect the central government's need to pacify the population in the east. In that remote region, Indigenous peoples had waged a war for self-determination against the Sandinistas in the 1980s. The legacy of that violent uprising and the potential for its recurrence motivated a pact in 2006 between Daniel Ortega and Brooklyn Rivera,[1] the antagonists of the 1980s, for Indigenous land titling. Having regained power in 2007, Ortega executed the pact in haste to prevent a repetition of the turbulent history. In terms of the model proposed in Chapter 3, the threat of internal turmoil increased dramatically in 2007, when Ortega, the Sandinista leader who fought—but could not defeat—Indigenous belligerents in the 1980s, returned to power. As the perceived threat of instability rose, state elites titled Indigenous lands quickly to guarantee internal order where they perceived a high threat. In nonthreatening places, namely Nicaragua's western regions, the government has ignored Indigenous land claims.

I divide this chapter into three subsections to argue that state interests motivated Indigenous land titling in the east, but not the west; after 2007, but not before. First, I briefly articulate the limitations of alternative explanations for the Nicaraguan case. Second, I discuss the historical context that informed Indigenous land titling in 2007. By showing that state elites formally adopted communal property rights for Indigenous peoples and ethnic groups as an anti-insurgent mechanism in 1987, I set the stage to discuss what prompted the Sandinistas to implement this strategy twenty years later. The chapter systematically shows that state elites titled Indigenous lands only when and where the legacy of inter-ethnic conflict was politically potent and potentially incendiary. I use extensive qualitative evidence—mainly in-depth interviews with high-ranking political decision makers from the central government and Indigenous political elites—to show that Indigenous land titling in Nicaragua is a time-bound strategy to lower the levels of internal threats in a given area. Third, the chapter shows that *how* state elites title Indigenous land matters as much as whether they do it. State elites designed and titled multi-ethnic land blocks to prevent the concentration of Miskito territorial power within demarcated areas. In addition, state elites created new intermediary institutions that are tied to the central government to rule Indigenous peoples more easily.

This analysis demonstrates that state elites view Indigenous land titling as a way to deflate potentially destabilizing Indigenous collective action. By solving communal land claims, the issue that had caused the war for self-determination in the 1980s, state elites sought to diminish the levels of internal threats in the east. To account for the regional patterns of Indigenous land titling, I present a matched comparison of two provinces that experienced different levels of internal threat. In the analysis, I control for other factors typically associated with Indigenous land demands and outcomes, such as the existence of external pressure and economic, demographic, and contextual factors. The analysis isolates the effect that differences in location and the legacy of Indigenous resistance has on titling. Where the state has more presence but there is no recent history of Indigenous insurrection, political elites ignore Indigenous titling demands.

Limitations of Extant Approaches

Dominant theoretical frameworks are hard pressed to explain the sudden outburst of titling in 2007, its systematic spread through a third of Nicaragua's territory, and its exclusive geographical concentration in the east. Analyses that point to the power of transnational activist networks or grassroots mobilization can account for neither the timing nor the regional gap in outcomes. In the early 2000s, external pressure had been strong after the Inter-American Court of Human Rights and the World Bank pushed center-right governments to pass specific communal property rights legislation. However, these administrations dragged their feet when it was time to implement the law. Despite high levels of external pressure, there was virtually no political will to engage in Indigenous land titling in the east before Ortega came back to power in 2007. In terms of the regional gap in outcomes, the central government continues to lack the political will to recognize the ancestral land claims of twenty-two Indigenous communities (roughly about 333,000 people) in the west. A World Bank country report notes, "there is no explicit policy to title the lands of the Indigenous communities in the [western] Pacific and Central regions" (Attorney General's Office 2009, 23). Despite decades of transnational normative and material campaigns to further democracy and Indigenous rights, the observed geographical pattern suggests that the state fails to view Indigenous land titling as an opportunity to deepen democracy and bolster the Nicaraguan state.

Economic structuralism does not persuasively explain why state elites in an agrarian society—where land is at the very center of economic, social, and political life—would allocate vast resource-rich areas to poor and marginalized Indigenous and ethnic groups. According to Evelyn Taylor, the first director of the Communal Titling Unit in the Attorney General's Office (2007–2011), the biggest obstacles to titling Indigenous lands relate to regional economic elites with logging investments and municipal authorities interested in securing Mestizo votes.[2] In particular, cattle ranchers seeking to increase their economic activity in the east and landless peasants from the west sought to secure private property rights for themselves (Wilson 2012). Undeterred, the Ortega administration created the Mother Earth Program to resolve Indigenous land claims in the east (Attorney General's Office 2009). In less than a decade, at a rate of over 481,000 hectares per year, the central government completed the program (see Figure 4.2).

In addition, economic structuralism is hard pressed to account for the scope of titling. According to the Communal Property Regime Law (2003), it is illegal to sell, mortgage, confiscate, or otherwise transfer communal property to outsiders (Article 31-33). Only local insiders can legally use, manage, or exploit the valuable cash-producing resources—such as timber and gold—that exist within the state-delimited communal areas. When the government allocates land to a specific Indigenous or ethnic group and removes it from the land market, ethnic outsiders competing for the same resource experience a setback (Acosta 2011). Although Indigenous lands restrain market forces, they extend over a large contiguous area and are not limited to environmental protection zones. Areas classified as Indigenous property are highly coveted by poor peasants, cattle ranchers, wealthy private investors, and transnational companies alike (Ampié and Carrión 2017; Lorío 2014). Newly created communal property regimes now encompass land that is ideal

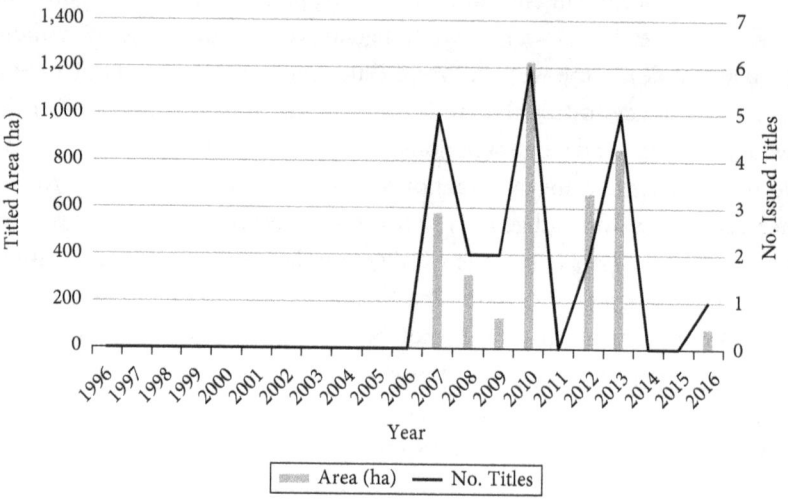

Figure 4.2 Total Number of Communal Titles Issued (Annually) and the Land Area Covered (Hectares) in Eastern Nicaragua.

for agricultural production, logging, gold extraction, and maritime trade. If economic structuralism were correct, the central government would not have created Indigenous areas over such an enormous, resource-rich part of the territory.

Finally, administrative theory is unable to account for the onset, incredible speed, and enormous geographical scope of Indigenous land titling in remote localities with feeble state presence. For over a decade (1990–2006), center-right governments claimed that the absence of a legal framework and insufficient financial resources prevented communal land titling in the east. Betty Rigby, representative for the Creole community in the regional Titling Commission (2002–2004) and officer in the United Nations Development Program at Bilwi, explains: "The titling process in that period [2002–2004] was difficult. The state lacked the resources and the results were limited. The process was not fluid and systematic."[3] If these factors were insurmountable obstacles, the central government would not have been able to title over 3.8 million hectares in eight years starting in 2007. Titling was accomplished by the same weak administrative agencies that existed in the 1990–2006 period and a bureaucracy that lacked internal coherence and is permeable to corruption and patronage (Acosta 2010; Finley-Brook and Offen 2009, 315). Contrary to the expectations of administrative theory, political appointees, rather than meritocratic office holders, directed and coordinated the entire titling process until its successful completion. Moreover, administrative theory postulates that poor countries are simply unable to identify, delimit, and title areas that are located in remote, mountainous, and sparsely populated localities (Brook 2005). This line of reasoning suggests that the government is willing to title Indigenous lands but that the bureaucratic apparatus lacks the requisite geographical projection to do so in remote areas. Observed geographical patterns disprove this argument. In fact, the central government chooses to ignore land claims in the proximate west and title in the distant east. Although theorists of administration expect otherwise, the geographical patterns suggest that titling co-varies with low population density and scant state presence.

Because the patterns of Indigenous land titling observed in Nicaragua do not conform to the expectations of dominant frameworks, I show, through a mix of primary evidence and secondary sources, that state interests are a central piece of the explanation. First, I detail the conditions under which Indigenous land and resource rights were adopted in the Constitution and the Autonomy Law. A discussion of the origins of the formal institutions establishes the baseline for understanding why the Sandinistas chose to secure internal order in the east by titling Indigenous lands, rather than establishing electoral institutions and social services (health and bilingual education) that Indigenous groups also demand. I demonstrate that the Sandinistas' hegemonic attempts in the east during the 1980s caused a vicious inter-ethnic conflict that continues to inform political decision-making today. In particular, I show that state elites titled Indigenous lands proactively to prevent the replication of a painful historical precedent.

Legal Origins: Formal Institutions as Anti-Insurgent Strategy

In 1987, Nicaraguan state elites formally recognized communal property rights for Indigenous peoples and ethnic groups to prevent the creation of a separate Miskito nation. In the early 1980s, Miskito paramilitary forces had fought the Sandinistas for self-determination and control of their ancestral territory situated in present-day eastern Nicaragua. Sandinista land redistribution initiatives provoked a war in the east—which was essentially a fierce backlash amplified to a full-blown secessionist movement in the context of the Cold War. At the time, the Reagan administration funded, armed, and trained the Miskito, as well as ideologically driven paramilitary groups, as part of a military strategy intended to destabilize and overthrow the Sandinista revolutionary regime (ICJ 1986; US Congress 1987). For their part, the Sandinistas received generous support from the Soviet Union. Fearful for the territorial integrity of the state, the Sandinistas adopted communal property rights in the Constitution and the Autonomy Law because they could not defeat the Miskito insurrection. In what follows, I will substantiate the claim that state elites adopted these property rights as an anti-insurgency strategy to prevent the dismemberment of the state.

In the 1980s, the Sandinistas' hegemonic goals in the east had prompted an insurrection. Soon after overthrowing the Somoza dictatorship (1937–1979), the Sandinistas attempted to integrate the eastern territory—an underdeveloped and geographically isolated region—with the more populated and developed west (Hale 1994, Chs. 3–6). The revolutionary regime designed and implemented nationwide policies to consolidate power. Efforts to invest "large amounts of economic resources there [in the east] to try and integrate the Atlantic region socially, economically and politically into the rest of Nicaragua," explained Daniel Ortega in July 1981, responded to "the latent danger that exists because the Somozistas [supporters of the overthrown dictatorship] have pinpointed the Atlantic region as a favorable zone in which to develop counter-revolutionary activity... For this reason, we are obliged to double our efforts to consciously integrate the Atlantic inhabitants into the revolutionary process" (Ortega cited in Ohland and Schneider 1983, 160–61).

The efforts at integration included the implementation of the Agrarian Reform Law (1981), whose Article 30 declared, "The State shall make available the amount of land necessary so that the Miskito, Sumu, and Rama communities can work them individually or collectively and so that they benefit from their natural resources."[4] Based on this law, which treated all rural land as state property (Roldán Ortega 2000, 63–66), the central government attempted to allocate small plots of land to individual landowners and cooperatives directly, but not based on ancestral territorial claims. The agrarian reform initiative collided head-on with the preexisting communal land structure. In the words of Patrick Thornberry (2005, 276), "tensions rose after the rise to power of the Sandinista regime. Miskitos opposed attempts by the government to reform their way of life and tribal organization." The prospect of expropriation and dispossession threatened Indigenous peoples' land tenure systems, as well as their way of life.

Local power structures rooted in the control of communal lands had developed historically in the eastern territory. Until the nineteenth century, the British Empire had erected and maintained a system of indirect rule by creating the Miskito Kingdom (IACHR 1983, Part I-A; Dennis and Olien 1984; Jenkins 2013, 192). In the Treaty of Managua (1860), Great Britain recognized Nicaraguan sovereignty, eradicated the title of "king," created a Miskito Reservation, and established a "hereditary chieftaincy" (Helms 1986). In 1894, Nicaraguan President José Santos Zelaya (1893–1909) secured U.S. military support to expel the British from the eastern lands and quell Miskito resistance (Colby 2013, 54; Weaver 2014, 98; Hale 1994, 41–44; Hooker 2010, 261–64). About a decade later, Great Britain and Nicaragua signed the Harrison-Altamirano Treaty (1905) to reinforce Nicaraguan sovereignty, while reiterating the rights of Miskito and Creole people to communal land (Article 3.c). Subsequent government administrations maintained and co-opted local communal structures—known as *síndicos* and communal boards—to rule the eastern territory (Goett 2016, 213). Over time, the notion of Miskito ancestral lands and resource rights became entrenched (Goett 2016, 208–11). By the late 1970s, local Indigenous leaders held considerable *de facto* political authority.

Therefore, in 1981, when the Sandinistas attempted to implement the Agrarian Reform Law, Brooklyn Rivera, representative of the Miskito political organization MISURASATA,[5] forcefully rejected any claims from the state to ownership of the land and resources in the east. In the middle of the Cold War, Rivera unhesitatingly demanded official recognition of a Miskito homeland and the titling of a single territory of about 3.2 million hectares.[6] According to Marcos Hoppington, Rivera's lieutenant in the 1980s and close political ally, "the idea to create a single block [of land] was to have our own government. The Moskitia had been its own state. As Indigenous peoples, we have the right to self-determination."[7] The primary ground upon which Miskito elites claimed political control over the east was the region's distinctive history.

Ancestral possession—land tenure predating the creation of the modern state—and aboriginal rights to natural resources were the basis of Miskito territorial claims. In July 1981, MISURASATA presented the following political arguments in demanding self-determination and territory for the Miskito people:

> "The right of the indigenous nations over the territory of their communities holds more importance than the territorial right of the state." Therefore, any sovereign and highly nationalistic country should recognize, without any discrimination, the inalienable right of territory belonging to the indigenous nations ... Our fundamental right to self-determination is an "aboriginal right." The indigenous peoples had this right from the outset, and it has been the dominant immigrant peoples who violated this right ... The right of indigenous peoples to land includes the rights to the surface and the subsoil, to inland waters and the coast, as well as the right to appropriate them, even including the coastal economic zones. Thus, the indigenous peoples can freely control the land's riches and natural resources ... To reiterate, [MISURASATA's] main objective is the recuperation of our alienated territories, which through age-old inheritance belonged to our ancestors and have been stolen from us, as we have already indicated. This age-old right of inheritance and possession of our territories is counter to that of property rights on a community basis, which they [state elites] have always tried to impose upon us. We are not in agreement with this because it is

against our interests and beliefs as peoples who possess their own rights. (Ohland and Schneider 1983, 163, 165, 169, 175)

As the representative of MISURASATA, Rivera claimed that the 1981 Agrarian Reform Law "denigrate[s] the authentic struggle of our Indigenous peoples for their lands and autonomy" (IACHR 1983). In 1982, Rivera denounced the law before the Inter-American Commission on Human Rights as an affront to Miskito ancestral ownership:

> [T]he government has decide[d] to deny us our basic Indigenous land rights, the most important matter in the crisis ... the government decreed [the] Agrarian Reform Law[,] which announced that the government would "give" to Indigenous people defined parcels or sections of land which each village would hold under an "agrarian title." This decree denied Indigenous ownership of all the lands of the Indigenous territory of the east coast of Nicaragua. (IACHR 1983, G.2)

The revolutionary regime strongly rejected Miskito territorial demands. The Sandinistas interpreted MISURASATA's initial claim to over 4.5 million hectares as a serious threat to the state's territorial integrity and feared that it would spur an attempt at separatism (Ohland and Schneider 1983, 171). Sandinista-Miskito tensions over land blew out of proportion and caused an inter-ethnic war. In Rivera's words:

> [T]he struggle started in the year 1980–1981 when the Sandinistas, faced with the communities' claim to the recognition and legalization of land, closed all avenues and refused to open space for dialogue with the indigenous organization MISURASATA, making us take-up arms to fight ... We presented a demand to title land to the FSLN [Sandinistas] ..., when presenting the claim, [the Sandinistas] labeled it as separatist and counter-revolutionary.... The 1980–1981 proposal of a single block of 32,000 km^2 scared the government and sent us to war.[8]

From the Sandinista perspective, Miskito land demands posed a serious challenge to the state's power and territorial control because leaders demanded a single territory based on ancestral Miskito possession (Brook 2005). A transnational Indigenous group extending into neighboring

Honduras and concentrated in northeast Nicaragua, the Miskito are the second largest Indigenous group in the country (Carrión 1983, 239; INIDE 2005). Ethnic insurrectionaries had ample U.S. support in the form of weapons, training, and funding to capture and hold the eastern territory (Jenkins 2013, 182–86). Together with the other U.S.-funded counter-revolutionary forces operating in Honduras and Costa Rica, the Miskito were formidable opponents (Brands 2012, 211–13). In fact, the Sandinistas expected the United States to orchestrate a large-scale military invasion from Honduras and secure control of the eastern territory (Honey 1994, 229). In 1981, William Ramírez, then minister of the Atlantic Coast for the Sandinista government, fumed before the United Nations:

> [W]e are currently harassed by North American imperialism which utilizes the indigenous problem as an ideological weapon to destabilize the revolutionary process... MISURASATA's position [i.e. land demands] left the organization open to imperialist manipulation, which could have resulted in the division of the national territory... [A MISURASATA political leader] has been inciting the Miskito population to rebellion, urging them to come to Honduras to join the *imminent* invasion of Nicaragua. (My emphasis, Ramírez 1983, 222, 229)

Luis Carrión, the Sandinista representative for the eastern territory in the National Assembly at the time, used similar terms to assess MISURASATA's territorial demands: "they claim a portion of 45,000 km² of national territory ... thus passing [transforming] a legitimate proposal [for land recognition] to a separatist proposal ... [MISURASATA's goal] is a general uprising of the Miskito population of North Zelaya following a military take-over of the settlements of the Río Coco by counter-revolutionary bands" (1983, 260). The Sandinistas were indeed convinced that the United States would manipulate the "Indigenous Crisis"—to use Rivera's words—to win the Cold War in Nicaragua. Map 4.2 shows the location and geographical extent of the contested territory of the 1980s.

The Miskito-Sandinista conflict lasted nearly a decade (Hale, Ch. 7; Nietschmann 1995, 12). In the end, the Sandinistas could not crush Miskito resistance. A stalemate and the fear of territorial dismemberment led Ortega to begin peace talks with Rivera in 1984 (IACHR 1986, Ch. 4). During the negotiations, the Reagan administration sabotaged an amicable agreement (Pineda 2006, 197). Therefore, to prevent the creation of

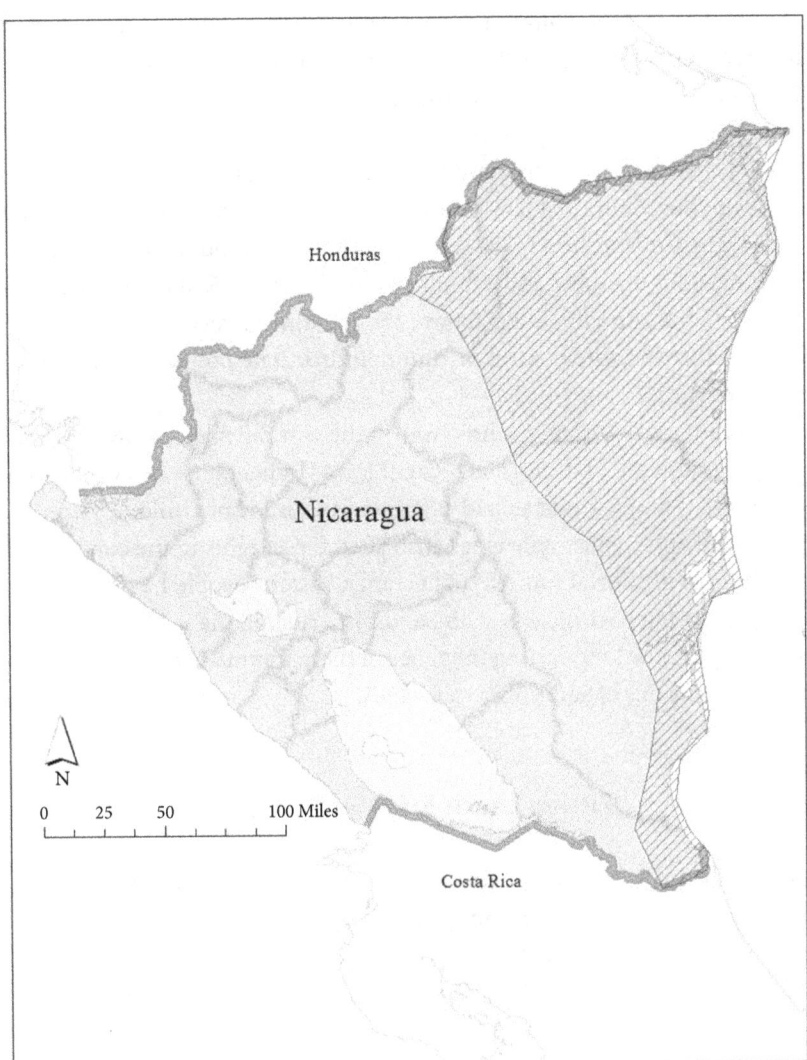

Map 4.2 Miskito Territorial Claims in 1981, Nicaragua
Sources: Carrión cited in Ohland and Schneider 1983, 171.

a separate Miskito nation, the Sandinistas acknowledged the importance of cultural particularities in the east, apologized for the mistakes committed in attempting to implement the Agrarian Reform Law, and offered regional autonomy as a solution to the conflict (Hannum 1996, 210; Pineda 2006, 194). In that context, a Sandinista-controlled legislature engineered the passage of a series of fundamental laws: the Autonomy Law and a new Constitution.

State elites codified communal land rights based on ethnicity as part of an anti-insurgency strategy. Although Rivera demanded a national homeland for the Miskito peoples (but not other Indigenous groups, afro-descendants, or Mestizos), the central government rejected that proposal (Hannum 1996, 222–23). Instead, the Autonomy Law recognized full property rights over non-alienable communal lands for *all* ethnic groups in the east (Articles 9, 11, 36). The Constitution (1987) also guaranteed communal property rights for Indigenous peoples and ethnic groups (Articles 5, 89–90, 107, 180). Fearful of Miskito collective action, the Sandinista revolutionary regime did so to recover state control of, and reinforce state power in, Nicaragua's eastern territory.

To summarize, the inter-ethnic war in the east during the 1980s was the fundamental cause of the formal recognition of Indigenous and ethnic property rights. The Sandinistas had instigated the war but could not win the conflict outright. Thus, state elites enshrined these rights in the constitution to guarantee territorial integrity. Thereafter, eastern people have associated the legacy of inter-ethnic war with Sandinista rule. In the following section, I demonstrate the long-lasting influence of these traumatic memories on the political decisions of Sandinista state elites.

Titling Lands for Internal Order

Two decades after formally adopting property rights, Nicaragua experienced a sudden outburst in Indigenous land titling in the east. Unlike the land titling initiatives of the 1980s and the early 1990s, which allocated small plots of land to individuals and communities for agricultural production, disregarding Indigenous claims, the 2007 titling program predominantly titled communal land claims based on ethnicity. Although in late 2005 the government had titled communal land for strictly environmental conservation purposes (UNDP 2011), the 2007 program had an impressive geographical range that quickly extended beyond forested areas. In the following subsection, I will demonstrate that the temporal and spatial patterns of titling stem from the motivation of political elites to prevent internal conflict, maintain control over rural people, and reinforce the power of the state in the eastern periphery. Institutionally motivated state elites acted proactively in titling Indigenous lands to curtail any potential for violent collective action.

State Interests and the Timing and Rate of Titling

Between 1990 and 2006, Nicaragua's central government resisted Indigenous land titling. Center-right governments were not motivated to title communal lands because the danger of insurrection dropped precipitously when Ortega lost the 1990 presidential elections. The subsequent center-right governments took a hands-off approach in the east. For instance, the administration of Violeta Barrios de Chamorro (1990–1997), focused on guiding the country from war to peace by implementing a demilitarization program, distributing private property to ex-combatants on both sides of the conflict, and securing high-ranking government positions for Miskito political elites. Presidents Arnoldo Alemán (1997–2002) and Enrique Bolaños (2002–2007) also had a detached attitude toward the east. These administrations considered the eastern territory available for future agricultural expansion or as a natural resource reservoir (Acosta 2011; Goett 2016; Wiggins 2002). When privatizing land or granting concessions for the extraction of natural resources, the central government carried out these initiatives on a case-by-case basis, rather than as a sweeping land titling and registration program. Therefore, the politicians in power ignored land claims without provoking severe repercussions. To be sure, Miskito political elites kept demanding territorial rights (Brook 2005). However, liberal governments had a noninterventionist approach in dealing with the Miskito question. State elites did not have the political will to engage in a far-reaching, politically costly, and technologically difficult land titling program (Finley-Brook and Offen 2009, 354). This trend changed dramatically with Ortega's return to power in 2007.

State interests in preventing radicalized Miskito land demands explain the timing and rate of titling. As mentioned in the discussion of economic structuralism, Indigenous land titling is a time-bound strategy intended to guarantee internal order. The shift of political power in 2007 raised the specter of ideological struggles over land and political power in the east. Because the legacy of Indigenous secessionist war is inexorably entwined with Sandinista political rule, Ortega's return to the presidency revived old concerns that land conflicts could turn violent again. The government quickly titled Indigenous lands to forestall any challenges to the state's authority. Whereas the center-right governments had claimed insufficient administrative capacity or lack of a legal framework to title Indigenous lands for sixteen years, the Ortega administration completed the task in less than a decade, beginning with the northeast—the contested territory of the 1980s.

From the Sandinista perspective, their government had caused a long and costly war in the 1980s. Fierce Miskito resistance to Sandinista policies almost split Nicaragua in half. Paul Oquist Kelley, private secretary for national policies and Ortega's closest political advisor, emphasizes that:

> The Nicaraguan state has titled about 37,000 km² as communal lands, twice the size of El Salvador and nearly that of Belgium. [Indigenous land titling has happened] in such a spectacular way because of the mistakes the FSLN committed in the 1980s. The revolution had good intentions but lacked knowledge about the indigenous question. The revolution pushed a socialist vision to create industry and wage labor that clashed with the lifestyle of the [people of the eastern] Coast . . . YATAMA and another group resisted with the support of the CIA [Central Intelligence Agency], financed by Norwin Meneses' drug money. The result was a costly war that persisted for 8 years . . . Titling communal lands [in the east] is fundamental to guarantee national unity. . . . The historical lesson [learned] is that Nicaragua is hard to govern . . . [The central government titles Indigenous lands] to prevent conflict, it is a way to govern the country.⁹

The essence of Oquist Kelley point is that Indigenous land titling is a political strategy to prevent the repetition of the historical precedent of the 1980s. Upon taking power again in 2007, Sandinista elites expected Miskito resistance, with increasing political and ethnic tensions and possibly renewed secessionist attempts. In particular, state elites in Ortega's administration were apprehensive about YATAMA's political edge, which could incite radicalized mobilization. For Lumberto Campbell, the top decision maker for eastern political affairs and Ortega's lieutenant in the 1980s, titling Indigenous land guarantees national unity and is an essential mechanism to prevent insurrection. Referencing the conflict of the 1980s, Campbell himself explains that Sandinista political elites anticipated the Miskito "to rebel" without concessions to land claims:

> [In the 1980s, the United States'] aggression made progress difficult [in the eastern territory] and an important part of the population fought for autonomy. The recognition of Indigenous land rights guarantees territorial unity . . . Without respect for communal lands, they [the Indigenous communities of the east] rebel . . . In 2007, Daniel Ortega made the political decision to implement ethnic communal property rights . . . The political

will [to title Indigenous lands] responds to an actual historical demand...
A fundamental factor for implementation is Daniel Ortega's political will;
the goal is to make the Coast [eastern territory] a functional part of the
country to ensure national unity; if not, they will rebel.[10]

The Sandinistas had foreseen Miskito challenges because the inter-ethnic war of the 1980s continues to have enormous political resonance in the east (GiZ 2010, 3). As late as 2009, the Miskito Council of Elders—the political voice of the Mosquitia Nation—declared independence from Nicaragua and claimed a territory that spans from Honduras to Colombia as their ancestral homeland (Gibbs 2009; Schmidt and Lacey 2009; UNDP 2005, 133). For decades, the Council of Elders has worked to recover the territory of the Miskito Kingdom and has argued that Nicaragua seized that territory after 1894 (Gordon and Hale 2003, 370; Williamson Cuthbert 2003). In fact, Miskito social-political organizations maintain a cohesive militant base that demands territory and self-determination as a distinct nation (UNDP 2005, 50–51, 116–17, 133). The collective memory of armed struggle fuels territorial claims and permeates invocations of Miskito nationhood. Social anthropologists Edmund T. Gordon, Galio C. Gurdián, and Charles R. Hale (2002, 273) report that,

> The near unanimity of indigenous and Creole mobilization against the Sandinista government in the previous era has long since passed. Some organizations—most notably the *Consejo de Ancianos* (Council of Elders)—have carried on the ideological mantle of that mobilization, making control over a vast indigenous "territory" a nonnegotiable demand around which political struggle should proceed... demands for autonomy have animated the anti-Sandinista mobilization and served as a common thread in Miskitu social memories of struggle since the last century.

Aside from the potent legacy of the war, three factors are indicative of the potential for radicalization and the possibility for renewed violent mobilization during a Sandinista administration. First, individuals that self-identify as Miskito manifest loyalties as Indigenous people, rather than with the nation-state. Second, Indigenous communities from the east consider that the respect of communal lands is essential for peaceful coexistence within the contemporary state. Finally, members of these communities hold the Sandinista responsible for their marginalization.

A survey of rural communities conducted by the former Central American University in 2004 provides the most compelling evidence of the primacy of Miskito identity in the communities of the east, the importance of communal land rights, and views about discrimination and unequal treatment. Table 4.1 shows the results of a representative regional survey administered in the eastern territory in respondent's native languages.

The evidence reveals that members of Miskito communities have very strong in-group loyalties. In addition, people that self-identify along ethnic lines (such as, Miskito, Rama, Garífuna, Mayangna-Sumu, Kriol, and Ulwa) show nearly universal support for communal property rights and point to the existence of discriminatory practices against them. As shown in the second column (Yes), more than 80 percent of Miskito rural villagers explicitly identify with that Indigenous group. Over 85 percent of easterners have a strong regional identity, as opposed to a national one. The vast majority of communities in the east (88.6 percent) believe that respecting communal property is a precondition for peaceful coexistence in the eastern territory. As the authors of the survey explain, "the respect of communal property is a fundamental issue" (Ortega Hegg, Daza, and Venerio 2006, 53). Finally, over 75 percent of the respondents believe that Nicaraguans

Table 4.1 Views of Rural Populations in the East about National Identity, Communal Property Rights, and Discrimination, 2004

Question	Yes	No	Doubts/No Comment
Identifies more or equally as Miskito than Nicaraguan (%)	84.7	10.7	4.5
Identifies more or equally as eastern than Nicaraguan, Miskito respondents (%)	87	6.8	6.2
Believes respect for communal lands to be fundamental for coexistence, all ethnicities (%)	88.6	2.1	9.2
Believes that eastern people have always been seen as second-class citizens, all ethnicities (%)	77.7	13.9	8.4
Believes there is racism against indigenous people, all ethnicities (%)	76.5	14	9.5
Believes there is racism against afro-descendants, all ethnicities (%)	77.2	13.2	9.7
Number of respondents: 950			

Source: Ortega Hegg, Daza, and Venerio 2006.

have always treated people from the east as second-class citizens and that racism exists.

The survey results provide unambiguous evidence about communities' views a few years before the Sandinistas regained power. In the lead up to 2007, any political development thought to encroach on communal land rights would have been very unpopular among eastern villagers. The deeply rooted sentiments of marginalization and alienation, in combination with communities' strong attachments to local land tenure regimes, was a powerful indicator of the potential for mobilization, especially against the Sandinistas. As stated above, Indigenous and other ethnic communities in the east hold the Sandinistas directly responsible for their marginalization. In 2005, the United Nations Development Program reported that:

> The devastating effects of forced migration during the war—associated with death, destruction of communities, separation of families, and material loss—are still present in the collective memory. In fact, for the Miskito or Sumu/Mayangna communities, the "ills of today" have roots in the effects of the [forced] migration caused by the military conflict of the 1980s. (UNDP 2005, 140)

From a Sandinista perspective, Miskito political elites could have easily tapped into the latent militancy of eastern communities to destabilize the state. As the UNDP (2005, 140) report notes, members of eastern communities, especially among the villages displaced during the war, shared an aversion to Sandinista leadership just before 2007. In a context of generalized indignation and grievance, the Sandinistas feared that their return to power could trigger protests and perceived the threat of resistance.

Even political elites of the opposition party in the national legislature view Indigenous land as a way to reinforce state power in the eastern territory. Table 4.2 shows the results of a survey on Indigenous land titling administered to legislators in June 2015. The survey results are not representative of the viewpoints of the Sandinista political party. The survey was administered to all of the representatives in the National Assembly but only the legislators of the opposition party block, the Independent Liberal Party (or "Partido Liberal Independiente") chose to participate in the study. Nevertheless, the evidence is revealing as it shows the viewpoints of opposition legislators in a Sandinista-controlled political environment. As shown in the second column (Agree), about half of the members of the opposition

Table 4.2 Views of Politicians in National Legislature about Indigenous Land Titling, Opposition Block, 2015

Question	Agree	No	Blank/No Comment
Indigenous land titling in the east strengthens the control of the state in that region (%)	55%	20%	25%
Supports Indigenous land titling although ethnic outsiders are evicted (%)	55%	5%	40%
Believes there is too much Indigenous land for too few people (%)	20%	0	80%
Number of respondents: 20 (out of 23) or 86.95 percent. Note: The general response rate was 21.97%.			

party agree that titling Indigenous lands strengthens the power of the state in the eastern territory.

Although titling Indigenous lands disempowers ethnic outsiders, 55 percent support titling. Interestingly, the overwhelming majority of legislators (80 percent) chose to ignore the politically sensitive statement about the disproportional allocation of land to minority groups. The survey provides evidence that during Sandinista times, Indigenous land titling reinforces state power in the east.

State elites worked fast and hard to resolve land claims in the east as quickly as possible. Once in office, Ortega played a decisive role. The primary objective was to cut Rivera's political edge, limit Indigenous elites' opportunities to stir up the masses again, and sap the impetus of territorial demands. Ortega ordered the restructuring of communal property regimes in the east to prevent serious governability problems.

To accomplish the objective quickly and systematically, Ortega created the Secretariat for the Development of the Caribbean Coast under Lumberto Campbell—Ortega's long-term ally cited earlier in this chapter—and with broad powers and discretion that made Indigenous land titling its top priority.[11] The secretariat determined the courses of actions that mid- and low-ranking government officers follow regarding the eastern territory. For instance, the secretariat oversaw the work of the Communal Titling Unit within the Attorney General's Office, which in turn coordinated and managed the technical aspects related to the titling and registration process. The regional government, the regional Titling Commission (CONADETI),[12] and the technical experts of the Institute for Territorial Studies[13] followed the directives and guidelines of the secretariat. To finance the operation, the central government used available funds from the World Bank and other international funding agencies, such as the Ford Foundation and the Catalan Agency for Cooperation to Development (UNDP 2011). Miskito legislative representative Evelyn Taylor, explained that:

> In January 2007, the fundamental mission was to delimit and title all communal property within the framework of a new program called Mother Earth headed by Lumberto Campbell. The most important priority was to title twenty-two territories quickly. High political will began then. The funds came from the World Bank. The leadership [*incidencia*] of the FSLN was necessary to finish the process in record-time ... [At that moment,] it was clear that titling communal land was the most important priority since the right to property is a fundamental right. The communities have historically demanded respect for collective property; they went to war against the FSLN for communal property rights ... All issues related to the east must pass through the door of Commander Campbell, whose topmost priority was to set the boundaries [*amojonar*] and title the communal lands in the east quickly and systematically.[14]

The Sandinistas consolidated the petition of dozens of villages into a manageable number of multi-ethnic communal blocks to quicken the pace of the titling program. That is, the Sandinistas chose not to title hundreds of communities individually and ignored already submitted petitions. In 2006, just before the Sandinistas regained power, the Titling Commission had received over 60 communal property claims[15] (Finley-Brook and Offen 2009). Political negotiations between Sandinista and Miskito leaders resulted in the final number of land blocks that the state would title.

During the negotiation, Rivera proposed titling thirteen land blocks. Given the precedent of the 1980s, the Miskito did not demand a single title for the entire Miskito territory. Miskito political elites, according to Hoppington, sought to "build trust with the Nicaraguan state [since] a single block looks like a country."[16] At the same time, the Miskito sought a relatively low number of land blocks to consolidate power and assuage criticisms from local Miskito elites, who had rejected the central government's authority outright and argued that titling communal land fragments the ancestral Miskito Nation (Offen 2003; Mendoza and Kuhnekath 2005).

The Miskito territorial strategy of power concentration was obvious to the local people of the east. Melba McClean, a member of the Awas Tingni community and head of the former Central American University research unit at Bilwi, explains, "YATAMA [the Miskito political party] sought to create a few Indigenous lands, manage a limited number of Territorial Authorities, and have more communities under their control."[17] Rivera himself uses a similar rationale to explain his role in the creation of the new communal property regimes: "There were more than 22 [to] 23 territorial [claims] during [the] Bolaños' [government] term; we merged territories [together with the Sandinistas] to move faster since some territories were too small, containing only three communities... [In addition,] we sought to have more strength and face the central government."[18] Rivera's point is that before the Sandinista regained power, communities had claimed smaller, but more numerous communal land plots. When the Sandinista returned to power, there was an agreement between the central government and Miskito elites to amalgamate smaller land claims. These negotiations resulted in larger land blocks that join several villages together.

The identification and titling of Indigenous lands did not result from a bottom-up technical process that took into consideration the initial preferences of villagers and communities. By the end of 2006, communities had made demands for about sixty titles directly to the Titling Commission. In early 2007, Miskito political leaders amalgamated communal land claims, causing a dramatic drop in the number of jurisdictional units that would result. Clearly, Miskito leaders made a significant effort, disregarding villagers' initial demands, to make a noticeably different type of territorial claim to the state. Thus, the state did not receive villagers' request in an unmediated manner. The state received a proposal designed and approved by intermediaries, Indigenous elites, not by the communities themselves. Moreover, the state also transformed and redesigned the proposal to meet its own objective. In addition to decreasing the initial number of land claims made in 2006 to quicken the pace of titling, the central government further increased the number of land blocks compared to what the Miskito proposed in early 2007, to break Miskito control over the communities. In essence, state elites reconfigured the boundaries of the new land blocks, rather than simply identify and certify villager's ancestral land claims. The resulting number of land blocks meets the twin goals of quickening the pace of titling and undermining Miskito elites' political advantage.

To prevent Miskito concentration of territorial power, state elites designed and titled twenty-three different land blocks composed of several multi-ethnic communities. Consequently, each land block has an average of about fourteen communities per title. Only two property titles include only one village and surrounding areas, namely the Mayangna communities of Awas Tingni and Sikilta (Attorney General's Office 2013, 2016).

By dividing the eastern territory into a greater number of multi-ethnic land blocks than those originally proposed by the Miskito leaders, the government signaled its traditional worries about a single Miskito homeland. Table 4.3 contains information about the number of titles awarded per year, the composition and number of communities enclosed within each title, and the percentage of the country's total territory that each title represents. The information in the table evidences that the state purposely divided the eastern territory into a controllable number of jurisdictional units.

In sum, Ortega and the Sandinista political elite fully understood the relationship between Indigenous land titling and the territorial integrity of the state. The potential for renewed resistance was the single most important factor motivating Sandinista elites to title Indigenous lands. But the government was careful to subdivide the ancient "Miskito Kingdom" and to draw lines that aggregate multi-ethnic communities, in order to defuse both separatist aspirations and the power of Miskito elites. The state took decisive action in the east, not the west. In the next subsection, I show how the legacy of inter-ethnic war in the east informed political decisions to create communal property regimes there but not in the west.

Table 4.3 Indigenous Lands in the East, 2007–2013

Year	Communal Lands (No.)	Communities (No.)	Communities per Title (avg)	Area (ha)	As %, Eastern Territory (ha)
2007	5	85	17.00	575,602	4.8
2008	2	17	8.50	314,701	2.6
2009	2	19	9.50	131,676	1.1
2010	6	93	15.50	1,225,873	10.2
2012	2	29	14.50	659,967	5.5
2013	5	78	15.60	857,911	7.1
2016	1	2	2.00	88,468	0.7
Total	23	323	14.04	3,854,198	32

Sources: Attorney General's Office 2016; Álvarez 2016.

State Interests for the Spatial Pattern of Titling

The preceding historical analysis suggests that the threat of internal turmoil in the east triggered political elites' institutional interests to title Indigenous lands quickly and systematically. Sandinista leaders designed, delimited, and titled land blocks to clip the wings of potential mobilization and prevent the repetition of a painful precedent.

To provide further evidence of the political elites' motivations and to eliminate other explanatory factors, I undertake a controlled matched comparison of two provinces in Nicaragua with varying levels of internal threat: Madriz and the North Caribbean Autonomous Region ("North Caribbean"). In particular, I compare the outcomes of Indigenous land claims from the Miskito and the Chorotega, the two largest Indigenous groups in Nicaragua (INIDE 2005; Olguín Martínez 2006). The Miskito claim land in the North Caribbean, a remote, sparsely populated, and mountainous province in the northeast. The Chorotega claim land in Madriz, a poor, agrarian, and mainly Indigenous province in the west.

The North Caribbean and Madriz have comparable economic and demographic conditions that are typically associated with land titling processes. Both provinces are similar in their levels of economic development, the size of the rural population, and the percentage of Indigenous peoples. Similarly, all communal land claims are based on colonial titles or customary tenure, cultural distinctness as Indigenous peoples colonized by a Mestizo nation-state, and the experience of historical oppression. Civil society organizations formed by the Miskito and Chorotega receive financial support from external sources and work with NGOs that have dense links to international networks advocating for Indigenous rights. Finally, all Indigenous leaders couch land claims in the Constitution (1987) and ILO Convention No. 169. Table 4.4 shows the levels of poverty and demographic characteristics, as well as the number, area, basis, and outcome of land claims per province.

Despite the many similarities, the provinces differ in outcomes. In the North Caribbean, the state solved all Miskito land claims at a breakneck rate: in six years, the state titled over two million hectares. The state divided about 65 percent of the province's total land area into eleven Indigenous lands. In contrast to the experience in the northeast, the state has ignored all of the claims from the west. Indigenous peoples from Madriz, just like all others from western Nicaragua, continue to have unclear communal

Table 4.4 Socioeconomic Conditions, Indigenous Land Claims, and Outcomes by Province

Province	Ethnicity	Poverty*	Rural Pop. (%)	Indigenous Pop. (%)	Land Claims (ha)	Claim Basis**	Outcome
North Caribbean	Miskito	Severe	69	57	11 (2,078,558)	Customary tenure	Titled
Madriz	Chorotega	Severe	72	77	6 (75,317)	Colonial titles	Ignored

Sources: INIDE 2005; Olguín Martínez and ILO 2006; Attorney General's Office 2016; author's compilation from CONADETI files.
Notes: *The central government considers anything over 50 percent as severe poverty.
**Claim basis is defined as the legal argument that Indigenous peoples use to substantiate claims.

property rights. Although the Constitution recognizes communal property rights for Indigenous peoples and all ethnic groups in Nicaragua regardless of place of origin, the government is not attempting to bridge the gap in implementation between the east and the west. How can Indigenous groups from two halves of the same country, under the same political leadership, have such radically different outcomes? I argue that state elites' motivation to title Indigenous lands is rooted in the need to prevent instability based on a historical lesson: Miskito people can resist land dispossession and defy the central government violently.

The two provinces have significantly different histories of political mobilization and insurrection. Whereas communities from the east threatened the integrity of the state in the 1980s, such a separatist threat did not emerge in the west. The North Caribbean province, the bastion of Miskito militancy, has a long history of antistate mobilization and secessionist claims. State elites are aware that under a Sandinista government, radicalization is a stone's throw away in the east—as substantiated earlier in the chapter. Because of the palpable memory of concerted resistance against state rule, Miskito elites could incite their militant base to destabilize the eastern region where the state has little institutional presence. Madriz, by contrast, lacks a recent history of insurrection against state rule. Moreover, Madriz is located in the western part of Nicaragua, where the state has a strong presence. A comparison of these two provinces reveals why the threat of turmoil, instead of other potential explanatory factors, triggered the state's institutional interests to design and title Indigenous lands. Table 4.5 shows the contextual similarities and differences in outcome.

Table 4.5 Contextual Similarities and Differences in the Provinces, per Indigenous Group

Ethnic Group	Province	Land Claim	Subject of Law*	External Support**	Potential Local Resistance	State Interest	Titling
Miskito	North Caribbean	Yes	Yes	Yes	Yes	Yes	Yes
Chorotega	Madriz	Yes	Yes	Yes	No	No	No

Sources: Olguín Martínez and ILO 2006; Attorney General's Office 2009.

Notes: *Subject of law means that formal communal property rights apply to the Indigenous or ethnic groups demanding secure property rights.

**External support indicates support from international financial institutions or international NGOs. For instance, the World Bank and the International Land Coalition—a large global NGO network—support the Chorotega.

The North Caribbean Autonomous Region

As the historical analysis in this chapter shows, the North Caribbean province is a remarkable case of swift and systematic titling rooted in a history of ethnic war and violent struggle against the state. The legacy of Miskito secessionist aspirations triggered the institutional concerns of Sandinista leaders, which led to the quick resolution of claims. Through the design and titling of Indigenous lands, state elites created new jurisdictional units and a system of hierarchical rule that they can co-opt and wield to restrain Indigenous self-determination and reinforce the state's territorial power. After titling communal lands and installing new ethnic communal property regimes, the government has sidelined or co-opted traditional Indigenous leaders. In 2015, a Sandinista-backed coalition stripped Rivera, the Miskito representative in the National Assembly, of his immunity and legislative seat (Montez Rugama 2015). Other representatives from the east, such as Loria Raquel Dixon and Evelyn Taylor, are either part of or under the control of the Sandinista legislative block. In addition, the Ortega administration fails to protect Miskito communities affected by ongoing land conflicts (IACHR PM505/15, IACHR Resolution 2/16; Miranda Aburto 2016; Newman 2018). In what follows, I use extensive in-depth interviews with Sandinista ruling elites, experts, and Indigenous elites to show that state elites create new communal property regimes as governing arrangements akin to indirect rule. State elites seek to manage and co-opt these new institutional hierarchies to secure internal order and territorial control.

The Making of New Communal Property Regimes

Upon regaining power in 2007, the main concerns of Sandinista political elites were twofold, to (a) avoid an uprising, and (b) exert political control over Indigenous peoples in the remote east. For that purpose, the central government created a new institution called the Territorial Authority to take advantage of mechanisms of social control that existed—and can be reinforced—at the local level. When state elites designed, delimited, and titled Indigenous lands, they created new subnational jurisdictions called Indigenous Territorial Government (or "Gobierno Territorial Indígena," GTI) that have as boundaries those geographical coordinates established by the communal property title. The new governing units lump together all of the people and communities that are officially listed in the property title. The Territorial Authority is the legal representative of the Indigenous Territorial Government with the capacity to make a wide range of political and economic decisions in the name of the people and the communities that are inside the new jurisdictional units. The Territorial Authority serves as the intermediary between local rural people and the state, and the Indigenous Territorial Government cements the control of Indigenous political elites over the population.

Paul Oquist Kelley, Ortega's top political advisor quoted earlier in this chapter, is explicit about the importance of creating communal property regimes and the crucial role that these new institutions play for governing the east:

> The new [communal] institutions are a fundamental piece to ensure unity. They are an integral part of the political and developmental process that Nicaragua is experiencing. When there is a Territorial Government and a Regional Council, the central government can talk and negotiate with those representatives about the [Inter-Oceanic] Canal or other projects. The Territorial Government, Regional Council, and central government can reach a consensus ... The society as a whole and the [central] government benefited from the new [communal property] institutions. The new institutions are a mechanism to govern via consensus, if not the problems

become unmanageable. Titling communal land prevents conflict and establishes new institutions that facilitate the governability of the region.[19]

In talking about Indigenous lands as new institutions, Oquist highlights that state elites view communal property regimes as a mechanism to govern Indigenous peoples. That is the case because state elites—after titling land blocks and creating a new governing structure in these land blocks—attempt to cement alliances with the Territorial Authority and control decisions about the use and management of resources inside Indigenous lands. Unsurprisingly, the Regional Council—a governing apparatus under the reigns of the central government—certifies the Territorial Authority. Figure 4.3 illustrates the hierarchical levels of government in the east; in bold are the new political structures that the state created by titling Indigenous lands.

The Territorial Authority is a new institution introduced by the central government in the Communal Property Regime Law (2003), the interlocutor par excellence between the state, on the one hand, and rural local villagers and communities on the other. Whoever holds that position, has political control over the management of natural resources and the distribution of power within the new jurisdiction. While the Communal Property Regime Law expressly seeks to enhance local autonomy and Indigenous self-government, in practice the central government attempts to monitor and influence local political life through the Territorial Authority. Carlos Alemán, the Sandinista representative in the Regional Council, explains, "The communities are joined into blocks according to geographical areas. Some [blocks] are ethnically mixed, so the challenge now is to manage the communities internally."[20] In fact, the Sandinista administration controls both the Regional Government and the newly created Territorial Authority in a top-down fashion.[21] As Melba McClean, a Mayangna leader cited above, puts it, "the Sandinista government has created national and regional level

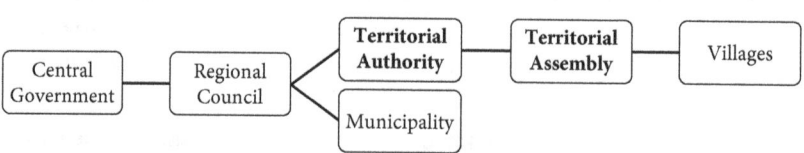

Figure 4.3 Levels of Government in the Eastern Territory.

positions for the indigenous people. Nevertheless, these people only receive orders and do not represent the communities."[22]

Betty Rigby, a respected member of the Creole community, explains:

> The idea was to have local level communal demands rise to the regional level but that does not work in practice . . . The FSLN [Sandinistas] have been in power for two periods in the central government. Now, they [the Sandinistas] hold power in the regional government . . . The central government has increased its presence in the region with programs and projects from the Ministry of Environment, Ministry of Health, and the Forest Institute. The central government now penetrates the communities and has more presence than in the 1980s.[23]

In sum, Indigenous land titling does not simply help resolve communal land claims and pacify restive communities, defusing separatist claims, but it also helps create new common property regimes designed to govern the region through intermediaries that state elites monitor in a top-down fashion. The creation of communal property regimes is a noncoercive way of sorting and settling the local population into state-designed areas and creating decision-making structures to govern local social and political life. The state establishes the administrative framework to control the local population and prevent the recurrence of a massive insurrections.

Madriz

There has been no Indigenous land titling in Madriz in contemporary times. That fact grants a unique opportunity to assess directly—in a controlled manner—whether the threat of insurrection or other concerns motivate political elites to create communal property regimes. The Chorotega experience is a striking case of undefined property rights in an Indigenous agricultural province that suffers from severe poverty levels. The Sandinista government has disregarded Indigenous land claims from Madriz while the Chorotega, an overwhelming majority of the province population (76 percent), demand titles to about 75,000 hectares of their ancestral land (INIDE 2005; Olguín Martínez and ILO 2006). The main reason behind government inaction is that these land claims are not rooted in what state elites perceive as a secessionist attempt. Moreover, the Indigenous population is located in the west, where the state's institutional apparatus has had considerable presence and exerts direct control. Because the Chorotega do not pose an acute threat to the state's power, the central government does not need to create a differentiated governing system to control the rural population. Therefore, the state has ignored Indigenous land claims in the west.

Currently, Indigenous peoples constitute the majority of the population in Madriz. The Chorotega political elites demand Indigenous land titles emphasizing an indigenous identity and distinct cultural rights. In particular, local leaders demand secure property rights based on Colonial Indigenous land titles. These colonial titles are property titles to communal land that the Spanish Empire issued as royal decrees to Indigenous ancestors during the seventeenth and eighteenth centuries (Mechri Adler 2000). For centuries, community leaders have safeguarded these colonial titles by either hiding, restoring, or securing certified copies of the original royal decree (Olguín Martínez and ILO 2006; Monachon and Gonda 2011). In Madriz, only one land claim, namely Totogalpa, bases tenure demand on customary possession alone without having the support of a colonial title. Moreover, the communities have made enormous efforts to preserve the boundaries of those lands allocated under Spanish rule. A report by the International Land Coalition, written by David Monachon and Noémi Gonda (2011, 10), remarks that, "[t]he royal titles are the patrimony that the indigenous people use to defend their rights to the land left them by their ancestors." Table 4.6 details the name, area, number of communities, and basis of Chorotega land claims in Madriz, by municipality.

The Chorotega people do not pose a threat to the Nicaraguan state, which has traditionally had a stronger foothold in the west than in the remote east. Not only are there more roads and connections between the provinces of the west, but Madriz has always been an integral part of Nicaragua. Through centuries of state building, political leaders have been able to erect and maintain institutions that reinforce the nation-state's power. Therefore, state elites can more easily wield repressive power in Madriz to quell social movements and prevent radicalized land demands. Likewise, political leaders can manage local affairs more efficiently and directly through orthodox political means. For instance, state elites can manipulate local political leaders and destabilize incipient Indigenous communal structures using patronage and corruption (Monachon and Gonda 2011, 15–16). Finally, because of historical and enduring nation-building practices, political elites can put in place a system of private property without generating violent resistance from local

Table 4.6 Chorotega Land Claims in Madriz

Municipality	Claim Name	Claimed Area (ha)	Communities, (number)	Land Claim Basis
San Jose de Cusmapa	San Jose de Cusmapa	10,100	28	1652 Colonial Title
San Lucas	San Lucas	13,900	32	1662, 1673, 1737 Colonial Titles, 1901 Donation (Pablo Jose Moreno).
Somoto	San Antonio de Padua	270	4	1779 Colonial Title
Somoto	Santa Barbara	1,902	4	1737 Colonial Title
Telpaneca	LiTelpaneca	35,445	37	1622 Colonial Title
Totogalpa	Totogalpa	13,700	40	Lost Colonial Title (seventeenth century), 1860 Delimited, Customary Tenure

Source: Olguín Martínez and ILO 2006.

leaders. Because the state has more presence and control in the west, it is unlikely that the privatization of land that has already been parceled out would provide sufficient incentives for radical insurrection in Madriz.

The Sandinistas did not anticipate a Chorotega insurrection in Madriz, where the state has a more robust foundation. Hence, the levels of internal threat in the west are low. In the absence of a motivating factor to trigger state interests, political elites in the central government are not motivated to erect and maintain communal property regimes. There is no Indigenous land titling program in Madriz—or in the rest of western Nicaragua—because it is unnecessary to guarantee internal order there. In the absence of a strong precedent of resistance, the government does not need to—and does not—put in place communal property regimes through Indigenous land titling to control people and territory.

Conclusion

The overall goal of this work is to develop an explanation for the patterns of Indigenous land titling in Nicaragua, where a titling program began in 2007 and spread systematically with dramatic speed in the remote eastern portion of the country. This chapter has shown that transnational constructivism, economic structuralism, or administrative theory cannot fully account for the onset, rate, and geographical concentration of titled Indigenous lands. First, external pressures were low in 2007, which indicates that transnational pressure is not necessary for titling action. The regional gap in outcomes between the east and the west also suggests that external pressure did not motivate state action. Second, titling occurred in huge expanses of resource-rich lands despite opposition from powerful economic groups, which is indicative of the limitations of economic structuralism. Finally, while the state's bureaucratic capacity remained limited, Indigenous land titling spread quickly where the state has very little institutional presence. Clearly, weak state capacity is not an insurmountable obstacle for titling.

Because of the limitations of extant explanations, I draw on the framework outlined in Chapter 3 to argue that state interests, triggered by high levels of internal threats, affect where, at what pace, and how titling happens. I showed that the Nicaraguan state proactively identified, delimited, and titled twenty-three communal land blocks in the east to prevent the resurgence of Indigenous resistance. The security interests motivated the unexpected move toward rapid and systematic titling. State elites' fears of civil unrest activated their institutional interests and prompted titling to thwart potential uprisings. High internal threats in 2007 resulted from the return to power of Daniel Ortega, the revolutionary leader who instigated the inter-ethnic war of the 1980s. The vivid memory of armed conflict in the east and the threat of political reversion posed by Ortega's 2007 election to the presidency might have radicalized Indigenous groups to embrace their historical claim to an ancestral homeland, rise in arms to fight for self-determination, and demand independence from state-rule. Because the legacy of inter-ethnic war is particularly potent in the eastern territory, the Sandinista leaders were cognizant that their return to power increased the potential for renewed radicalized land demands. Once in power, state elites were determined to title Indigenous lands quickly to prevent the repetition of a painful turbulent history.

While the state has ignored Indigenous land claims in the west, the central government has channeled international financial support to title lands in the east. The dramatic differences in outcomes between the east and the west suggest that political elites title Indigenous lands where the state has little institutional presence. By titling Indigenous lands, state elites create new jurisdictional units, represented by a Territorial Authority. By co-opting the

Territorial Authority, the central government can manage the distribution of power and resources inside Indigenous areas. Where the state has a strong presence and there is no potent history of insurrection, the state does not need to create a new arrangement to govern the rural population. For this reason, the state ignores Indigenous land claims in the west.

The preceding analysis shows that high levels of internal threats activate state interests to title Indigenous lands. In the Nicaraguan case, these high levels of internal threat stem from the political salience of self-determination struggles in the eastern territory and the increased potential for renewed resistance with Daniel Ortega's reelection in 2007. In Chapter 5, I show that medium-high levels of internal threats are sufficient to trigger state interests. In the Honduran case, I identify escalating organized criminal activity in the east, rather than the potential for Indigenous resistance, as the source of the internal threat. In doing so, I emphasize that state interests—and not bottom-up demands from Indigenous peoples—are key to explaining Indigenous land titling.

5

Honduras

Mine Not Yours: Indigenous Land Titling to Recover the Eastern Territory

The central government has not been present in La Mosquitia [the eastern Gracias a Dios province], which paved the way for drug trafficking. Two years ago, drug traffickers provided basic services, like healthcare and so on, in La Mosquitia ... This is why we invest heavily there in social programs, to keep drug traffickers out.
(Vice Admiral Rigoberto Espinoza Posadas, May 25, 2015, Tegucigalpa, Honduras)

Drug traffickers threatened to substitute the state because they have abundant economic resources, controlled a territory, and subjected or controlled the population... They controlled part of that [eastern] territory... The state intervenes to regain control.
(General Julián Pacheco Tinoco, June 19, 2015, Tegucigalpa, Honduras)

Titling Indigenous lands is necessary because we cannot solve the [drug trafficking] problem using only repressive tactics; logically, titling Indigenous land is good so that people cooperate [with anti-narcotics operations].
(Infantry Colonel Gustavo Adolfo Paz Escalante, June 18, 2015, Tegucigalpa, Honduras)

The preceding chapter explained why, starting in 2007, the Nicaraguan government implemented Indigenous land and resource rights quickly in the east but not the west. My analysis showed how the potential for Indigenous mobilization, perceived as an internal threat, prompted state elites to advance in Indigenous land titling. A few years later, a similar process unfolded in eastern Honduras. From 2009 onward, eastern Honduras suddenly became a haven for organized crime, creating a state inside the state. Seeing its monopoly over legitimate coercion drastically challenged, the Honduran state soon felt compelled to respond and retake control over this territory. State elites used Indigenous land titling to reinforce state power. In 2012, under medium-high levels of internal threats, the central government quickly implemented a generous Indigenous land titling program in Gracias a Dios—the isolated province known as La Mosquitita overrun by organized crime. In only four short years (2012–2016), the state allocated about 12 percent of the total land area in Honduras to Indigenous peoples and ethnic groups there. By 2015, the center-right governments of Porfirio Lobo (2010–2014) and Juan Orlando Hernández (2014–present) had titled the largest amount of land in forty years. Figure 5.1 illustrates the number of hectares that the central government has titled as Indigenous lands since 1982, when the state recognized communal property rights in the Constitution.

Tellingly, the state only titled large expanses of communal land in Gracias a Dios province. In other provinces, which had not fallen under the control of organized crime, titling takes a radically different form. The state has titled micro-territories to Indigenous groups located in the coastal regions to the north, the mountainous forests of the west, and the central plains. Although political leaders from eight other Indigenous groups claim property rights over large areas based on the constitutional provisions and ILO Convention No. 169, the central government has only given them title to small land plots. Map 5.1 illustrates the location and area of titled Indigenous lands in Honduras.

The Honduran government's titling of extensive resource-rich areas as Indigenous lands in such a short time period was highly surprising for three reasons. In Honduras, the military has considerable political power over civilian affairs, socioeconomic elites are inordinately influential in political decision-making, and social movements are fractured and severely repressed. For three decades, the central government had ignored the demands of Indigenous leaders for secure property rights in Gracias a Dios province. Historically, this province was part of a Miskito territory known as the Miskito Kingdom, which spanned eastern Honduras and Nicaragua. The state vehemently resisted the recognition of Miskito land claims based on possession predating the creation of the modern state. Yet, in 2012, state elites unexpectedly recognized sixteen inter-communal land blocks and decided to title each to a Territorial Council or local political organization on behalf of Indigenous communities. What explains the sudden political decision to title Indigenous lands in the east? Why is titling so radically different

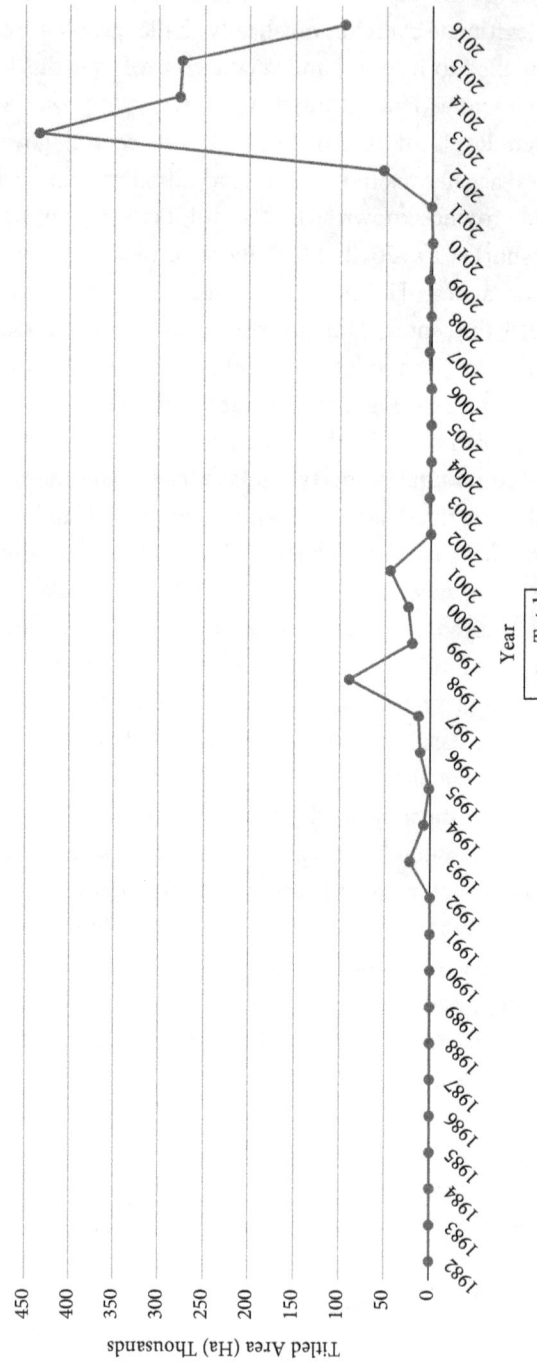

Figure 5.1 Indigenous Land Titling in Honduras since 1982
Sources: IP 2016; Forest Trends 2015.

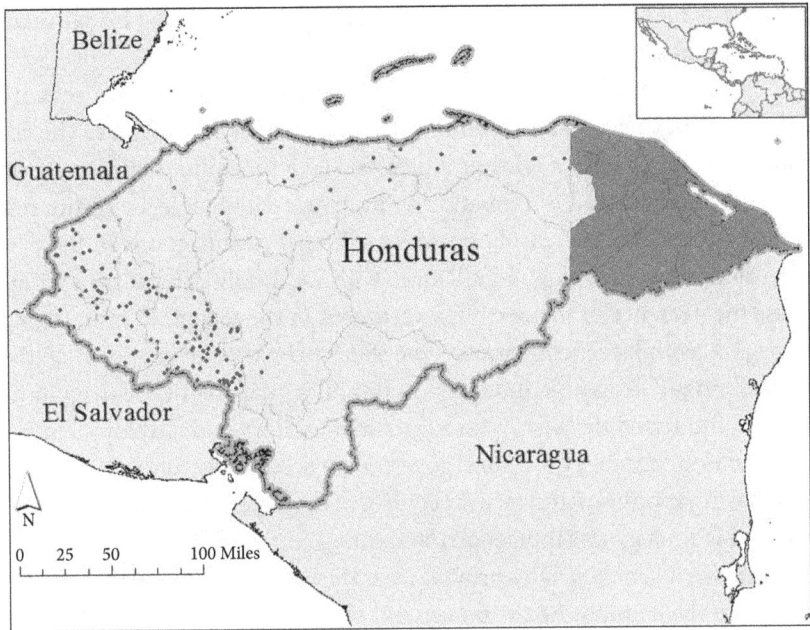

Map 5.1 Titled Indigenous Lands, Honduras
Sources: Anderson 2009; Forest Trends 2015; National Agrarian Institute 2016; ICF 2016.

in other regions? What accounts for the distinctive features of Indigenous land titling in Honduras?

Based on primary evidence collected during fieldwork, this chapter demonstrates that state interests in recovering military and political control of the eastern territory account for the dramatic burst in Indigenous land titling there. Titling is part of a military and political program designed to reduce the flow of narcotics into the country and to tame the power of criminal organizations that threaten the state. In 2010, state elites devised and implemented a full-blown anti-narcotics strategy that included the titling of Indigenous lands, the provision of local healthcare services, and the construction of education centers to curtail the growing influence of drug trafficking organizations in the east. Following the advice of military strategists, the center-right government installed communal property regimes to govern the Gracias a Dios province because that depressed and stateless region had become an operating base for organized crime. Thus, like Nicaragua, internal threats drove the sudden burst in titling. Yet, unlike Nicaragua, internal threats did not stem from the perceived threat of

Indigenous mobilization but from real security threats arising from organized criminal activity.

In 2009, a serious political crisis created the opportunity for a massive amount of cocaine to enter Honduras through the eastern province. The cocaine flooding Gracias a Dios province caused a precipitous surge in drug trafficking activity and a dramatic rise in drug-related violence in the rest of the country. The increasing power of criminal organizations in the east motivated state elites to build alliances with local political leaders and increase the presence of the central government in the region. In militarizing the region, with local acquiescence, the state's primary aim was to crush the political might, economic influence, and military capabilities of drug lords that had infiltrated the east. With substantial military and development aid from the United States, the central government acted decisively to destabilize criminal organizations and recover control of the eastern region. One crucial part of this strategy was Indigenous land titling.

The eastern Gracias a Dios province was the source of internal threats, not the rest of the country. As the power and control of criminal organizations increased and threatened the state's power in the east, state elites devised a military and political strategy to repossess that infiltrated territory. By contrast, in places where the state has had a firmer presence, namely outside of Gracias a Dios province, the central government has severely restricted the titling of communal property and has alienated Indigenous political organizations that are demanding the application of the same Indigenous land and resource rights.

This chapter, which is divided in three subsections and a conclusion, will substantiate the argument that state interests motivated political elites to title large areas as Indigenous lands in Gracias a Dios province in the 2010s, while titling only micro-territories in the rest of the country. In the first subsection, I show that standard accounts do not fully explain the distinctive titling patterns found in Honduras. In the second subsection, I demonstrate that a rise in drug trafficking activity triggered the institutional interests of state elites to incorporate the eastern region into the rest of the country, albeit in a highly differentiated way. By showing that violent conflict between criminal groups created serious security and governability problems for the state, I pinpoint what prompted state elites to build alliances with local Indigenous leaders, title extensive areas as Indigenous lands, and augment the presence of the central government in the east—both militarily and politically. In the third subsection, I explain the reason the central government has employed a radically different approach to land demands in the east compared to the rest of the country. State elites only titled extensive Indigenous lands when and where organized crime threatened the state's territorial control, and neither before nor elsewhere.

To account for the timing and rate of titling, I use extensive qualitative evidence, mainly in-depth interviews with military leaders and government officials, as well as the results of an original survey administered to military officers enrolled in postgraduate courses at the Honduran University of Defense in May 2015. I show that Indigenous land titling in the east is part of an anti-narcotics strategy intended to undermine the power of criminal organizations. The analysis that follows conclusively shows that the military elite, and other key decision-makers, viewed Indigenous land titling as a fundamental piece in a broader military and political program that envisioned the integration of the eastern territory with the rest of the country. By providing a modicum of public goods—namely, land tenure security, healthcare, and education—state elites have sought to displace the political power of drug lords and diminish the level of internal threats originating from Gracias a Dios province. To account for the spatial patterns in titling, I present a matched comparison of two regions that have experienced radically different titling outcomes, while controlling for external pressure, as well as other economic, demographic, and contextual factors that are normally associated with these outcomes. The analysis isolates the effect that internal threats posed by criminal organizations have on titling extensive Indigenous lands. I emphasize that where the state has a firmer hold on the territory and criminal organizations do not pose a direct threat to its power, political elites limit the allocation of communal land to Indigenous peoples.

Limitations of Extant Approaches

Established frameworks provide important contextual information about the nature of Indigenous land titling in Honduras. However, these perspectives have a hard time explaining the timing, rate, and manner in which the state has titled Indigenous lands in eastern Honduras. Transnational constructivism is hard pressed to account for the timing and striking regional difference in titling outcomes. In 2010, President Porfirio Lobo was not responding to external pressure when he decided to title Indigenous lands in Gracias a Dios province. Rather than focusing on Indigenous lands, the international community was concerned with the violent aftermath of the military coup against Manuel Zelaya—a democratically elected center-left president (2006–2009)—and was demanding free and fair elections (UN 2010; IACHR 2009, 2010, 2015). Although all Indigenous and ethnic groups demand the implementation of the same rights to communal land and resources, using the same strategies (i.e. peaceful marches and demonstrations), only those from the east received preferential treatment. In the east, the central government joined several villages together along with their surrounding lands in a single title; in the rest of the country, the central government separated Indigenous communities and only titled micro-territories surrounding single villages without including their surrounding areas in the land title (National Agrarian Institute 2016; Forest Trends 2015).

Similarly, social movement theories cannot explain the repression that land rights activists have endured outside Gracias a Dios province, along with the central government's neglect. Notably, the central government failed to protect Berta Cáceres, an award-winning environmental activist from western Honduras and leader of the Council of Popular and Indigenous Organizations of Honduras (COPINH), Honduras's strongest Indigenous political organization (IACHR 2010, par. 94; IACHR 2015b, 40–47). In March 2016, Cáceres was assassinated for opposing illegal logging and hydroelectric dams in Lenca territory, despite the central government having been ordered to ensure her protection in 2009 by the Inter-American Commission on Human Rights (Rivero 2016; Malkin and Arce 2016; Shoichet, Griffiths, and Flournoy 2016; BBC 2016; Palencia and Pretel 2016; COPINH 2016; *The Guardian* 2016; Lakhani 2019). Although tragic, Cáceres's assassination is not an isolated event. Despite precautionary measures issued by the Inter-American Commission, members of a Xicaque (Tolupán) Indigenous organization from central Honduras, the Broad Movement for Dignity and Justice (MADJ), have also been threatened, harassed, and assassinated (Global Witness 2015, 20–21; IACHR 2013). As United Nations Special Rapporteur for Indigenous Rights Victoria Tauli-Corpuz observed in reaction to Cáceres's death, "[T]here is a clear tendency for indigenous campaigners and human rights activists to be killed [in Honduras]" (cited in *The Guardian* 2016). The media, including *The New York Times*, *The Washington Post*, and *Reuters*, similarly reported that land rights activists in Honduras face severe risks, repression, and intimidation (Miroff 2016; Becher and Powis 2016; Nuwer 2016; Fears 2016). Since 2009, more than 130 land and environmental activists have been assassinated in Honduras (Puentes Riaños

2016; IACHR 2016; IACHR 2015, para. 77; Global Witness 2015, 2017, 2020). A study conducted by Global Witness, an international NGO, notes that Honduras is "the deadliest country in the world to be a land and environmental defender" (2015, 16). Paradoxically, the death toll of Indigenous land activists relative to the population is higher *outside* the drug-infested Gracias a Dios province.

Economic structuralism does not persuasively explain why the central government would title an extensive cash-producing region with timber, and potentially oil, to economically and politically marginalized Indigenous groups, effectively removing it from the land market and vesting power to manage and allocate resources on local Indigenous elites, not ethnic outsiders. According to the 2004 Property Law, it is illegal to sell or otherwise transfer communal property rights (Chapter III, Article 100). In fact, the communal land title allocated to Indigenous peoples and ethnic groups based on customary possession is "inalienable, imprescriptible, not subject to liens [*inembargable*], and indivisible" (National Agrarian Institute 2016). To be sure, ethnic outsiders can invest in agriculture, logging, cattle ranching, and other economically productive industries inside Indigenous lands but only under contract with state-sanctioned local representatives (Property Law, Article 100). Despite going against economic interests, the central government divided Gracias a Dios province into sixteen inter-communal land blocks and declared it an "Indigenous Territory" (Executive Decree PCM-023, 2013). During only four years (2012–2016), the central government titled over 1.4 million hectares as Indigenous lands in the eastern province (National Agrarian Institute 2016; ICF 2016). Surprisingly, about one million hectares (roughly 80 percent) of these newly titled lands are ripe for economic exploitation (ICF 2016; National Agrarian Institute 2016); these areas are rich in natural resources, including pastoral land and fishing grounds (Cuéllar et al. 2012, 42–54). Before titling the inter-communal land blocks, the Honduran state remarked, "La Mosquitia [or Gracias a Dios province] is the most important 'continuous flat valleys' [sic] in the country and a reserve zone with *incalculable value* for our [country's] future" (Honduras, 2010, 87–88). The very pattern of titling, especially its striking speed and vast geographical scope, contradicts the observable implications of economic structuralism, which expects the state to move slowly and allocate lands to Indigenous groups only in areas with little to no economic value.

Finally, theories of administration make it difficult to make sense of the timing, impressive rate, and geographical scope of land titling in an effectively abandoned territory that is hard to reach. In Honduras, the titling rate increased dramatically in 2012 although the quality, technical capacity, and lack of cohesiveness of the Honduran bureaucracy remained the same. In only four short years (2012–2016), at a rate of 347,000 hectares per year, the state identified, delimited, and titled all of the Miskito inter-communal land blocks. This impressive outcome occurred in a country notorious for its weak institutional capacity, where there is widespread corruption and routine use of patronage and non-meritocratic hiring practices in ministries and public offices. In addition, no single agency has control of the titling process: responsibility for titling rests jointly with the Property Institute, the National Agrarian Institute, and the Forest Conservation Institute. Despite the cacophony of overlapping mandates between institutions, and without guidance from a specific titling law, the central government made impressive strides in the east (IP 2016; National Agrarian Institute 2016, ICF 2016). The sudden move toward titling is not only surprising, it also challenges the official argument, maintained by political elites for thirty years, that the government lacked the resources, legal framework, and technical expertise to title Indigenous lands in the east.

The following sections demonstrate that state interests—the institutional interests of political elites in government to combat an acute internal threat—are key motivation for the generous allocation of land to Indigenous peoples and ethnic groups in Gracias a Dios province.

Titling Indigenous Lands to Recover the East

The central government decided to title vast Indigenous lands in eastern Honduras to regain territorial control. The main objective of state elites was to displace criminal organizations that had infiltrated Gracias a Dios province and to incorporate that remote and underpopulated province into the rest of the country. Indigenous land titling has been part of a strategy to rule the eastern territory through state-sanctioned intermediaries; the central government has titled Indigenous lands to secure local acquiescence and cooperation while implementing heavy-handed military operations intended to cut off the drug supply of trafficking organizations. Heightened levels of internal threats triggered state elites' interest in implementing Indigenous land and resource rights. To be clear, the security challenges do not stem from the perceived ability of the Miskitos to resist nation-building policies, as is the case in Nicaragua. Instead, state elites were concerned about the serious security and governability problem posed by criminal organizations that had started to use the eastern province as an operating base.

In the following two subsections, I demonstrate that the central government's decision to integrate the eastern province with the rest of the country was a response to increased levels of internal threats. To document the causal connection between titling and internal threats, I use in-depth elite interviews and the results of an original survey administered to mid-ranking military officers. I present a controlled matched comparison of two otherwise similar regions that faced radically different levels of internal threats to demonstrate that sovereignty concerns drove a generous form of Indigenous land titling in the east. The comparative analysis shows that in the east, where drug lords threatened the power of the state, the central government titled Indigenous lands to build alliances with local elites and reinforced state power by using a few state-vetted intermediaries. In the west, by contrast, where the state has more presence, the central government has titled micro-territories and has enacted a land administration policy that produces the proliferation of local intermediaries, maintaining state power by fragmenting the territorial base of Indigenous political organizations. Put succinctly, state elites only titled vast areas as Indigenous lands where criminal organizations threatened the state's power.

The Centrality of State Interests in Titling

In the 2010s, the Honduran state began classifying vast stretches of rural land as communal property in Gracias a Dios province. That's three decades after Honduras formally recognized communal property rights in the constitution[1] and over a decade after ratifying ILO Convention No. 169.[2] As mentioned earlier, the Honduran state had ignored Miskitos' decades-long demands for a title over the historical Indigenous territory known as La Mosquitia, which included Gracias a Dios province and parts of the neighboring provinces of Colón and Olancho (Unidad Técnica de MASTA 2013, 9). Then, in September 2012, President Porfirio Lobo unexpectedly ordered the government's agencies to work with Miskito political elites to title twelve Territorial Councils, each amalgamating several villages into a single Indigenous land. By 2016, the state had met its objective: the government had identified, delimited, and titled thirteen Miskito land blocks. Both Lobo and his successor, Juan Orlando Hernández, traveled to Puerto Lempira, the largest village of Gracias a Dios province, to hand deliver the land titles to the presidents of the newly formalized Territorial Councils (Presidency Press Office 2016).

To be sure, state elites divided the original land claim, rather than issue a single title for the Miskito land, as the local political elites had initially demanded.[3] In this way, the state sought to prevent the concentration of territorial power in a single political organization.[4] But the Miskito received much larger land allocations compared to Indigenous groups outside of Gracias a Dios province (such as the Garífuna, Pech, and Tawahka). In fact, the newly titled Miskito lands are the most extensive communal areas officially recognized by the state in the entire country: their inter-communal land blocks extend, on average, over 100,000 hectares (National Agrarian Institute 2016; ICF 2016; Presidency 2016). Together, the Miskito lands sum to over 1 million hectares, which is equivalent to about 80 percent of the land area covered by the other 500 Indigenous lands in the country. Moreover, the Miskito lands represent 80 percent of the area of Gracias a Dios province and over 12 percent of the national territory (National Agrarian Institute 2016; ICF 2016; Presidency 2016). Put another way, the state has officially sanctioned about a dozen people, the heads of the Territorial Councils, to allocate and manage the natural resources in 1 million hectares of the eastern territory. Why would the central government suddenly title vast Indigenous lands?

I propose that large-scale Indigenous land titling is part of an anti-narcotics strategy to increase state presence in the eastern territory. By responding to local demands for secure property rights—as well as healthcare and education—state elites sought to marginalize drug traffickers and reestablish their control in Gracias a Dios province. As part of the strategy, state elites made alliances with local political leaders,[5] while increasing military presence and enacting counter-narcotics operations unencumbered. According to Infantry Colonel Gustavo Adolfo Paz Escalante, commander of FUSINA, a highly trained anti-narcotics unit, "the state intervenes directly [militarily] and with social [goods] provisions . . . to defeat drug traffickers and take back La Mosquitia [as Gracias a Dios province is known]."[6]

President Porfirio Lobo took the decision to combat criminal organizations in 2010 (Mejía 2010; Bosworth 2011, 87). Accepting the military's advice,[7] Lobo and Juan Orlando Hernández, his successor and the head of the legislature at the time,[8] focused on securing military aid and information from the United States.[9] Honduras' strategy to recover state power in the east had congealed by early 2012, when Lobo and Daniel Ortega met to discuss security threats in Central America (Consejo de Comunicación y Ciudadanía 2012). "I was in Nicaragua observing the process and spoke with President [Daniel] Ortega and Comrade [*Compañera*] Rosario [Murillo], we talked a lot about what they had done," remarked Porfirio Lobo. "We enrich ourselves with the experiences that our neighboring countries have regarding common issues."[10] But why title large Indigenous lands in 2012 and not before? After all, Honduras has served as a cocaine bridge since at least the 1980s (Bunck and Fowler 2012, 265, 271). A surge of cocaine entering Gracias a Dios province in 2009 caused mayhem in the rest of the country and forced state elites to pay attention to the east.

State elites had completely neglected Gracias a Dios province for decades. Since the end of the Cold War, the state had barely invested in developing infrastructure and providing public goods and had only maintained a nominal presence there. Over time, the unguarded province became a hotspot of organized crime and drug traffickers. In 2009, however, the drug trafficking problem suddenly worsened. Organized crime took advantage of the political crisis triggered by the successful overthrow of President Manuel Zelaya and used Gracias a Dios province as the main entry point for drugs destined for the U.S. market (UNODC 2010, 239). After the coup d'état, the repressive arm of the state (i.e. the police and the military) focused on controlling dissidents in the major cities of the country and neglected the east even further (ICC 2015, para. 61–65). Moreover, in response to the coup, the United States suspended crucial economic assistance, information exchange, and anti-narcotics aid to the country (UNODC 2012, 15; Bosworth 2011, 86–87). The resulting abandonment turned the eastern province into a hub for drug traffickers. According to the United Nations Office on Drugs and Crime (UNODC), "much of this air traffic appears to have been rerouted to Honduras after 2007, particularly following the Zelaya coup in 2009" (2012, 32). By 2010, according to U.S. estimates, about 260 tons of cocaine, worth roughly US$2 billion (or 13 percent of Honduras's GDP), had landed in Honduras for transshipment to the United States (UNODC 2012, 43).

The eastern province offered ideal geographic and strategic conditions for drug trafficking organizations. Geographically located in the middle of the drug path to the United States, Gracias a Dios province is flat, traversed with rivers, has a deep-water port, and is virtually inaccessible except by small planes or boats. The state had very little military presence there to begin with and only few police officers. Furthermore, the province had already served as a popular refueling stop for vessels moving cocaine northward. The region became the perfect place for drug lords looking for an unencumbered path to the north when Mexico began cracking down on the drug cartels from 2006 onward (UNODC 2012, 3).

Since 2009, criminal organizations used Gracias a Dios province as the single most important port of entry for northbound drug cargoes transported in small aircraft,[11] speedboats, and even makeshift submarines (UNODC 2012, 37; Bosworth 2010; Cuéllar et al. 2012, 46; Bunck and Fowler 2012, 297; Mendoza 2014). When shipments arrived in the east from South America, they "were then broken down into smaller loads for onward transit" (INCSR 2011). Its location, remoteness, and lack of police presence made Gracias a Dios province "the most risk-free zone for aerial-trafficking schemes" (Bunck and Fowler 2012, 301, 307). As the U.S. Department of State reported, in 2012, "La Mosquitia region [i.e. Gracias a Dios province] of eastern Honduras remained vulnerable due to its remoteness, limited infrastructure, lack of state presence, and weak law enforcement institutions" (INCSR 2012).

The U.S. government has estimated that nearly 80 percent of the cocaine trafficked to the United States stops first in Central America (INCSR 2011–2015). In 2011 and 2012, 80–87 percent of all cocaine smuggling flights destined for the United States first landed in Honduras (INCSR 2012–2013). Moreover, 80–90 percent of cocaine arrived in Honduras via maritime shipments (INCSR 2014–2015). Figure 5.2 shows the number of suspected cocaine-carrying flights detected by U.S. authorities before and after the 2009 coup, an increase from 75 in 2008 to 150 in 2009. By 2011, the United States detected 233 flights. The graph also shows estimated northbound cocaine movements using Honduras as a bridge, which also increased from 2008 to 2013, though they peaked in 2011.

The drug surge added to the de facto power of criminal organizations affiliated with the Sinaloa Federation in Honduras (United Nations Office on Drugs and Crime (UNODC) 2010, 21). Given the transshipment of large amounts of narcotics, transnational criminal networks permeated the economic life of the local population and created a drug-based economy. In the remote and unpopulated eastern province, where there are few livelihood options, drug trafficking became an important source of income. Without economic alternatives, the villagers performed menial tasks for drug lords, such as transporting cocaine out of the province, guarding storehouses,

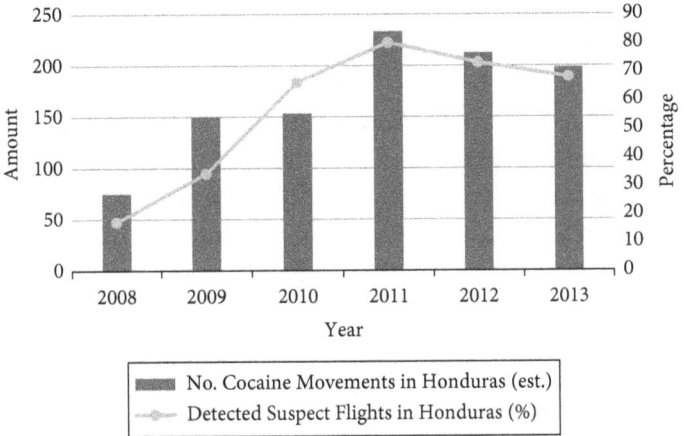

Figure 5.2 Suspected Drug Flights Detected Landing in the East and Cocaine Movements, 2008–2013
Sources: INCSR 2011–2013; UNODC 2012.

maintaining clandestine airstrips, or getting rid of trafficking evidence (Miralda Bulnes 2012; Cuéllar et al. 2012, 46; Bunck and Fowler 2012; Alava 2015). Bunck and Fowler (2012, 302) describe how, "to conceal evidence, drug traffickers had paid local people [in the east], often compensating them with drugs, to dispose of dozens of planes. Some were helicopters; others were one- or two-propeller light planes; still others were cargo aircrafts."

While cocaine flowed into the east, the more developed, populated, and affluent cities of the north and west suffered the violent consequences of the trade. Heavily armed criminal groups, ready to profit from the narcotics boom, fought to control strategic territories—the prime transshipment real estate for drugs (UNODC 2010a, 19). As the UNODC explained in a 2010 study, "The wealth associated with cocaine trafficking has created large and powerful organized crime groups. These groups command manpower and weaponry sufficient to challenge the state when threatened, including access to military arms and explosives" (UNODC 2010a, 21). Rivalries between these drug trafficking rings, in turn, caused mayhem in the country's major cities (UNODC 2010, 239–240; UNODC 2010a, 23–24). By 2011, "the national murder rate (92 per 100,000) . . . was one of the *highest recorded in modern times*" (my emphasis, UNODC 2012, 15). Drug lords targeted each other but also police officers and high-ranking military officials. For instance, in late 2009, the Sinaloa cartel assassinated "anti-narcotics czar"

General Arístides Gonzales, the director of the national office for combating drug trafficking, who had gone on a campaign against illicit airstrips linked to that criminal organization (Bosworth 2010, 7). The influx of great volumes of cocaine raised the economic incentives for criminal groups to maintain control over larger geographic areas, tax all activity therein, and "act like a state within the state," as the UNODC remarked (2012). To put it succinctly, criminal organizations affiliated with Mexican cartels usurped state power in key strategic localities and, in the process, destabilized the country. Figure 5.3 shows the homicide rate in Honduras (per 100,000) since 2005.

State elites viewed the trafficking problem as a serious threat to the state and the lack of state presence in the east as the fundamental cause. From the perspective of state elites, the local population were victims of criminal organizations, not the main perpetrators. During the 2012 meeting with President Daniel Ortega mentioned before, President Lobo remarked:

> Without a doubt a factor that greatly affects [drug trafficking] is the economic situation of our people. That is, it [our country] is sometimes fertile ground because of the needs people have to endure. We observe that in part of our population where it [drug trafficking] is frequent now, they [local people] go out to defend the smugglers that bring drug cargoes. We [state officials] were surrounded about a week ago, a unit in the Naval Base of Honduras was surrounded by the community, [they were] defending the drug cargo, and this is due to the same [economic] situation.[12]

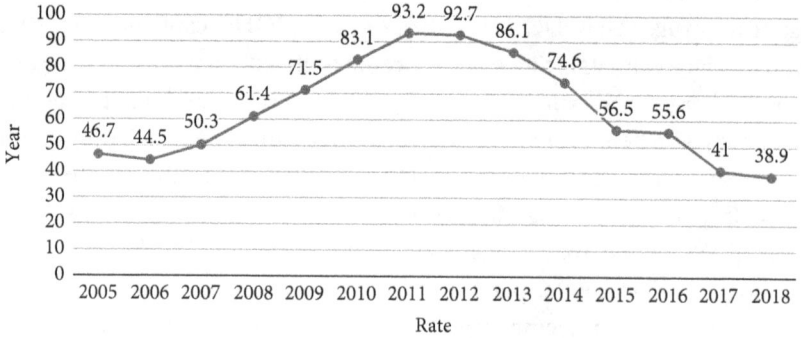

Figure 5.3 Homicide Rate in Honduras (per 100,000), 2005–2018
Source: UNODC 2005–2018.

Juan Orlando Hernández, then serving as president of the Honduran Congress, also described criminal organizations as threats to the state. In January 2012, he noted, "As we have said that we could very well lose the country, now with the support that is being given to us by friendly nations [i.e. the United States] we can say that we will be able to reclaim peace and tranquility in Honduras."[13] Top-ranking military officers supported the idea that criminal organizations operating from Gracias a Dios province threatened state sovereignty. For instance, Vice Admiral Rigoberto Espinoza Posadas, deputy chief of the Armed Forces (2014–present), explained that,

> Two years ago, drug traffickers used to provide basic services, like healthcare... La Mosquitia [Gracias a Dios province] is a depressed zone without presence from the government. For that reason, drug trafficking activity flourished there. Organized crime was rooted in La Mosquitia... that is why all of the [military and political] activities are happening there to ensure that drug traffickers do not return.[14]

In similar terms, General Julián Pacheco Tinoco, head of the Bureau of State Investigation and Intelligence during Lobo's administration and minister of security under Hernández's tenure, described the narcotic trafficking problem:

> In that zone [the east], the state has only rarely exercised sovereignty... In the United States, drugs are a public health concern... In Honduras, *drugs jeopardize the survival of the state*... Drug trafficking generates serious governability and security problems... which is why President Lobo and President Hernández focused on that issue... Many people began to depend on drug trafficking, directly or indirectly. We had to deal with that, *if not, drug traffickers were going to substitute the state* because they have abundant economic resources, control territory, and subjected or controlled people... They [organized crime] controlled part of La Mosquitia [Gracias a Dios] territory; so we intervened to drive them out and to recover state control over that territory.[15]

The essence of Vice Admiral Espinoza Posadas' and General Pacheco Tinoco's explanation is that drug lords infiltrated Gracias a Dios province because that territory was unguarded. As criminal organizations threatened the state, state elites designed a military and political strategy to regain control of the eastern territory and displace drug traffickers from the region. The military viewed drug lords as outsiders who either employed Miskito villagers as hired hands or bought large expanses of land to launder drug-money or build clandestine airstrips, storage facilities, and training grounds (i.e. complete drug transshipment camps). For instance, General Ronald Rivera Amador,[16] director of the School for Commanders and Generals, and Infantry Colonel Alfonso Reyes,[17] director of the National Defense University, believed that government neglect of the eastern province paved the way for drug trafficking to become "a way of life" there. Local villagers began to protect the drug trade and to refuse collaboration with anti-narcotic agents, who were viewed as threats to the only profitable source of livelihood in the region.[18] As General René Osorio Canales, chief of the Armed Forces during Lobo's administration, puts it, "The [eastern] sector has been the platform of drug traffickers ... it is a flat region where an airplane can easily land ... humble local people have seized the opportunity to earn a living transporting drugs and making do because there are no other opportunities."[19]

Thinking that the state's absence in Gracias a Dios province caused the drug boom, Presidents Lobo and Hernández decided to invest considerable military and administrative resources to reestablish and effective state presence there. The state's anti-narcotics approach intertwined a military and a political component. The military plan hinged on stopping the drug flow by intercepting cocaine cargoes landing or docking in Gracias a Dios province. The political strategy, which had military support, centered on building alliances with local political leaders. In fact, military officers viewed Indigenous land titling as a way to reinforce state power in the east. Table 5.1 shows the results of a survey administered in May 2015 to active military personnel enrolled in graduate courses at the Honduran University of Defense at Tegucigalpa, Honduras. Although the survey results are not representative of the entire military, the evidence reveals the attitudes of mid-ranking military officers in training to become future commanders.

The survey results provide the most compelling evidence that the military has an overwhelmingly positive view toward Indigenous land titling. More than 70 percent of the respondents believed that titling reinforces state power. Moreover, respondents overwhelmingly supported the view that the armed forces could act inside Indigenous lands without consulting

Table 5.1 Views of Active Mid-Ranking Military Officers in Training at the National Defense University about Indigenous Land Titling, 2015

Question	Agree (%)	Disagree (%)	No Comment/ Blank (%)
1 Indigenous land titling in the east strengthens the control of the state in that region	70.77	21.54	7.69
2 Believes Armed Forces can act inside Indigenous lands without consulting local communities	70.77	26.15	3.08

Number of respondents: 100 percent (65 out of 65).

local communities. This shows that military officers are perfectly comfortable with communal titling because the policy reinforces state power in the east and the military can act freely inside these areas. In short, active mid-ranking military officers are avid supporters of the policies. For the military, Indigenous land titling fosters local cooperation. General René Osorio Canales, the former chief of the Armed Forces cited above, explained,

> Logically, we [the armed forces] need more presence and authority [in the eastern province], but we need more health, education, and sources of livelihood... Indigenous land titling does not violate sovereignty... The idea of the President was to foster local cooperation for government projects to be successful... Titling Indigenous lands and investing in government services builds a sense of belonging to the nation-state.[20]

The state used Indigenous land titling as a way to win the war on drugs. State elites fully supported titling as a policy to reinforce state power in the eastern territory. The military and government elite viewed titling as an essential component of a political strategy employed to meet security objectives—specifically to displace criminal organizations in the east. I further support the argument that Indigenous land titling in the east responds to internal threats with a controlled matched comparison between titling practices in the east and the west. In the following section, I use in-depth interviews that show the beliefs and expectations of military and government elites about Indigenous land titling in the east.

State Interests and the Spatial Pattern of Titling

The preceding analysis suggests that threats to state control of the eastern territory posed by criminal organizations triggered political elites' institutional interests to title Indigenous lands in the east—the gateway to drugs bound for the United States and the operating base of heavily armed criminal organizations. To substantiate the point that state interests explain the spatial titling patterns in Honduras, I present a controlled matched comparison in this subsection. I compare two Indigenous regions in Honduras that face very different levels of internal threat: the Lenca provinces to the west and the Miskito province to the east. In particular, I contrast the outcomes of Lenca land claims, the largest and most politically cohesive Indigenous group in the country, and the Miskito, the second largest but less organized group (INE 2013, Forest Trends 2015). As the preceding subsection described, the Miskito had claimed land and resource rights in Gracias a Dios province since the late 1980s, decades before the state paid attention to their demands. The Lenca had demanded ancestral land and resource rights in Lempira, Intibucá, and La Paz—three poor, agrarian, mainly indigenous, and mountainous provinces to the west for nearly three decades.

The Lenca and Miskito regions have comparable economic and demographic conditions that are typically associated with titling practices (INE 2013). Both regions have similarities in the levels of economic development, size of the rural population, and percentage of people that self-identify as Indigenous. Moreover, local political elites from both regions claim land based on customary possession, the constitution, and ILO Convention No. 169. While Lenca civil society organizations are stronger and more cohesive,[21] the political organizations of both groups receive financial support from external sources and are part of a dense national and international network of NGOs advocating for Indigenous land rights. Table 5.2 shows poverty levels and demographic characteristics, as well as the number, area, and average land area (in hectares) for each group per region.

Despite the many similarities between the two regions, the provinces have radically different titling outcomes. In Gracias a Dios province, the state issued communal land titles over enormous areas at a very quick pace. In only four years (2012–2016), the central government titled thirteen intercommunal land blocks for the Miskito, totaling nearly 1.4 million hectares and encompassing over 80 percent of all state-classified Indigenous lands in the country. In stark contrast, the state has titled small land plots to the Lenca

Table 5.2 Socioeconomic Conditions, Indigenous Land Claims, and Outcomes by Province

Region	Ethnicity	Poverty Index	Rural Pop. (%)	Indg Pop. (%)	Land Titles (No.)	Area (ha)	Outcome (Avg. Ha)
East	Miskito	50+	65.74	82	13	1,388,980	106,844
West	Lenca	50+	82.96	90	301	156,059	518

Sources: INE 2013; National Agrarian Institute 2016; ICF 2016; Presidency 2016.

in the west, and only after a very slow and administratively cumbersome process. In the past twenty-three years, the state has issued about 300 titles, each averaging roughly 500 hectares, for the Lenca. Because each Lenca micro-territory encompasses only a village and its immediate surrounding area, together they add up to about 156,000 hectares or 11 percent of all titled Indigenous lands. The percentages of Lenca versus Miskito territories in comparison to the national territory exemplify the state's divergent approach to titling between regions. Whereas the Lenca lands represent barely 1 percent of the country's total land area, the Miskito lands encompass a whopping 12 percent. How can Indigenous groups from the same country, demanding the implementation of the same land and resource rights over their ancestral territories, have such radically different outcomes? What causes the remarkable contrast in titling practices? I argue that state elites' motivation is rooted in the need to regain territorial control in the east and dismantle the power base of drug trafficking organizations operating there.

The two provinces have significantly different levels of state presence and histories of state-building practices. Whereas eastern communities are mostly disconnected from the centers of political power, those in the west are located in regions where the state has a more robust presence. The central government has long neglected Gracias a Dios province, which became the operating base of drug trafficking organizations. Because that area turned into a crime haven, state elites built alliances with local political elites, increased public goods provision, and heightened military operations there.

The western provinces, by contrast, have not posed a major threat to state sovereignty from the military's perspective. Indigenous groups are located where the state has a fairly strong presence, and the region has not become a major gateway for northbound drugs entering the country. A comparison of the two regions reveals how state interests in combating organized

Table 5.3 Contextual Similarities and Differences between Regions, per Indigenous Group

Group	Region	Land Claim	Subject of Law*	External Support**	Internal Threat	State Interest	Type of Title
Miskito	East	Yes	Yes	Yes	Yes	Yes	Inter-Communal
Lenca	West	Yes	Yes	Yes	No	No	Single-Village

* Subject of Law means that formal property rights apply when demanding land titling.
** External support indicates that the Indigenous group received support from international financial institutions or international nongovernmental organizations.

crime motivated the demarcation and titling of extensive Indigenous lands. Table 5.3 shows the contextual similarities between regions and differences in outcome.

The Eastern Province

In a longitudinal perspective, Gracias a Dios province is a remarkable case of a dramatic shift in Indigenous land tiling practices driven by a sudden increase in internal threats. To recover the eastern territory—the operating base of organized crime—the center-right governments of Porfirio Lobo and Juan Orlando Hernández decided to implement a two-pronged strategy that hinged on militarizing the region and building alliances with local political elites.

Repressive state action alone threatened to alienate the local population, who viewed government officials as outsiders and anti-narcotic operations as mechanisms to push them even further into abject poverty. In 2011, when General René Osorio Canales took over the Armed Forces, he advised President Lobo that the "root of the security problem [in the eastern territory] was the lack of opportunities . . . If the state enters with social projects and new opportunities, the culture changes and guarantees security."[22] Likewise, Infantry Colonel Paz Escalante, head of the specialized anti-narcotics unit, explained, "titling Indigenous lands is necessary because we cannot solve the [drug trafficking] problem using only repressive tactics; logically, titling Indigenous lands is good so that people cooperate . . . The state wants to pave the way [*agilizar el terreno*] to operate."[23] Displacing drug lords from the eastern territory became the priority target for military elites.

To win the acquiescence and even the collaboration of the local population, the Lobo and Hernández administrations began a campaign to title Indigenous lands, provide health services, and guarantee education in the east. In this context, the military elite supported increasing direct government intervention and state-building policies. In the words of Vice-Admiral Espinoza Posadas:

> The armed forces need to gain the trust of the Miskito to displace organized crime from the region. Titling Miskito land helps the state protect the territory... To prevent drug traffickers from acquiring land... we [the armed forces] need to destroy the standing that organized crime has in the region.[24]

From the military's perspective, working with local intermediaries was crucial to reinforcing the state's power in the region. General Rivera Amador, Director of the School for Commanders and Generals, said, "It is a necessity to title Indigenous lands; it is important because the state seeks to have more influence in that remote zone."[25] In similar terms, Colonel Gustavo Adolfo Amador Fúnez emphasized that, "Titling Indigenous lands is a way to establish [state] presence in those remote regions ... The [central] government is interested in having security there."[26] General Mario Villanueva Reyes, advisor at the Ministry of Labor, also remarked that, "The central government titles Indigenous lands to integrate La Mosquitia [Gracias a Dios] and recover that territory from the control of drug traffickers."[27]

In Honduras, where the armed forces continue to be "entrenched in national life" (Bunck and Fowler 2012, 255), military assessment of the nature of the security threat and its solution strongly influenced political elites' views about the eastern territory. For instance, Rigoberto Chang Castillo, a high-ranking center-right politician and former secretary of human rights, justice, government, and decentralization, agreed with the military prescription: "Drug traffickers had invaded the [eastern] region, by buying or taking land from the local population, because the state had abandoned it for decades... We will gradually incorporate that population by providing them with basic services."[28] For state elites, the strategy to integrate the Miskito through social goods provision served to ensure the success of government security operations at the local level. From the military's viewpoint, the drug traffickers had exploited the failure of the state to guarantee security and provide basic services. Therefore, the central government would come in to dislocate those criminal organizations as providers of public goods.

Moreover by titling Indigenous lands, state elites built new hierarchical governing structures that are prone to political manipulation and co-optation. The central government worked closely with local political elites to identify the exact area that the state would title as Indigenous land. Once the boundaries were identified, the state issued communal property titles to Territorial Councils on behalf of multiple villages. The Territorial Council, headed by one appointee, became the official representative of the communities specified in the land title. A dozen state-sanctioned local political leaders, the Territorial Council representatives, are the key intermediaries between the state and communities. Importantly, the presidents of the Territorial Council have the prerogative to allocate and manage the natural resources within the newly demarcated areas. Put differently, state elites built communal property regimes that hinged on alliances with local elites in the east to have an institutional apparatus to command and manipulate in that remote region. In Figure 5.4 the new governing structures that the state built and bolstered by titling inter-communal lands are highlighted with bold text.

Political elites used the new communal property institutions to build a patronage system that generated local political support. In fact, the central governments channeled all the development programs and international aid through vetted political intermediaries. For instance, the Hernández administration worked with local leaders to implement the "Plan of Action for the Development of La Mosquitia" (Proceso Digital 2016). The plan contained new projects intended to gather detailed demographic and geographic information about the east. For instance, the central government worked closely with local Indigenous allies to carry out a comprehensive door-to-door survey in the entire Gracias a Dios province (SCGG 2015). The U.S. Department of Defense funded a detailed mapping project of the eastern territory, called Indigenous Central-America, conducted by the University of Kansas with the help of the very same local intermediaries (Minerva Initiative 2013).

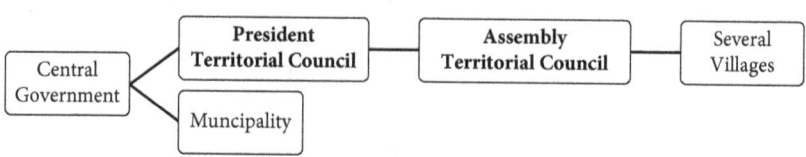

Figure 5.4 New Hierarchical Governing Structure (in Bold Text)

Furthermore, the central government used these new institutions to mute widespread criticisms about the heavy use of military power to ensure state dominance in the eastern territory. After all, local elites, rather than common villagers, are the ones connected to national and international NGOs that could openly criticize the government for the militarization of Gracias a Dios province. In the east, there is no clear dividing line between civilian and military functions. The center-right governments militarized police work and public security in Honduras by decrees that authorize the armed forces to issue and carry out arrest orders, undertake search and seizure activities, and conduct anti-narcotic operations (Honduras Decrees PCM-075-2011, PCM-009-2012, PCM-020-2012, PCM-037-2012; Cajina 2014; International Criminal Court 2015, 99–112). Moreover, the central government has given the military the responsibility of providing local public goods in the east; these are normally, in other countries, civilian tasks. For instance, the armed forces are in charge of the only regional hospital in the eastern province, in Puerto Lempira. The army also monitors environmental reserves and acts to control environmental crimes within these areas (Decree 41-2011). The central government has even welcomed U.S. military assistance to build basic infrastructure. President Hernández himself said, "U.S. troops are going to help us build new educational centers, health care centers, and they will probably assist in the construction of the Mosquitia Agricultural University" (Pelcastre 2015). Without making a distinction between military and civilian functions, the central government uses the armed forces for police work, social goods provisions, and anti-narcotics operations.

In sum, Indigenous land titling in the east helps create new governing institutions to control the underpopulated, remote, and geographically extensive eastern territory through local political intermediaries that state elites can co-opt and manipulate. The central government creates communal property regimes and responds to local demands for public goods to secure the state's security objectives. Through greater government intervention, the state seeks to build local acquiescence and political support to displace drug trafficking organizations from the east and reach anti-narcotic objectives.

The Western Provinces

In the western provinces of Lempira, Intibucá, and La Paz—a land-locked and mountainous region where drug cargoes cannot dock or land—the majority of the population self-identifies as Lenca. Through powerful local political organizations, Lenca activists have peacefully demanded secure property rights based on customary use or historical possession since the late 1980s. In the mid-1990s, COPINH, the strongest Indigenous political organization in Honduras, organized a massive protest to push for land rights, in which between five thousand and eight thousand people marched about 125 miles from Intibucá to Tegucigalpa. The demonstrators demanded the implementation of constitutionally and internationally recognized rights to communal property, education, and healthcare (McCann 1994; Anderson 2009, 127–30; Barahona 2005). That is, social movements have been demanding basic public goods and land rights for nearly three decades.

As Berta Cáceres, the internationally renowned Lenca activist, murdered in early 2016 for her land rights activism, explained, "Our communities are the rightful owners of the entire territory, including the rivers, forests, and ceremonial sites, on the basis of possession and customary law [*derecho consuetudinario*] even if the central government does not title our ancestral territory. We simply demand respect for our rights."[29]

The crux of Cáceres's explanation is that Lenca political organizations have fought not just for titles over small plots of land, but for the official recognition of Lenca *territorial* rights, which refer to a geographic area that encompasses the total environment that Indigenous peoples use, including rivers, forests, and mountains (Anaya 2004, 307). In other words, the Lenca people demand title over vast areas, akin in geographical scope to the Indigenous land titling that occurred in the east. But the state has practiced a radically different communal land titling policy in the western provinces. The Lenca experience is a striking case of drawn-out titling of micro-territories in provinces that do not suffer from internal threat.

Since the early 1990s, the state has disregarded the ambitious territorial demands of Lenca political elites. Instead, the central government has engineered the proliferation of local political organizations. Unlike the intercommunal property regimes of the eastern territory, the state has only titled small plots of land that surround a single village. In other words, the state has fragmented, rather than fostered, the territorial and political concentration of power of Lenca political organizations. I posit that the firm state presence in the west and the absence of powerful drug cartels account for the radically different land titling policy enacted there. Because the Lenca are not located in a region where state elites fear the loss of state power, the central government does not implement a generous land titling program. Where the state has a more robust presence, and internal threat is therefore low, the central government weakens, rather than bolsters, local indigenous organizations.

In fact, for over two decades, the state has applied a strategy intended to parcel out Indigenous territorial claims and to foster the multiplication of small land-based organizations. In 1993, the National Agrarian Institute began titling lands to Lenca, Garífuna, and Xicaque (Tolupán) villages. The state agency issues the communal property titles to state-sanctioned local political organizations on behalf of villagers. As is the case in the east, the representatives of these new territorial organizations become the interlocutors between the state and villagers. Since the state titles each village individually, the policy encourages the proliferation of local organizations. Not surprisingly, by March 2015, over 260 different civil society organizations officially represented Lenca communities. In that way, the central government restricts the territorial base of Lenca political organizations; this fragmentation limits their collective clout. Figure 5.5 contains information about the number and area of titles, per province.

The state employs a radically different Indigenous land titling policy in localities with low internal threats. The western provinces are mountainous regions where drug traffickers do not have a significant presence. State elites do not feel threatened by criminal organizations in the west. Hence, the central government lacks the incentives to accommodate and give concessions to Indigenous groups. In fact, because of the numerical and organizational strength of social movements in the west, state elites had the incentive to fragment their organizational capacity to resist state power. The central government implements limited land rights in the western provinces—and anywhere except Gracias a Dios province—because it already has a firm grip in these areas. In the absence of heightened internal threats to state power, the government limits the influence of local political elites by titling small land plots.

Conclusion

In Honduras, titling of vast tracts of resource-rich Indigenous lands began in 2012 and spread only within the eastern Gracias a Dios province. This chapter has shown that transnational constructivism, social movement theories, economic structuralism, and theories of administration do not fully account for the timing and regional concentration of titling. Indigenous land

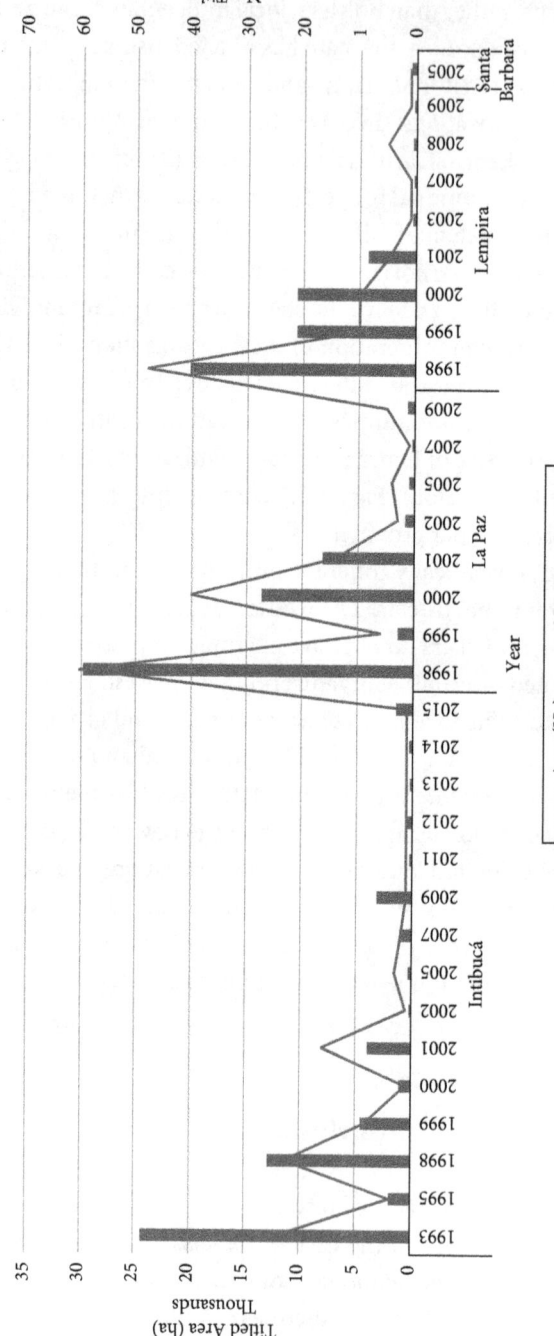

Figure 5.5 Lenca Lands in the West, per Province
Source: IP 2016.

titling responds to internal threats. In 2009, after the military coup against Manuel Zelaya, the international community was pressuring for democratic elections, not Indigenous land and resource rights. The substantively different way the government titles Indigenous land in the east versus the west also suggests that external pressure and bottom-up social pressure did not motivate state action. As regards economic structuralism, the state titled vast areas rich in timber, fishing grounds, and potentially oil in the east, disregarding the interests of powerful economic groups. As regards administrative theories, the state finished titling all of the Miskito lands in only four years in the remote, sparsely populated, and drug-flooded eastern region. Because agencies retained their limited implementation capacity, the impressive speed with which the state titled the Miskito lands shows that state weakness does not preclude titling.

I draw on the framework explained in Chapter 3 to argue that state interests, triggered by heightened levels of internal threats, drove the central government to title large Indigenous lands in the east. I showed that the state, after ignoring Miskito territorial claims for three decades, suddenly moved to identify, delimit, and title about 12 percent of its territory as Indigenous land to reinforce state power. A drug boom in 2009 caused mayhem in Honduras and activated the institutional interests of political elites. In the aftermath of the coup against Zelaya, the military and police, which focused on maintaining internal order in major urban centers, left the remote eastern territory unguarded. In addition, the United States, the source of substantial military aid and intelligence, briefly stopped supporting the government. Consequently, the eastern province became a haven for drug trafficking organizations. As criminal organizations battled with each other and the state to control strategic transshipment areas, the homicide rate in the country skyrocketed. The cocaine bonanza that entered the country from Gracias a Dios province forced state elites to implement measures to stabilize the country. Medium-high levels of internal threat stem from drug lords' control of the east.

Motivated by the need to extend military control and displace organized crime in the east, the central government paid attention to long-standing local demands for secure property rights, education, and healthcare. The anti-narcotics strategy not only contained a weighty military component, but also a political component designed to build alliances with local political elites. Instead of attempting to title small plots of lands around single villages—a strategy that would alienate Miskito leaders—the central government applied a more effective, generous method to gain local cooperation.

The chapter also showed that the state has taken a radically different path to Indigenous land titling in the western Lenca provinces. There, as in other places outside of the eastern province, the state only titles small plots of land surrounding a village. The distinct regional variation in titling practices suggests that political elites are generous when they need allies to resist an acute threat. By titling lands, state elites created new jurisdictional units, represented by the presidents of the Territorial Council, amenable to co-optation and manipulation. By contrast, where the state has a strong presence and faces little threat, the central government does not need to build alliances with Indigenous leaders. Instead, state elites thwart mobilization and limit the power of Indigenous political organizations by titling micro-territories and fracturing the territorial base of Indigenous organizations.

In sum, the preceding analysis shows that high levels of internal threat activate state interests to title vast areas as Indigenous lands. In the Honduran case, the source of the internal threat did not originate from the legacy of a secessionist war, but from the increased strength of criminal organizations in the east after the 2009 military coup. The increasing power of drug traffickers in the country made the government pay close attention to the historically marginalized east.

In Chapter 6, I show that state interests help explain how, where, and at what rate, Indigenous land titling takes place. In the Brazilian case, I identify state interests as a necessary condition for Indigenous land titling.

6

Brazil

On My Terms: Creating Indigenous Lands to Control the Borderlands

> Indigenous lands are not a problem for national security as long as there are no restrictions on the interests of the state.
> Retired General Rubens Bayma Denys, Secretary-General, National Security Council (1985–1990), March 20, 2015, Brazil

> The army has jurisdiction in the frontier zone. The military frontier units transmit Brazilian pride to trans-boundary indigenous people and help to consolidate Brazil.
> General Ubiratan Poty, Chief, Amazonia Military Command, October 26, 2015, Brazil

> [T]he armed forces have the duty to monitor and protect Indigenous lands, especially those located in the frontier zone.
> General Carlos Alberto Mansur, Chief, 1st Infantry Brigade, October 30, 2015, Brazil

As in other countries of the Americas, in the last three decades the Brazilian state has titled vast resource-rich areas as Indigenous lands. Most of the land allocated to Indigenous communities is located in Amazônia Legal (or Amazonia), a socio-geographic division created in the late 1940s that spans over 3.2 million square miles. The standard way of thinking about Indigenous land titling in Brazil is that the state grants communal land to native groups as a result of successful transnational environmental and human rights activism. Anthropologists, environmentalists, and members of domestic and international NGOs, the argument goes, have focused on Amazonia for decades and have used moral and economic pressure to push state elites into titling vast areas as Indigenous land. From that perspective, transnational activists amplify the voices of Indigenous peoples, a small minority of the

Brazilian population that is vulnerable to land dispossession and cultural assimilation. Activists resist the marketization of land, the advance of the agricultural frontier, the commodification of land-based resources, and capitalist accumulation in Amazonia. In this common-sense understanding, transnational social pressure drives titling to ensure Indigenous peoples' cultural survival and to further their self-determination.

In Chapter 3, I developed an alternative explanation for Indigenous land titling. In my assessment, transnational social activism is an important but insufficient factor to account for the distinctive titling patterns observed. Even strong and sustained external pressure is not enough to push state officials to title vast, valuable, and unexploited areas as Indigenous land. I suggested, rather, that the central government safeguards the state's sovereignty interests first before using Indigenous land titling to extend state power into strategically important borderlands. Guaranteeing state interests is a crucial condition for state agents to implement Indigenous land and resource rights.

In Brazil, the state's security interests mediate external pressure. The resulting titling model differs substantially from transnational activists' demands. The institutional architecture that is put in place prioritizes military prerogatives inside titled areas, which allows military officials to reinforce state control over Indigenous peoples and territory. In fact, Brazil's titling model guarantees the right of the military to oversee Indigenous lands and encourages federal officials to slowly incorporate Indigenous groups into the Brazilian nation via government policies and programs. Moreover, the military has overarching jurisdiction in Indigenous lands located inside the northern frontier zone, a porous international border in Amazonia with feeble state presence. The federal government can build, maintain, or reinforce military bases; erect administrative offices; monitor activities inside the territory; and reinforce state sovereignty over Indigenous peoples. Put succinctly, state elites use Indigenous lands as the most effective method to guarantee military presence and restrict Indigenous self-determination. Over time, the state extends its infrastructural power in remote localities, gradually absorbing into the modern state disparate Indigenous groups scattered across an immense geographical area.

In my alternative account, state elites reconfigure Indigenous land titling to benefit military interests: the state allays external pressure, which government officials perceive as security challenges that expose vulnerable regions, while extending military functions in otherwise stateless regions. Thus,

I posit that the largest concentration of titled Indigenous lands will be in areas where state elites have security interests they want to protect without inciting resistance. In stateless borderlands, Indigenous land titling serves to expand and intensify the role and presence of the state. State officials erect new institutions and create governing mechanisms that serve to consolidate military control and reduce Indigenous peoples' de facto autonomy. By contrast, in localities where the state already has a stronger foothold and state officials more confidently penetrate society, state elites restrain Indigenous land titling.

Brazil affords the perfect conditions to assess the persuasiveness of transnational constructivism, economic structuralism, and state capacity arguments, as well as the explanatory power of my own account. For over three decades, transnational activists have pressured Brazilian state elites to title Indigenous lands as a way to ensure the cultural survival of Indigenous peoples as well as their self-determination. Such a prolonged exposure to external pressure allows me to gauge the extent to which transnational activism is effective. In addition, Indigenous lands are filled with abundant wealth-producing resources. The largest areas that state elites have confirmed as Indigenous land are located in remote localities accessible only by air. These two facts, plainly observable in available and reliable geospatial records, allow me to evaluate rival accounts that emphasize competing economic interests or state incapacity as elements that frustrate titling efforts.

In this chapter, I draw on the Brazil Database—a new geospatial dataset I constructed about Indigenous land titling using official sources—to illustrate broad spatial patterns of Indigenous land titling. In Appendix A, I conduct additional statistical tests of my state-centric argument as well other competing explanations. Appendix A also contains a detailed description of the sources of data I used to compile the Brazil Database. To my knowledge, I carry out the first attempt at empirically testing rival hypotheses using fine-grained geospatial data on Indigenous land titling that cover the entire Brazilian territory since 1988. By investigating existing titling patterns, I am also assessing the explanatory power of transnational constructivist approaches, since they rely on Brazil as a case to support their transnational pressure theory (Keck and Sikkink 1998, Ch. 4; also in Stocks 2005).

In the first part of this chapter, I analyze the location of titled Indigenous lands to show that alternative accounts cannot fully explain the observed geographical patterns. In particular, transnational constructivism does not fully explain where titling occurs. I show that titled lands are overwhelmingly concentrated in the northern section of a military area called the frontier zone (Faixa de Fronteira)—a national security buffer extending 93.2 miles along the international border. This fact suggests that state elites chose to approve titling proceedings in localities where the military has complete jurisdiction, rather than approving Indigenous lands uniformly across the Amazon River Basin, as transnational constructivism expects. I also show how the empirical record challenges the temporal and substantive predictions of transnational constructivism, as well as those of economic structuralism and administrative theories.

In the second part, I explain why and how state elites focus on titling lands that overlap with the northern frontier zone in Amazonia. To do so, I provide a historical overview of state elites' decision-making process about the redesign of the Yanomami Indigenous Land, a case that became the decisive precedent to resolve subsequent cases. As transnational pressure formed and reached an all-time high, state elites reacted by radically transforming the traditional land titling model in place since the 1960s in a way that expands, rather than limits, military power in Indigenous areas. The result was unchecked military power inside Indigenous lands.

The third part of this chapter discusses the results of a controlled comparison of subnational regions within Amazonia. The case studies examine the trajectories of Indigenous lands located in two distinct regions: the Brazil-Colombia-Venezuela Frontier Zone (the northwestern quadrant of the northern frontier zone), and the Heart of Amazonia (100 miles from Manaus, the capital of Amazonas). These subnational regions have similar levels of untapped economic potential and environmental value but differ in the extent to which state elites have an interest in reasserting state control. In addition, I will discuss an outlier case: the Xingu Cluster. The analysis of the titling trajectory in the Xingu Cluster—located north of the Xingu National Park—discloses crucial information about the effect of external pressure on titling. In the analysis, I include the results of a survey administered to federal legislators, which shows that politicians view titling Indigenous lands as a way to mark state presence in areas distant from the centers of power. In the final section, I conclude with a discussion of the contribution of this chapter to the understanding of Indigenous land titling in the Americas.

In Appendix A, I present the result of a statistical model that tests whether location in the frontier zone (as an indicator for military interests), external pressure, the existence of mineral, gas, or oil deposits, or overlap with environmental conservation units correlate with Indigenous land titling in Brazil. The results show an unambiguous and strong relationship between location in the northern frontier zone—the military buffer zone along the international border—and the official approval of titling proceedings. This evidence suggests that military jurisdiction plays a key role in Brazil's titling pattern: Indigenous land claims originating from the center of the Amazon Region have considerably lower approval levels. After controlling for a number of important factors, such as the size of the Indigenous population, news coverage of international NGO activity, and mineral and agricultural potential of the land, the results consistently show that land claims located throughout the Amazon River Basin have lower titling rates than those located in the northern frontier zone. Finally, the evidence demonstrates a strong relationship between the existence of untapped mineral deposits and higher levels of Indigenous land titling in the northern frontier zone. State elites disregard the interests of domestic economic interest groups in places where the armed forces have complete jurisdiction. In sum, the military's preeminence in the frontier zone contributes to the spread of Indigenous land titling in Amazonia.

Limitations of Extant Approaches

Established approaches point to useful factors that enrich our understanding of Indigenous land titling in Brazil. Social movement theory has less relevance in Brazil, where Indigenous peoples are widely dispersed across the Brazilian territory and, together, constitute only a small minority of the population (0.5 percent). They lack the material, technical, and strategic resources to confront the Brazilian state. Because of this structural fact, I focus mainly on transnational constructivism, which mixes both local and global activism, as the standard account. While external pressure is an important factor that I include in my explanation, transnational activism alone cannot fully explain the distinct spatial clustering, timing, and attributes of Indigenous land titling in Amazonia. I also look at economic structuralism and administrative theories closely. In what follows, I provide further detailed information to show how the observed outcomes in Brazil do not fully conform to the expectations of the main alternative explanations and why we need another perspective to make sense of Indigenous land titling.

Transnational Constructivism

The geographical patterns of Indigenous land titling in Brazil do not fit the predictions of transnational constructivism, which expects titling to disperse across the Amazon River Basin where Indigenous peoples claim land and resource rights. The Brazil Database, which contains all 655 Indigenous land proceedings from January 1989 to February 2016, shows a nonrandom spatial autocorrelation in Indigenous land titling (the outcome of interest). I employed Moran's I statistic, a popular indicator of geographical clustering in the aggregate, to formally evaluate the strength of spatial dependence.[1] My analysis shows that the spatial dependence of titled Indigenous lands is positive and statistically significant: Moran's I has a value of 0.66 and a variance of 0.10 (z-score: 2.01; p-value < 0.05). This high value, which is closer to the maximum of 1, indicates a strong positive geographical clustering of titled Indigenous lands. That is, given the z-score of 2.01, there is less than 5 percent likelihood that the clusters observed are the result of random chance.

In Brazil, titled Indigenous lands are geographically clustered in the Amazonian borderlands. Map 6.1 shows that these areas are packed into the northwestern quadrant of Amazonia. The map shows statistically significant spatial clusters of high values (or "hot spots"). Indigenous lands with darker shades have a higher confidence level, which indicates greater assurance that the observed spatial clustering is more pronounced than expected in a random distribution. Lands shaded in black reflect a statistical significance with a 99 percent confidence level; in dark gray, a 95 percent confidence level; and in light gray, a 90 percent confidence level. Other Amazonian states like Acre, Amapá, and Rondônia have experienced much less titling. Other than one cluster of titled lands in southern Pará and northern Mato Grosso, the most intense concentration occurs in the north: four of the five darkest hot spots overlap with the Amazonian borderland.

Even in Amazonia, where the expectations of transnational constructivism should hold, titled lands cluster in a small number of municipalities. As shown in Map 6.2, titled lands concentrate in only eight municipalities. Only fifteen municipalities register moderate levels of titling, and another twenty-five municipalities experience some clustering. This shows that titled lands clustered in fewer than fifty out of more than seven hundred municipalities in Amazonia and over fifty-five hundred municipalities in the country. Map 6.2 also illustrates that most titled lands are located in the frontier zone. Within the frontier zone, most lands are tightly crammed

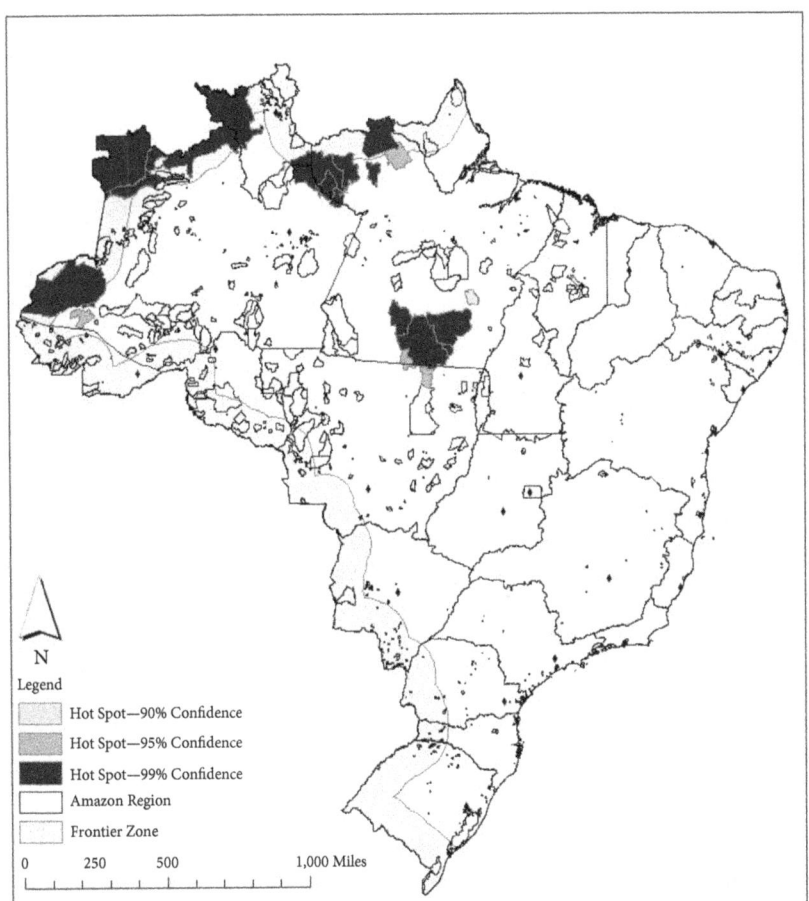

Map 6.1 Spatial Clustering of Titled Indigenous Lands, Brazil
Source: FUNAI 2016.

in the northwestern quadrant of Amazonia, a region bordering Colombia and Venezuela known as Cabeça do Cachorro (Dog's Head). I dubbed this subnational region the Brazil-Colombia-Venezuela (BCV) Frontier Zone. Other sectors of the frontier zone (in Rondônia, Acre, and Amapá) have lower levels of titled lands. Finally, I label as the Xingu Cluster the concentration of lands outside of the frontier zone, which is an outlier according to the results of the statistical analysis presented in the penultimate section of this chapter.

In addition, the observed patterns radically depart from transnational constructivist predictions of titling as a function of demographics. According

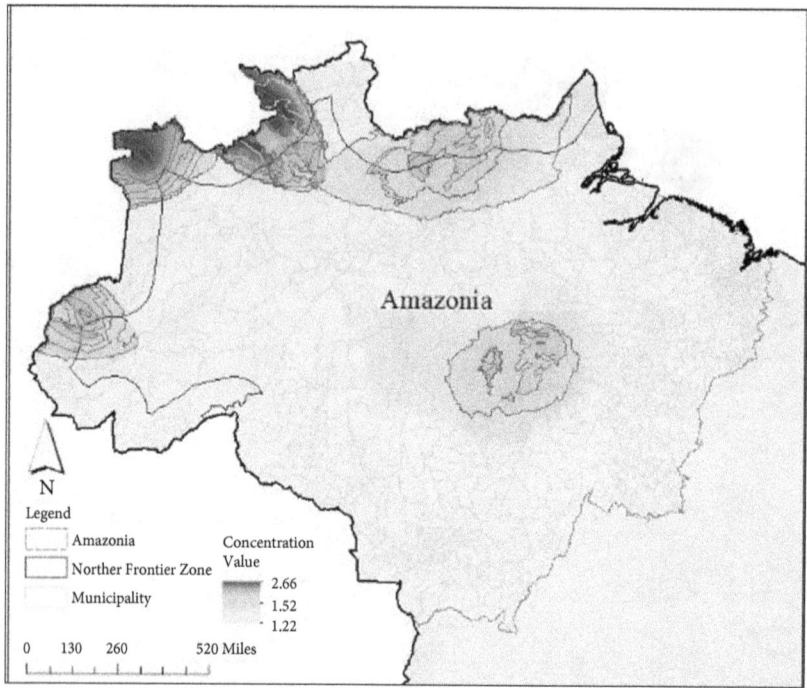

Map 6.2 Clusters of Titled Indigenous Lands in Amazonia, per Municipality
Source: FUNAI 2016.

to constructivists, state officials allocate land to Indigenous groups regardless of their location. But, in fact, state elites have a tendency to ignore land claims from the states located outside of Amazonia.

As shown in Figure 6.1, Indigenous lands are overwhelmingly located in Amazonas (AM), Mato Grosso (MT), and Pará (PA). Importantly, over 50 percent of titling proceedings from the non-Amazonia states of Mato Grosso do Sul (MS) and Rio Grande do Sul (RS) are pending, although three of the five largest Indigenous groups in Brazil have their ancestral lands in these very states. In fact, the northeastern and southern states have the lowest titling levels in the country, although half of the Indigenous population lives there (IBGE 2011). Map 6.3 shows the disassociation between titling rates and the location of Indigenous peoples in rural Brazil. The light gray dots represent the concentration of Indigenous peoples per municipality, the dark gray circles illustrate Indigenous land claims pending in the administrative pipeline, and the dark gray areas show the titled areas.

BRAZIL 141

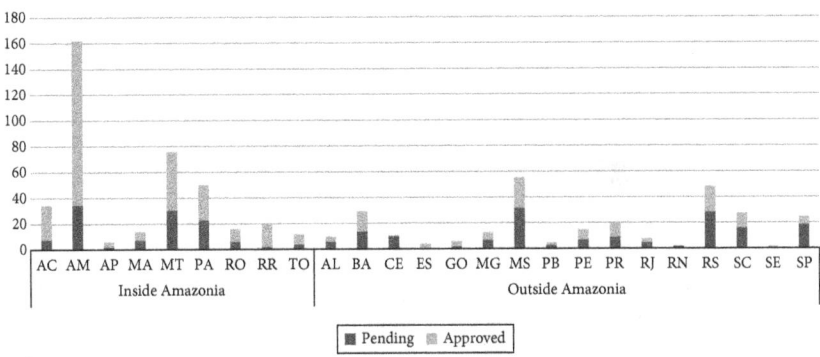

Figure 6.1 Count of Indigenous Lands in Brazil by State, 1989–2015
Source: FUNAI 2016.

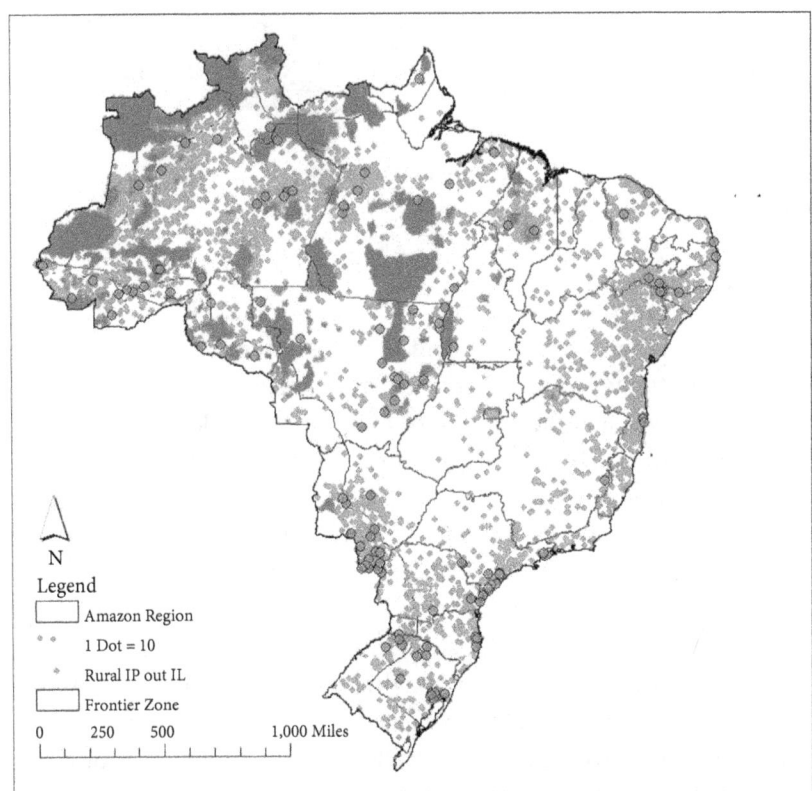

Map 6.3 Indigenous Lands and Indigenous Peoples, Brazil
Source: IBGE 2010; FUNAI February 2016.

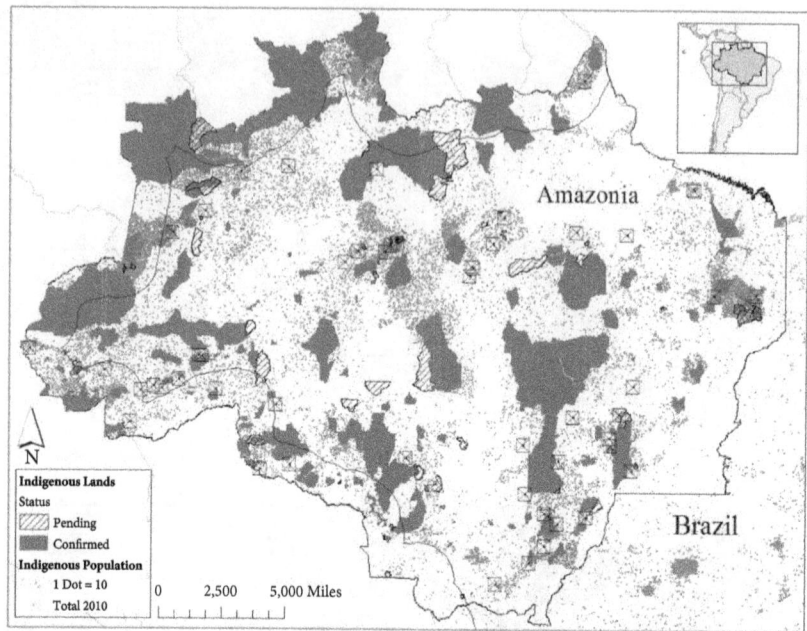

Map 6.4 Indigenous Lands and Indigenous Peoples, Amazonia
Source: IBGE 2010; FUNAI February 2016.

Map 6.4 below shows that, even in Amazonia, there is no close correspondence between Indigenous land titling and residence of Indigenous peoples. The tremendous disparity between titled lands, those that are pending approval, and the location of Indigenous peoples run against the predictions of transnational constructivism. These theories have a hard time accounting for the large number of untitled lands found across Amazonia. While Indigenous peoples are dispersed across the region, titled lands are predominantly located in the northern borderland. If transnational constructivism were correct, we would see titled lands evenly dispersed, if not uniformly, across Amazonia. In short, evidence from the Brazil Database confirms that transnational constructivism over-predicts titling. It is clear that the state does not title based on where Indigenous peoples are.

In addition, transnational constructivism cannot account for the observed temporal titling patterns. This approach expects efforts to occur in response to transnational activism. Thus, state elites should react during moments of strong transnational activist pressure. In the case of Brazil, we should see a spike in 1990–1992 and in 2005, when transnational activists were especially

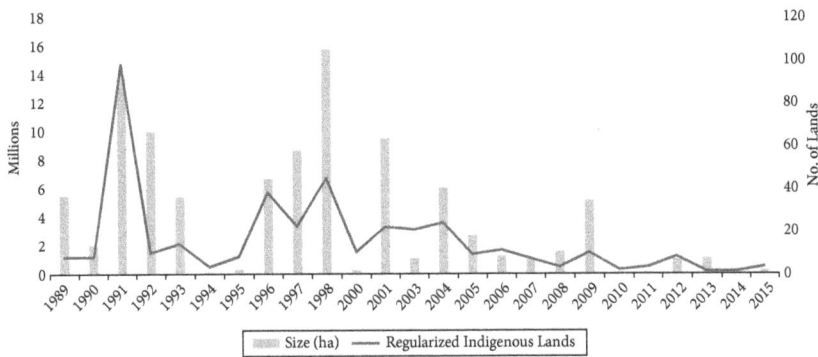

Figure 6.2 Rate of Indigenous Land Titling in Brazil by year, 1989–2015
Source: FUNAI 2016.

potent, but not at other moments. The empirical record shows that there was an increase in titling in the early 1990s but that titling took a downward turn in 2005. Moreover, there was an important spike in the 1996–1998 time period and in the early 2000s that cannot be attributed primarily to transnational campaigns (see Figure 6.2). At that time, transnational pressure had subsided, and Indigenous land titling was no longer the hot-button topic for national and international news headlines.

In fact, only a few, well-publicized Indigenous land claims receive transnational attention. Most land claims are submitted by nearly invisible Indigenous communities and never make international news headlines. Under exceptional circumstances, some communities manage to obtain the support of transnational activists with access to world leaders, who can generate sustained news coverage. For instance, in the early 1990s the Yanomami ruled the headlines. In 2005, it was the Kayapó and Macuxi that figured prominently in national and international media. In very few cases, transnational activists manage to solve overwhelming logistical problems and orchestrate highly publicized global titling campaigns.

Scholars of transnational political dynamics have seen large Indigenous land titling campaigns as a major sign of the organizational maturity and influence of international NGOs. I agree. But in the case of most indigenous groups in Brazil, international attention is intermittent, and the strategies of global NGOs are transitory. In her book, *Brazil's Indians and the Onslaught of Civilization*, anthropologist Linda Rabben maintains that, "most of Brazil's indigenous people live in a state of silent deprivation. When they do call for help, few hear them" (2004, 9). The evidence from the Brazil Database

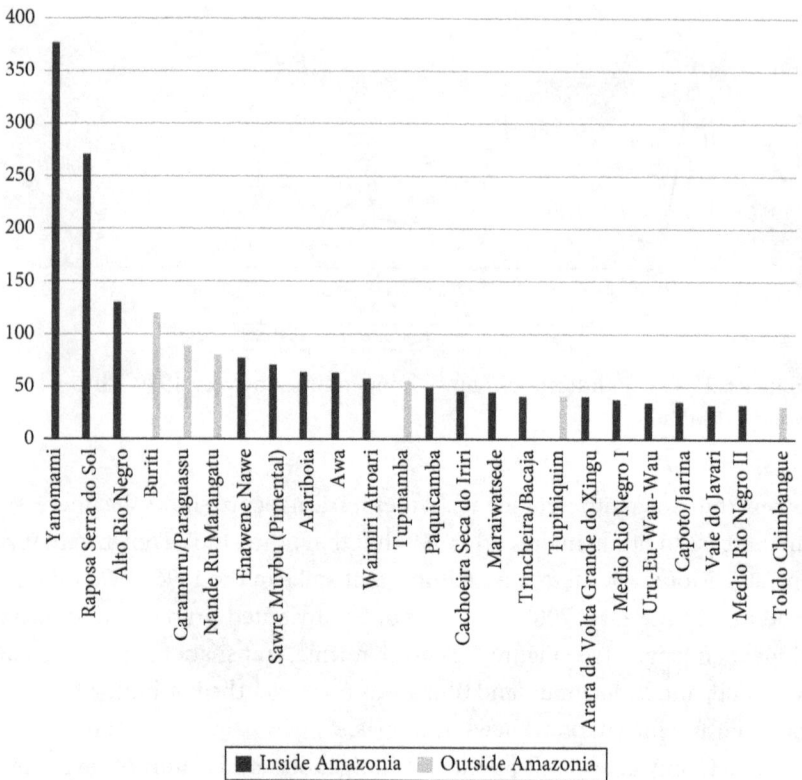

Figure 6.3 Top Ten Indigenous Lands with Highest Number of News Coverage, per Location
Source: Brazil Database, 2016.

supports Rabben's assertion by showing that most of the Indigenous lands are off the news radar. In the Brazil Database, there are a total of 3,416 news items covering pro-indigenous land rights activism. Most Indigenous lands (52%) are not covered by even a single news report. Figure 6.3 shows the Indigenous lands that receive over 55% of NGO-generated news coverage in Brazil. The most popular Indigenous land is the Yanomami area (news count, 376), followed by Raposa Serra do Sol (270), and Alto Rio Negro (130); all of which overlap with the northern frontier zone. Next are Buruti (119) and Caramuru/Paraguassu (88), both in Mato Grosso do Sul.

Last but not least, Brazil's implementation of Indigenous land and resource rights differs substantially from the expectations of constructivism. The Brazilian state elites did not acquiesce with the demands made by transnational activists in the 1990s. Instead of adopting a property regime that would guarantee full political and cultural autonomy to Indigenous peoples, state elites transformed the Indigenous land titling model in a way that limited indigenous self-determination. They redesigned the titling model so that the new lands serve to consolidate military power, rather than restrict it. In fact, state elites disregarded the preference of transnational activists for Indigenous self-determination and restricted military authority inside Indigenous lands. Instead, they vested property rights in the state, gave the military full discretion over their actions inside Indigenous lands, and rejected the right of Indigenous peoples to manage resources inside Indigenous lands, especially mineral and energy-producing resources. Moreover, rather than title a single, continuous area per Indigenous group, the preferred option of transnational constructivists, the state has divided into several lands the territories of Indigenous peoples dispersed across large areas. Three of the five largest Indigenous groups in the country, for instance, the Guarani, Terena, and Kaingang, have been scattered across 160 Indigenous lands. This fact alone suggests that the Brazilian state can determine the shape and size of Indigenous lands and create different jurisdictional units to amalgamate or separate Indigenous groups according to state elite preferences, not activists' demands.

The Indigenous land titling model adopted in Brazil tames indigenous self-determination and safeguards the military's core interests. Even at a time of democratic opening, following two decades of military rule, when civil society clamored to restrict military power, transnational activist pressure could not achieve its fundamental goal of securing full autonomy for native groups (Survival International 2000; Meirelles Filho 2006, 15). The institutional interests of state elites overrode the preferences of pro-indigenous voices, especially their call for severely restricted military authority inside all state-designed Indigenous lands. As a result, pro-indigenous activists and their international allies had only limited success. Above all, they could not limit military functions and prerogatives inside the frontier zone and Indigenous lands. International NGOs and their lobbyists simply did not have sufficient leverage to impose their substantive normative preferences on Brazil.

Economic Structuralism

Accounts that emphasize economic interests and influence find it difficult to explain the extraordinary geographical extensions of titled Indigenous lands in mineral-rich zones. This approach predicts that state elites will not demarcate large areas with wealth-producing potential. The size and economic potential of titled lands in Brazil falsify these expectations. In fact, the Brazilian state has demarcated and titled the largest Indigenous lands—in terms of size—in the northern frontier zone, a region with copious and untapped amounts of gold, uranium, and niobium. The Yanomami Indigenous Land, the most extensive Indigenous land in the country, is located in Amazonia's northwest borderlands, a region renowned for its awe-inspiring deposits of easily exploitable gold, tin ore, uranium, and niobium. Closely behind are the Vale do Javari Indigenous Lands with 8.5 million hectares and the Alto Rio Negro Indigenous Lands with 7.9 million hectares, which contain diamond, gold, and niobium deposits. Map 6.5 depicts Indigenous

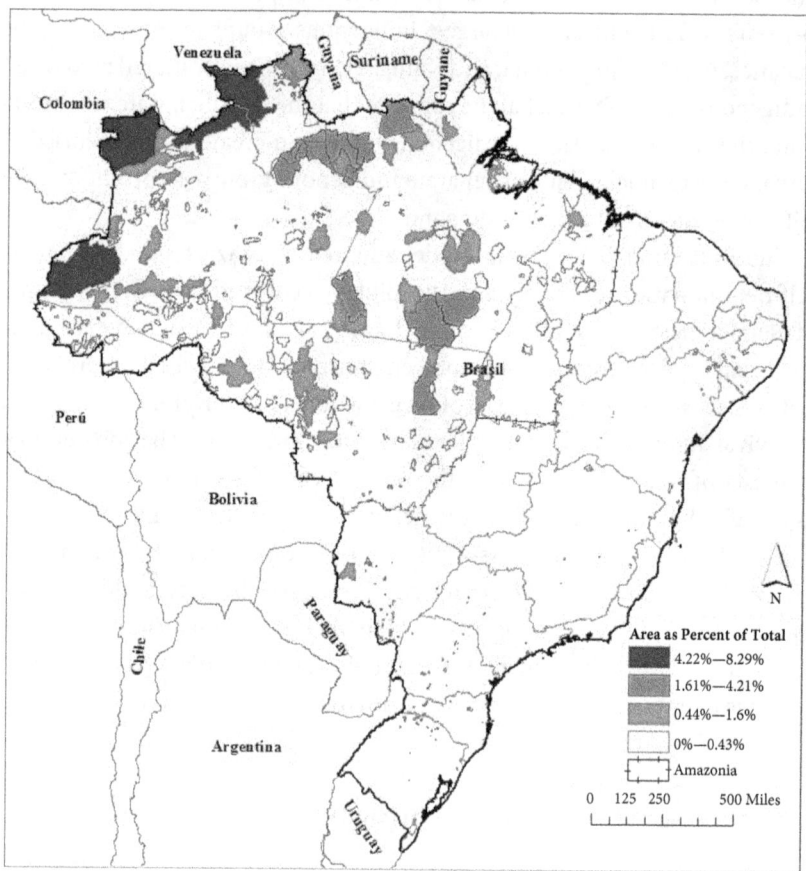

Map 6.5 Size of Indigenous Lands as Percentage of Total, Brazil
Source: National Indigenous Agency (FUNAI), February 2016.

lands, but represented as a percentage of the total amount of Indigenous lands in Brazil, in hectares. The Yanomami, Vale do Javari, and Alto Rio Negro Indigenous Lands are the solid dark areas; each represents 4.22–8.29 percent of all Indigenous lands in Brazil; medium grey areas indicate 1.61–4.21 percent of the total; light grey areas signify 0.44–1.60 percent of the total; and finally, hollow areas are less than 0.43 percent of the total. The solid dark and medium gray areas, which represent the above-mentioned Indigenous lands, are some of the country's most resource-rich lands.

Contrary to economic structuralism, which predicts very limited Indigenous land titling in resource-rich areas, the state titled lands holding enormous mineral wealth and over contiguous territories, thereby banning all economic activity therein. Titled lands do not overlap with environmental conservation units either. In fact, titled lands are highly coveted by transnational mineral companies, wealthy domestic investors, and poor small-scale miners alike. State elites title Indigenous lands in areas that are enticing not only for mineral extraction but also for logging and agricultural production. If economic structuralism were correct, state elites would not approve Indigenous lands over such a resource-rich part of the territory. In sum, economic structuralism cannot easily explain the vast geographical scope of Indigenous land titling in Brazil's economically viable areas.

Administrative Theories

Theories that invoke state capacity as a crucial determinant for Indigenous land titling cannot account for observed outcomes either. Administrative theories expect the state apparatus to simply be unable to identify, physically delimit, and approve the classification of vast Indigenous lands in distant and sparsely inhabited localities of continent-size countries like Brazil. The empirical record, however, runs against the argument. Titled lands are mostly located in the Amazonian borderlands, a region that is hard to access and where the state maintains only a minimal presence. The evidence shows that Indigenous land claims closer to the centers of power have considerably lower titling rates. In fact, titling is correlated with low population density and scant state presence, not the other way around.

Moreover, the state invests scarce resources in drawing and redrawing the boundaries of Indigenous lands. Indigenous peoples claim areas that encompass enormous territories as ancestral homelands. State officials draw the extent of land reserved for Indigenous use and map out the perimeter of the new jurisdiction. State elites do not simply identify and confirm ancestral lands as demanded by Indigenous peoples. Rather, the state continuously invests considerable administrative and technical resources to engineer at the grassroots level the institutional base that establishes a governing relationship with Indigenous communities. Whatever land state elites have classified and reclassified as Indigenous is the byproduct of political choices about which groups to lump together, what identities to incentivize or suppress, and whom to classify as an Indigenous person, who is a ward of the state and subject to a differentiated set of federal policies. If administrative theories were correct, the state could neither adjust their boundaries nor manage these jurisdictional units. In that sense, administrative theories cannot explain the constant investment that state elites make to title and manage Indigenous lands.

To summarize, transnational constructivism provides useful contextual information about Indigenous land titling but only partially accounts for the spatial clustering, temporal regularities, and substantive features of titled Indigenous lands. Economic structuralism and administrative theories do not expect the size and location of economically valuable titled Indigenous lands. Because the observed titling patterns run against the expectations of dominant frameworks, I show, through a mix of primary evidence and secondary sources, that state interests are a central piece of the explanation. The state has managed to build an institutional architecture that guarantees and extends its control over a vast and almost impenetrable territory through the allocation of Indigenous land to state-recognized Indigenous groups. State elites have devised a suitable and highly effective model to design and redesign communal property regimes as a way to govern the distant areas. The next section focuses on the Yanomami case, a watershed case in Indigenous land titling in Brazil, in which anthropologists and Indigenous rights activists claimed a large territory on behalf of four distinct groups that share the Yanomamo linguistic family (IBGE 2010). The Yanomami case is the referent for Indigenous land titling in Brazil.

The New Titling Model: Extending the State's Reach in the Borderlands Effectively

As transnational pressure came to a head, the state's reaction, in addressing the Yanomami issue, resulted in a new Indigenous land titling model that guaranteed military interests inside Indigenous lands. The case became a crucial precedent that shaped all subsequent Indigenous land titling in Brazil.

In 1992, Fernando Collor de Mello (1990–1992), the first democratically elected president after two decades of military rule, decided to allocate over 9 million hectares to the Yanomami people to contain a major international campaign centered on cultural survival in the Amazon (Survival International 1991; Albert 1992; Ramos 1978; IACHR 1985). Because of external pressure, the president redesigned the area that had been previously reserved for individual communities by grouping several villages together and titling a large macro-territory for the Yanomami and the Ye'kwana people. Crucially, the president also asserted military jurisdiction inside Indigenous areas, largely because the military derailed the efforts of transnational activists to restrict military functions (that is, guarantee full Indigenous autonomy) inside Indigenous lands.

Transnational activists had demanded that the president title the Yanomami ancestral homeland as an "Indigenous Park" following the precepts of the 1988 Constitution and the rules set out in the 1973 Indian Statue (Law 6001). Under the traditional titling model, the military's power was circumscribed inside Indigenous reserves. The statute established that the military could access Indigenous lands as a measure of last resort under exceptional circumstances and only with official authorization by presidential decree (Indian Statue, Article 20). In other words, activists had two specific goals: (a) enlarge the area designated for Indigenous communities, and (b) restrict the influence of the military inside titled areas. Their mission was to ensure that the "Yanomami maintain autonomy as distinctive peoples" (Indian Law Resource Center 1980, 11).

Despite strong external pressure, the president rejected anti-military demands and settled on an adjusted titling model that allows for continuous demarcation but reinforces military power. In particular, the president assured the unrestricted access, presence, and function of the military and other federal authorities inside Indigenous lands, especially those located in the northern borderlands.

The history of the Yanomami case is instructive to pinpoint the change in the titling model that occurred in the early 1990s. Since the late 1960s, FUNAI had made a series of unsuccessful attempts to design a continuous indigenous reservation for the Yanomami and other recently contacted, and uncontacted, Indigenous groups (FUNAI 1984–2005; Ribeiro 1970;

Lima 1995, 2010; Diacon 2004). The military government sought to design small indigenous areas to facilitate cultural assimilation and the implementation of state-led settlement, mining, and agricultural projects (FUNAI 1984–2005). In the mid-1980s, international outrage over Indigenous land rights and cultural survival engulfed Brazil. Transnational activists pushed to limit economic activities (especially mining) and military functions in Yanomami areas (Ramos 1998, Ch. 7; IACHR 1985, par. 3a, 3b, 3e, 10b; Davis 1980). Despite external pressure, the Calha Norte Program—a border fortification project that began in 1985 to populate the areas north of the Solimões and Amazon Rivers—created nineteen separate Indigenous reserves in 1988. According to retired General Rubens Bayma Denys, intellectual father of the Calha Norte Program and secretary-general of the National Security Council (1985–1990), the "government titled [the] indigenous areas to ensure that federal agencies take care [*"tomar conta"*] of that territory."[2] President José Sarney (1985–1990), a conservative ally of the military, approved the policy of titling micro-territories in 1989 (Presidency (Brazil) 1989, Serva 1989).

Shortly after taking office, President Collor repealed Sarney's decision and redesigned the Yanomami area. According to President Collor himself, the international media and policy discussion pitted developmental and security forces in one camp, with the military having the reigning voice, and environmental and pro-indigenous voices in the other.[3] The media had heavily criticized Brazil's failure to protect Indigenous communities from the depredations generated by unbridled economic development (Rabben 2004, Ch. 4). Likewise, Indigenous leaders, anthropologists, and connected NGOs like the Missionary Council for Indigenous Peoples (CIMI)—an organization linked to the Roman Catholic Church— systematically criticized Brazil's military presence in the frontier zone (Brooke 1989; Albert 1992, 48; House 1990; *Folha de São Paulo* 1986, 6; *The New York Times* 1990).

Meanwhile, President Collor had to cope with strong pressure from the Amazon caucus in Congress (Rabben 2004, 22). The Amazon caucus is a group of federal legislators from the states of Amazonia who defend mining interests, insist on lobbying for economic development projects for their states, support market-oriented agrarian initiatives, and demand the reduction of areas reserved for native people—because the state bans all types of economic activity by ethnic outsiders, including mineral extraction and logging, inside Indigenous lands (Ricardo 1998, 198). Despite counter-pressures form the Amazon caucus, pro-indigenous and environmental groups (i.e. transnational activism) prevailed over regional economic concerns.

Transnational activists achieved an important, albeit partial, victory. At that time, Brazil was exceptionally vulnerable to international public opinion as host of the 1992 Earth Summit. Government officials at FUNAI and Indigenous activists pushed President Collor to increase the size of the Yanomami area using the argument that a large continuous "park" would ensure cultural autonomy. Their goal was to condition military authority through presidential decrees by applying the Indian Statute (Art. 20). FUNAI also sought the authority to restrict the presence of all outsiders in Indigenous lands (FUNAI 1984–2005, Vol. 1). For instance, in March 1990, Airton Alcântara Gomes, interim president of FUNAI, published a report criticizing the Calha Norte Program in the following terms: "The Calha Norte Program marginalized the National Indigenous Agency (FUNAI)... the frontier zone is inside indigenous territory and it is the Agency's duty to protect and defend indigenous interests" (*Folha de São Paulo* 1990, A8). Likewise, anthropologist Isa Pacheco Rogedo, FUNAI officer in charge of redesigning the boundaries for the Yanomami area, petitioned to classify the area as a sanctuary for recently contacted tribes, thus completely barring the entrance of all ethnic outsiders in the area—including the military (FUNAI 1984–2005, 671). In political terms, President Collor was asked to choose between an indigenous policy informed by the military and a model preferred by transnational activists and their allies (Hunter 1997, Ch. 6).

To resolve the conflict, President Collor adopted a titling model that preserved the military's core interests. On the one hand, he made concessions to pro-indigenous voices by increasing the size of the Yanomami reservation (Brazil Presidency 1991; Brazil MJ 1991). Moving FUNAI from the Ministry of Interior, where it had little autonomy, to the Ministry of Justice, he signaled a political decision to grant the agency more independence. But, on the other hand, Collor maintained military power in the borderlands and ensured military activities inside Indigenous lands. When faced with the choice between ensuring military or indigenous rights in the frontier zone (both constitutionally protected), the president favored military prerogatives. Thus, rather than restricting military action inside Indigenous lands as the Indian Statute stipulated, the president upheld the rights of the military to access and operate inside these areas without restriction. While increasing the size of the reservation, Collor did not accede to an institutional arrangement that would further Indigenous self-determination. Instead, Indigenous lands became not only federal property but also territory under military control.

President Collor refused to enhance the political power of FUNAI and to increase the political, social, and economic independence of Indigenous subjects. Indigenous peoples remained subject to the policies designed and implemented by the federal government (AGU 2012). For instance, under law, Indigenous peoples are wards of the state and can only use land in reservations according to federally supported "custom and tradition" (Lima 2005, 246). In fact, Indigenous peoples are subject to the priorities and policies dictated by the central government, even inside titled Indigenous lands. Collor first ensured that the military had sufficient power to access, function, and guard all titled Indigenous lands. Only after securing military interests did he enlarge the area reserved for Yanomami use.

President Collor circumscribed the power of FUNAI to block military interests inside Indigenous lands. In fact, the Brazilian model for Indigenous land titling expands, rather than limits, military power. State elites insisted that all federal officers can enter Indigenous lands without authorization and guaranteed the permanent presence of military fortifications in so-called special frontier posts ("Pelotões Especiais de Fronteira"). Jarbas Passarinho, a former colonel who served as minister of justice during Collor's administration (1990–1992), prohibited the unauthorized entrance or permanent residence of outsiders in the Yanomami area, "*except* the presence and action of federal authorities" (my emphasis, MJ Order 580, November 1991). In an opinion issued in July 1992, the Ministry of Justice reiterated:

> [T]he presence and actions of federal authorities [inside Indigenous land] are always guaranteed, thus, administrative control and special authorization is not necessary for federal authorities, but only for individuals ... the state cannot remove permanent military fortifications from strategic areas that are necessary for the defense of our territorial integrity. (emphasis in original, FUNAI Proceeding Vol. 2, 686)

By ensuring the unrestricted access and presence of the armed forces in the frontier zone, President Collor embraced the preferences of military elites, who had long insisted on the supremacy of national interests inside Indigenous land.[4] Consider, for instance, Rubens Bayma Denys' views about Indigenous lands. Denys opines that Indigenous lands serve to secure order because state interests reign supreme:

Indigenous lands are not a problem to national security as long as there are no restrictions to the interests of the state ... Not demarcating [Indigenous lands] creates difficulty because a country's sovereignty, inside its territory, depends on the way in which national laws are obeyed and implemented . . . The state needs to be [physically] present to be able to protect [the area] ... The idea is to establish Brazilian presence to assist the population, as well as delimit and order jurisdictional boundaries [in that locality]. It is very important to demarcate [Indigenous lands] because in the future it reduces the possibility of conflict and even eliminates it through the presence and protection of the state. Demarcating Indigenous lands serves to determine which [federal] agency will be responsible to oversee [the area] and prevent social conflict ... [The state] demarcates Indigenous lands for the National Indigenous Agency (FUNAI) to oversee the area, to order the territory, to prevent conflict, and to ensure governability. Demarcating [Indigenous lands] is useful to the state apparatus ... The state must enter the [indigenous] areas since Brazilian Indians are not nations, they are tribes, men with a sense of Brazilian pride.[5]

In other words, Denys believes that Indigenous land titling serves as a state-building mechanism that prevents conflict and builds the state's administrative apparatus. Because state interests have primacy over Indigenous rights, titling marks the state's presence in the farthest and most remote sections of its territory. In similar terms, Jarbas Passarinho agrees that the Indigenous land titling, even over a continuous area, bolsters state power in the Amazonian borderlands:

Since there is overlap [of the Yanomami area] with the frontier zone, the state has *double ownership* [of the land]. The state exercises sovereignty over the Indians and guarantees the frontier, wholly safeguarding the integrity of the Brazilian territory... The army is present in the demarcated area (Surucucus army unit). We can install, if the government so determines, as many army units or military brigades as we wish without the need to hear Congress. We can install an air force base, if that is appropriate to secure the nation, since the state owns the land. The only restriction is the movement of nonindigenous people, except when federal authorities authorize it. The army, like the other armed forces, are "federal authorities." (My emphasis, quoted in Ricardo 1998, 209)

To be sure, members of the military dislike titling large areas as Indigenous lands and distrust NGOs that work in Amazonia (Hochstetler and Keck 2007; Zhouri 2002, 3).[6] For instance, Retired General Augusto Heleno, former head of the Amazon Military Command (2007–2009), insisted that "the problem [with Indigenous land titling] is the size of the land not the act of demarcation [per se]."[7] Aldo Rebelo, former minister of defense (2015–2016), has publicly criticized the presence of NGOs inside Indigenous lands.[8] However, the titling model that resulted from the Yanomami case, which radically departed from transnational activists' expectations, went a long way to alleviate military anxiety about protecting Brazil's territorial integrity.[9] Above all, President Collor ensured the right of the military to occupy Indigenous lands in the frontier zone. He agreed to design enormous Indigenous lands in the border region because the armed forces can act freely there.[10] In turn, the military—especially the army—operates inside Indigenous lands to monitor the influence of distrusted NGOs and gather intelligence from local inhabitants (Marques 2007, 65–69; Ministério da Defesa 2003). Collor created an institutional mechanism that enables state elites to govern from afar, erecting a few strategic military outposts to guard vulnerable territory and monitor its people.

State elites have applied the titling model that resulted from the Yanomami case to all other subsequent Indigenous land titling proceedings. Under the revamped model, the land is owned and managed by the federal government, not Indigenous peoples, and can only be used in accordance with federal policies. The armed forces have the responsibility and extensive power to access, monitor, and guard areas categorized as Indigenous land. In other words, the titling model allows state elites to slowly penetrate local society through a system of federal agencies, with the help of the armed forces. It is carefully tailored to reinforce state power inside Indigenous lands while dissipating external criticism about state colonization efforts in Amazonia. Therefore, I suggest that the contemporary titling method was designed to accommodate the core interests of state elites: the military's preeminence and power is assured.

Indigenous land titling allows the military to act inside titled areas. The state upheld the military's power to design and implement policies inside Indigenous lands without restriction. At the same time, titling curtails, to a great extent, the ability of anthropologists and human rights activists to successfully challenge state power at the international level. Through

Indigenous land titling, state officials dissipated transnational activist pressure intent on enhancing Indigenous self-determination.

In conclusion, external pressures by transnational activists were important for the titling of Indigenous lands over large, continuous areas for state-recognized Indigenous groups. High-level lobbying by international human rights and environmental activists proved important for redesigning the size of the Yanomami area. Overall, however, considering the tremendous opportunity that transnational activists had with the return of democracy, favorable international factors (such as the Earth Summit and its emphasis on protecting Amazonia), and the domestic opposition to military involvement in civilian affairs, external efforts had limited effects. International preferences certainly did not translate directly into domestic outcomes. The Brazilian government insisted on controlling Indigenous lands and maintaining the supremacy of military interests there, especially in the frontier zone. Because state elites are uneasy about limited state presence in the Amazonian borderlands, the allocation of usage rights to Indigenous groups happened only after state elites guaranteed military prerogatives.

In fact, President Collor only reserved enormous extensions of mineral-rich land in the frontier zone to Indigenous peoples after guaranteeing the military's complete access and power to occupy and protect the area. To be sure, the military elite would have preferred a fragmented set of small reservations to facilitate nation-building policies. In response to external pressure, however, civilian state officials overrode that preference. But they adopted a land titling model that increases the state's presence in the periphery relative to the status quo and contains international challenges to state power. The institutions that state officials created, maintained, and redesigned ensure the administrative occupation and militarization of Indigenous areas. Therefore, external pressure is not sufficient to explain the substantive features of the Yanomami case: military interests were a crucial, indispensable factor in the decision-making process. In the end, military and security interests reigned supreme inside Indigenous lands.

In the next subsection, I will present a controlled matched comparison of Indigenous lands that are located either inside or outside of the northern frontier zone. I show that state interests—i.e. the special need to reinforce territorial control in the borderlands—is necessary to explain the spatial titling patterns.

State Interests as a Crucial Condition for Creating Indigenous Lands: Qualitative Evidence

The qualitative analysis presented in this section aims to document that state elites use the existing, military friendly, Indigenous land titling model where state interests are at stake—the borderlands. The chapter showcases the difference in titling trajectories between Indigenous land claims that overlap with the military-controlled frontier zone and those that lie outside this border area. To gain a better understanding of the determinants of titling, I compare Indigenous land titling practices in two regions: (1) the BCV Frontier Zone and (2) the Heart of Amazonia. Compared to the Indigenous lands located at the Heart of Amazonia, Indigenous lands that overlap with the BCV Frontier Zone are bigger and have significantly higher titling rates. The BCV Frontier Zone, the westernmost quadrant of the northern frontier zone, has the largest concentration ("hot spot") of titled Indigenous lands in Brazil.[11] Where it maintains a presence through federal civilian institutions, namely in the Heart of Amazonia, the state resists the titling of large Indigenous lands.

I will also discuss a subnational case with unusually high titling levels: the Xingu Cluster. This is a compound of eight Indigenous lands north of the Xingu National Park and south of the famous Belo Monte Dam, the world's third largest hydroelectric dam. Although a hot spot for Indigenous land titling, these cases are not representative of the broader titling patterns in Amazonia and Brazil—as the statistical analysis that I presented above shows (similarly in Rabben 2004, 24).

Table 6.1 contains crucial information about the existence of external pressure; location in the frontier zone; potential for environmental conservation; type of wealth-producing resources; agricultural potential; as well as the number, total area, and average titling rate per subnational region.

Indigenous lands in these Amazonian sub-regions hold, or are adjacent to, unexploited mineral or oil and gas deposits. For instance, the Alto Rio Negro Indigenous Land, located in the BCV Frontier Zone, holds the world's largest deposits of niobium—a strategic metal critical for aerospace and defense (Klinger 2015). In the Heart of Amazonia, Indigenous lands are surrounded by oil and gas deposits. Finally, the Xingu Cluster holds a few gold deposits to the north and the land has great agricultural potential. Maps 6.6 A–D illustrate the type and location of wealth-producing resources inside or around Indigenous lands per subnational region. All of these land claims have been supported by pro-indigenous and environmental NGOs. Certainly, some of these lands have received more attention than others. The activists linked

Table 6.1 Location, Land Value, Indigenous Land Claims, and Outcomes by Region

Region	External Pressure	Frontier Zone	Environmental Conservation Potential*	Minerals** & Hydrocarbons	Agricultural Potential	Indigenous Land (No.)	Area (Mha)	Approval (Avg. %)
Brazil-Colombia-Venezuela	Yes	Yes	Yes	Uranium, Niobium, Gold, Diamond	No	34***	24.61	97
Heart of Amazonia	Yes	No	Yes	Oil, Gas	Yes	37	1.81	64.8
Xingu Cluster	Yes	No	Yes	Gold, Diamond	Yes	8	11.12	87.5

Sources: SGB/CPRM 2016; IBGE 2016; FUNAI 2016.

*Location in the Amazon River Basin; **Confirmed subterranean mines with mineral deposits; ***The state titled twenty-four small Indigenous lands—i.e., delimited by the military as model villages—before 1989.

158 SECURING TERRITORY

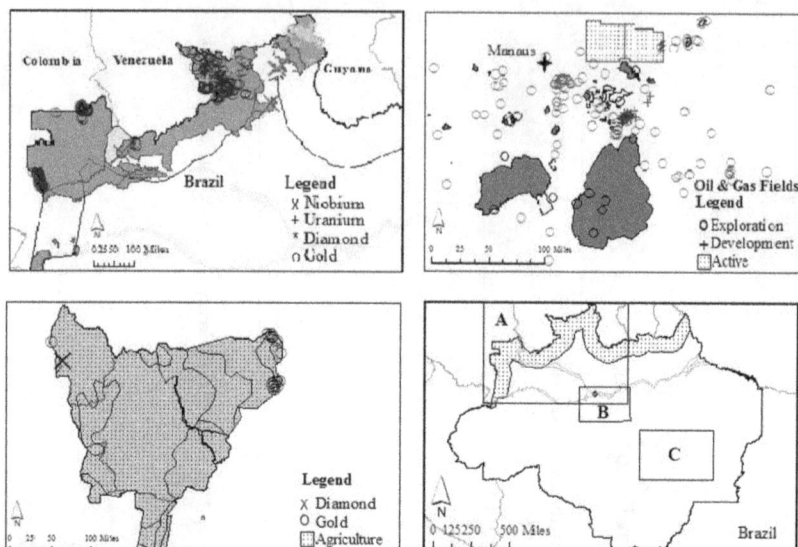

Maps 6.6 A-D Mineral and Hydrocarbons Inside or Around Indigenous Lands, per Subnational Region
Source: CPRN 2016; FUNAI 2016.

to the Xingu Cluster, for instance, are world famous because of their sustained defiance against developmental schemes, such as the Belo Monte Dam (Rabben 2004; Bratman 2015). The same holds true for the Yanomami, portrayed by the media as the quintessential guardians of the rainforest (Ricardo 1998; Graham 2003, 201–205; Ramos 2008; Milliken 2006).

As mentioned earlier, the sub-regions have significantly different titling outcomes. In the BCV Frontier Zone, the state has focused on titling enormous areas as Indigenous lands; titling rates are high at 97 percent. In stark contrast, the state has been less willing to title Indigenous lands in the Heart of Amazonia (100 miles from Manaus), where titling is about 65 percent; this may seem high, but Indigenous lands are much smaller than those in the BCV Frontier Zone. While lands in the Heart of Amazonia represent only 1.55 percent of all Indigenous lands in Brazil, those of the BCV Frontier Zone encompass a whopping 21.09 percent of the total. Finally, the lands of the Xingu Cluster have high titling at 87.5 percent (with about 11 years for completion). However, even the lands reserved for the world-famous Kayapó—strong critics of the Belo Monte Dam—are dwarfed in comparison to those located in the BCV Frontier Zone. The 11.12 million hectares contained in eight Xingu lands represent 9.53 percent of all Indigenous lands in the country; 23.61 million hectares contained in eight lands of the BCV Frontier Zone encompass 20.24 percent of the total. The variance in titling rates and size of Indigenous lands suggests that state elites have a strong preference for titling Indigenous lands in the frontier zone, rather than outside of it. Why do state elites prefer to title in the borderlands? Why do Indigenous peoples subject to the same rights have such different outcomes?

State officials are more willing to title Indigenous lands where the state has an interest in extending its reach. Because the military has overarching or unlimited jurisdiction in the frontier zone, state elites have less anxiety about controlling Indigenous lands there. State elites are less inclined to title lands in areas located in the center of the country where the federal civilian agencies serve to establish a state presence. A comparison of the two subregions I call the BCV Frontier Zone and the Heart of Amazonia reveals how state interests in controlling porous borderlands—rather than external pressure alone—motivate the creation, demarcation, and titling of extensive, resource-rich Indigenous lands.

The BCV Frontier Zone

Extensive in-depth interviews with high-ranking military officers, as well as conversations with bureaucrats from the Ministry of Defense and federal judicial opinions, reveal that titling Indigenous lands in the northern frontier zone serves to secure the state's objective of reinforcing its power in the borderlands. In what follows, I use this evidence to show that state elites uphold military interests inside the frontier zone and that state officials title Indigenous lands where the state needs to reinforce its presence. Otherwise, the state resists designating large Indigenous lands. In the Heart of Amazonia, state elites prefer to title micro-territories and leave open areas between Indigenous villages for other types of policies.[12]

Designating Indigenous Lands to Extend the State's Reach in the Borderlands

The military's main objective is to guard Amazonia and its abundant natural resources from international greed, especially along its porous international border. As anthropologist Linda Rabben puts it, "[The] 'Internationalization of the Amazon' became the nationalists' rallying cry" (2004, 19).[13] Fearing an international conspiracy "to invade the Amazon under cover of protecting the Yanomami Indians from genocide"—to use Rabben's phrase (2004, 19)—the military ensured that civilian state elites prioritized the power of the armed forces in the northern frontier zone.[14] Since the early 1990s, state elites have not only maintained but reinforced military functions in the Amazonian border.

Brazil has enhanced its military power in Amazonia and granted the armed forces overarching jurisdiction over the frontier zone. The military has forcefully insisted on the urgency of protecting Amazonia from international interference (Zhouri 2002; Bitencourt 2002; Marques 2007). To the chagrin of indigenous rights activists, the federal government has upheld constitutional provisions that grant the military unconstrained access and power inside Indigenous lands in the frontier zone (Rohter 2002; CIMI 2016). The Constitution of 1988 established that Indigenous lands are federal property and that national sovereignty interests have primacy inside these areas (Art. 231, especially §5). To be sure, Brazil retains the ownership of all titled Indigenous lands, regardless of their size and location. But the frontier zone is federal property deemed essential to secure the nation (Constitution, Art. 20; Furtado 2013). In the frontier zone the military has full power. In addition, the state only authorizes state-recognized Indigenous peoples to have usufruct rights over non energy producing resources on the land's surface, but not the subsoil—which is also federal property subject to military control (GSI 2004; FUNAI 2016).

Federal judicial authorities have maintained the supremacy of military power in the Amazonian frontier zone. On at least two occasions, the Attorney General's Office stressed that the military's constitutional mission to oversee the border is limitless, that the frontier zone is central to the defense of the national territory, and that the nation's security interests prevail inside Indigenous lands. In 1995, the Attorney General's office issued an opinion that emphasized the military's unlimited power: "Regarding the task of defending the Nation, a constitutional mission that rests on the Armed Forces (Art. 142), it cannot suffer any limitation, not even formal legal restraints. The frontier zone, also expressly created in the constitution, 'is considered fundamental for the defense of the national territory' (Art. 20, § 2)" (AGU 1995, para. 8). In 2012, the same federal body stated in no uncertain terms that:

[U]sage rights exclusive to Indians are *subordinate* to the political interest of national defense; establishing military bases, units, and posts or carrying out other types of military interventions, expanding a network of roads, exploring alternative energy sources deemed strategic, or controlling strategic resources shall be implemented, according to the opinion of competent federal offices (Ministry of Defense and National Defense Council), without the need to consult affected indigenous communities or the National Indigenous Agency (FUNAI)... The role of the Armed Forces and Federal Police inside indigenous areas, according to their functions, is guaranteed and will occur independent from consultation of affected indigenous communities or the National Indigenous Agency (FUNAI). (my emphasis, AGO 2012, par. V-VI)

As recently as 2009, the Federal Supreme Court, Brazil's court of last resort, has upheld the supremacy of national security interests inside Indigenous lands.[15] The decision reads:

The permanent allocation [of land] to the Indians [communities] in strategic areas [frontier zone] facilitates and requires that state institutions (especially, armed forces and federal police) maintain a presence in their surveillance posts, garrisons, battalions, command posts, and agencies. They [state institutions] do not need any type of authorization to do so [*"Sem precisar de licença de quem quer que seja para fazê-lo"*]. These mechanisms [of the military] are an opportunity to make our indigenous people aware, to instruct them (through conscription), warn against the influence of wrongful actions by certain foreign NGOs, mobilize them for the defense of national security, and reinforce in them the innate sentiment of being Brazilian [*"reforçar neles o inato sentimento de brasilidade"*]. (STF Pet 3388 2009, point 17).

In essence, according to Brazil's apex judicial authorities, state interests prevail inside Indigenous lands and the armed forces have the unencumbered ability, even duty, to design and implement defense and assimilationist policies there. State officials from the Ministry of Defense accordingly justify and assert military power over the frontier zone. "In many places [of the Amazon region], the military are the only presence of the state," said Jaques Wagner, minister of defense (January–October 2015), during an interview. "Countries like Brazil that do not suffer threats of war need to invest in defense to maintain the integrity and the sovereignty of the nation."[16] Colonel Rodrigo Prates, adviser in the Ministry of Defense, explained that "the military thinks in terms of the nation-state ... The armed forces are present and position themselves [in the frontier zone]; the army makes the decisions that protect [the nation]."[17] In short, the Federal Supreme Court, the Attorney General's Office, and state elites from the Ministry of Defense uphold the military's unfettered power in Indigenous lands that overlap with the frontier zone because that area is considered fundamental to national security.

Moreover, Brazil has passed a series of laws and decrees that bolster military power in Amazonia. For instance, Law 97 (1999), Decree 4412 (2002), and Decree 613 (2008) reaffirm the power of the armed forces to access Indigenous lands and their expansive jurisdiction inside the frontier zone (Silva 2008, Ch. 10). According to Brazilian law, the military need not coordinate with FUNAI, nor with local communities, to enter, remain, patrol, and recruit soldiers from Indigenous lands and the frontier zone. General Ubiratan Poty, Chief of the Amazon Military Command (2015), insisted that "the armed forces need not request authorization, or act in conjunction with, other government agencies to patrol, inspect, and make arrests in the frontier zone."[18] In addition, General Carlos Alberto Mansur, commander of the 1st Infantry Brigade, an army post with jurisdiction over the Yanomami and Raposa Serra do Sol Indigenous Lands, explained:

> [T]he armed forces have the duty to monitor and protect Indigenous lands, especially those located in the frontier zone ... In these [remote] localities, the state can provide social services only through the armed forces; only the military has that [logistical] capacity ... We [the military] have the responsibility to oversee activities in Indigenous lands. We ensure that everything is in order, especially in the frontier zone.[19]

In similar terms, General Antonio Manoel de Barros, commander of the San Gabriel de Cachoeira Army Base (Amazonas) in the BCV Frontier Zone, emphasized that, "issues of national defense have primacy in indigenous areas and the armed forces do not need authorization to act inside Indigenous lands."[20] In essence, military elites stationed in the northern border area can design and implement operations inside Indigenous lands without restriction by civilian institutions, including FUNAI. From the point of view of military officers, Indigenous lands in the frontier zone are far from being off-limits. Quite the contrary, in these areas the military is under control (*The Economist* 2017).

The Brazilian state has reinforced its power and extended control in Amazonia through military-designed programs and policies (Becker 2001; Nascimento 2006). The most prominent of these programs is the Calha Norte Program, an initiative that indigenous activists heavily criticized in the mid-1980s and 1990s for operating in indigenous areas. This program has intensified its operations in the region in the last two decades.[21] The program seeks to increase state presence in the region by funding municipal projects for socioeconomic development and by maintaining military infrastructure. President Fernando Henrique Cardoso (1995–2002) included the program in the National Defense Policy (1995) and President Luíz Inácio Lula da Silva (2003–2010) included it in the National Defense Strategy (2008). The Calha Norte Program's military budget has increased substantially, from 17 million reais in 2005 to 58 million reais in 2012 (an increase of 230 percent). In addition, the program's territorial reach has expanded over time. From 1985 to 2003, the Calha Norte Program operated in four states or seventy-four municipalities, covering 14 percent of the national territory and was mainly focused on the northern frontier zone. The Calha Norte Program covers areas outside of the frontier zone and has operations in two additional states: Acre and Rondônia. Since 2009, the program has operated in 194 municipalities, encompassing 32 percent of Brazil's land area. Importantly, the program serves as the "lifeline" (funding) for military fortifications and operations located along the Amazonian frontier zone. "The Calha Norte Program is fundamental for Amazonia," insisted Vice-Admiral Wagner Lopes de Moraes Zamith, commander of the 9th Naval District in Manaus, Amazonas. "Through the programmatic funding [provided] by the Calha Norte Program, Brazil takes care of the region. The navy, the army, and the air force are present in Amazonia to control [*tomar conta*]."[22]

In addition, the military operates three different programs to guarantee national security in the Amazon. The Amazon Surveillance System monitors the area using satellite imaging, ground-based radars, and control stations.[23] The army also launched the Integrated Frontier Monitoring System to strengthen military intelligence in the frontier zone. In 2011, the military put in place the Strategic Frontier Plan, a defense policy intended to extend state presence in the borderlands (Decrees 7.496, 2011; Decree 8.903, 2016; GSI 2016). These military programs demonstrate Brazil's insistence on guarding the national territory from foreign incursion (Romero 2012, A5).

Another salient feature is the intensification of the military presence in Amazonia. Since the 1990s, the army has transferred three brigades from the south (Rio Grande do Sul) and southeast (Rio de Janeiro) to the Amazon Military Command (Meirelles Filho 2006; Marques 2007, 79–81). The armed forces seek to increase active military personnel in Amazonia from 17,000[24] to 48,000 by 2030 (SAE 2012). The military also establishes the state's presence in the border with twenty-seven permanent special army units (or frontier posts), located 500 kilometers apart along the international border.[25] The state plans to increase the number of frontier posts to fifty-five by 2021, with most units expected to be installed inside Indigenous lands (Miranda 2012, 122). The units, for instance, provide social services like medical and dental care, assist in registering the civilian population,[26] and even engage in civic education. As General Poty explained, "The frontier posts are the only permanent presence of the Brazilian state in those places, especially for the communities. The frontier posts are erected in strategic areas... they [the military in the frontier posts] transmit a feeling of Brazilian pride to trans-boundary indigenous [people] to consolidate Brazil."[27]

In addition, the military designed the frontier posts to serve as a base of operations for other federal institutions. Aside from FUNAI, the Ministry of Health, the Ministry of Environment, and other federal agencies design and implement policies inside Indigenous lands, each within their own subject area. For instance, the Chico Mendes Institute for the Conservation of Biodiversity, an administrative arm of the Ministry of Environment, co-manages with FUNAI Indigenous lands that overlap with Environmental Conservation units (AGU 2012, par. VIII–IX).[28] To be sure, defense and military policies have supremacy over these and other federal agencies that act in the frontier zone. Yet, the military has envisioned using the frontier posts to allow federal officers to physically reach the remote Amazonian borderlands. Brigadier Roberto de Medeiros Dantas, Director of the Calha Norte Program, maintains that "military personnel are trained to work together with civilian federal agencies, such as the Environmental Agency, the National Indigenous Agency (FUNAI), the Federal Police, and others that are in the frontier... The military provides the logistical capacity and the frontier posts offer the infrastructure for federal agencies [to reach the borderlands]."[29]

The titling of Indigenous lands does not curtail the military's ability to recruit soldiers from local communities. A large portion of the mid- and high-ranking officers serving in Amazonia are not from the region.

However, the vast majority of low-ranking personnel are recruited from villagers surrounding military units.[30] In fact, the military "prioritizes conscription by young people native to indigenous communities" (Ministério da Defesa 2003, 2023). The military employs local Amazonian people for a period of eight years. Those who have special skills or are considered by high-ranking officers to provide an important link for the military unit with the surrounding Indigenous community can become career soldiers. General Mansur, in charge of the Yanomami territory, greatly approves of the military's recruiting strategy, "The military recruits Indians as soldiers. There is nothing better than an indigenous soldier working in a brigade that lives to protect the frontier."[31]

In Brazil, political elites have embraced the titling model that gives the military total access and control in Indigenous lands (also in Marques 2007, 70, 86–93). The titling of Indigenous lands allows state elites to simultaneously reinforce military control over indigenous areas and thwart external criticism. Put succinctly, Indigenous land titling makes it easier for state elites to govern indigenous areas. Table 6.2 shows the results of a survey about the titling of Indigenous lands administered in March 2015 to acting senators and deputies in Congress. Although the survey results are not representative of the viewpoints of the entire political elite in Brazil, the evidence reveals the attitudes of the vast majority of acting Senators (81 percent) and a third of the acting Deputies (35 percent) in the Brazilian Congress in 2015.

The survey results provide the most compelling evidence that politicians have a positive view of Indigenous land titling in the frontier zone. The survey reveals that the majority of respondents (over 60 percent) believe that titling in the frontier zone strengthens the control of the state in that region. Nearly the same percentage of Senators (62 percent) and Deputies (61 percent) supports that viewpoint. In addition, the survey results reveal that national legislators do not perceive a tension between titling Indigenous lands and military functions. As shown in the second column (Agree), nearly 70 percent of the respondents (69.07 percent) believed that the military and the federal police can act inside Indigenous lands without consulting local communities. Although half of the respondents agree that international pressure to title Indigenous lands has increased in recent times, the evidence demonstrates that only 30 percent thinks that the state titles too much territory as Indigenous lands. The data indicates that the majority of respondents are comfortable with Indigenous land titling in Amazonia because the military can act freely inside these areas. Legislators think in similar terms about

Table 6.2 Views of National Legislators about Indigenous Land Titling, per Chamber, March 2015

Question	Chamber	Agree	Disagree	No Opinion/Blank
1. Believes that Indigenous land titling in the frontier zone strengthens the control of the state in that region (%)	Senators	62.12	28.78	9.09
	Deputies	61.74	29.50	8.74
	Joint	61.84	29.31	8.83
2. Believes that the Armed Forces and the Federal Police can act inside Indigenous lands without consulting affected communities (%)	Senators	66.66	28.78	4.54
	Deputies	69.94	24.59	5.46
	Joint	69.07	25.70	5.22
3. Believes there is too much land for too few indigenous people in Brazil (%).	Senate	28.78	59.09	12.12
	Deputies	38.79	46.99	16.39
	Joint	36.14	50.20	15.26
	Chamber	Increased	Decreased	No Opinion/Blank
4. Believes that in recent times international pressure to title all Indigenous lands in Brazil (%)	Senate	51.51	10.60	37.87
	Deputies	51.36	2.73	45.90
	Joint	51.40	4.81	43.77

Number of respondents: Senators 66 (out of 81) or 81 percent; Representatives 183 (out of 513) or 35 percent.

Indigenous land titling as military elites. As Colonel Rodrigo Prates, adviser of the Armed Forces Joint Command in the Ministry of Defense, maintained, "the titling of Indigenous lands in the frontier zone serves the interests of the state. It is better to have indigenous peoples as allies since they help to protect the border."[32]

Federal officials govern Indigenous peoples by titling Indigenous lands in the frontier zone and guaranteeing the intervention of the military and other federal authorities inside these areas. Civilian state elites have upheld the armed forces' responsibility to monitor, inspect, and guard communities that are located in the border area. In addition, the military is responsible for providing public services, a task usually reserved for civilian agencies. State officials do not make a distinction between military and civilian functions in the borderlands because only the armed forces have the logistical capacity to reach that otherwise impenetrable region. For instance, the armed forces are in charge of the only regional hospital in San Gabriel de Cachoeira, a municipality located in the BCV Frontier Zone. The army also monitors and controls environmental crimes, drug trafficking, and illegal mining activities (including those activities practiced by Indigenous peoples).

In conclusion, the federal government goes especially far to title Indigenous lands in the northern borderlands. Despite strong external pressures, state elites have continued to prioritize military interests over indigenous rights. Titling Indigenous lands neither limits military power in the frontier zone nor ensures cultural autonomy and Indigenous self-determination. Through the titling model redesigned in the early 1990s, state elites have constructed an institution that thwarts international criticism but upholds military preeminence inside Indigenous lands. State elites put in place a differentiated institutional system that marks state presence, delimits jurisdictions, and implements federal policies in underpopulated, geographically extensive, and remote areas. In what follows, I highlight the different titling practices in the heart of the Amazonian River Basin.

The Heart of Amazonia

The Heart of Amazonia, a subnational region in the state of Amazonas, is located 100 miles from Manaus, its capital. Since the mid-1980s, Indigenous rights activists have demanded Indigenous land titling based on the Constitution and the Indian Statute (1973). The region has experienced lower levels of Indigenous land titling, despite having attributes emphasized by transnational activists: a scarce population, primarily Indigenous peoples, and abundant biodiversity (IBGE 2011, 2012). Indeed, Indigenous lands in the Heart of Amazonia are smaller, with a comparatively lower titling rate, than those overlapping with the northern frontier zone.

This subnational region exemplifies an instance of protracted titling of small areas. Since the early 1990s, state officials have demarcated Indigenous lands that divide a large Indigenous territory into smaller units. For instance, the Mura, an Indigenous community that traditionally occupied a vast area that spanned the waterways of the Madeira, Amazonas, and Purus Rivers, are separated into thirty Indigenous lands, each averaging about 19,370 hectares (FUNAI 2016; Ricardo 2016). Unlike the enormous Indigenous lands of the BCV Frontier Zone, where the state has joined multiple Indigenous groups into a single territory, in this subregion the federal government has titled small lands at the village level to split a single Indigenous community apart.

In other words, the state has restricted, rather than upheld, the territorial demands of Indigenous peoples that originate from the Heart of Amazonia.

I posit that state officials are less likely to title Indigenous lands in the Heart of Amazonia because they lie closer to a regional center of national power. State elites are less anxious about their control over territory closer to Manaus, a large city in the middle of the state and the headquarters of the federal government in the region. Because they can establish a state presence there through federal civilian institutions, the state does not have the incentive to establish large Indigenous lands that are designed to mark national power. For that reason, state elites title smaller Indigenous lands, and at a much lower pace, in the Heart of Amazonia.

To conclude, state elites are less willing to implement a generous Indigenous land titling strategy in the Heart of Amazonia. Because the federal civilian agencies play a large governing role closer to Manaus, state elites need not title large Indigenous lands there. In the following section, I present an outlier case: Indigenous lands with unusually high titling outside of the frontier zone because Indigenous groups have had exceptional success in attracting and sustaining significant international support.

The Xingu Cluster

The very high approval rates of Indigenous lands north of the Xingu National Park, along the Xingu River, needs further explanation. Even though this cluster of eight Indigenous lands does not overlap with the frontier zone, and even though two of the eight lands hold a number of valuable mineral deposits, the state has titled large Indigenous lands there (FUNAI 2016; Ricardo 2016). The case of these eight Indigenous lands is an exception that proves the rule in Brazil. Moreover, the case is noteworthy because such large-scale titling is found in northern Mato Grosso, the country's leading soybean producer and the power base of the influential Rural caucus in the National Congress—strong opponents of the Indigenous land policy since the early 1990s (Ondetti 2008, 107; EMBRAPA 2016).

A closer look at the strategies employed by the Kayapó, inhabitants of six of the eight lands in the cluster, provides clues for understanding state officials' unusual willingness to approve these titling requests. The Xingu Cluster is an outlier because of the unprecedented media attention and the presence of internationally linked NGOs that have focused on the area ever since João Café Filho, then vice-president under Getúlio Vargas (1951–1954), initiated a campaign to create the Xingu National Park in 1952 (Garfield 2004, 156). To be sure, transnational activists have been unable to guarantee Indigenous autonomy and self-determination; Indigenous peoples across Brazil continue to be wards of the state and are subject to federal policies—including conscription and military oversight. It is the case, though, that Indigenous lands in the Xingu Cluster are larger and have higher titling rates than other areas outside of the northern frontier zone.

The Xingu National Park has a long history. In the early 1950s, professional backwoodsmen ("*sertanistas*") Orlando and Carlos Villas Boas, academics like Darcy Ribeiro and Heloisa Torres, and military institutions like the Brazilian Air force lobbied the national congress to create a "national park" around the Xingu River. Getúlio Vargas, intent on preserving Brazil's national patrimony for its ambitious project of nation building, endorsed and supported the project. Part of the Estado Novo's nationalistic propaganda, the project attracted considerable media attention (Garfield 2004, 155).

In 1961, state officials approved the creation of the park, a large, continuous area, to safeguard the cultural diversity of native people from the effects of fast-paced economic development (Garfield 2001). Historian Seth Garfield explains, "Rather than conceiving of indigenous land in narrow terms of physical occupation, the park envisioned an integrated habitat capable of sustaining a community's physical as well as cultural well-being. Integration into Brazilian society would be gradual and limited" (2001, 64). For administrative ease, the state included sixteen Indigenous groups representing four aboriginal language families in the new area. Five groups were forcefully transferred from their traditional territory to the "park." In 1961, the Kayapó communities that had been in close contact with outsiders since the nineteenth century became part of the Xingu Park. The essentialist notion of Indigenous peoples, advocated by the proponents of the park, has had an enduring consequence in Brazilian indigenous politics. Since then, Xingu residents have "serve[d] as metonym for all Brazilian Indians" (Garfield 2004, 23).

In the late 1980s and early 1990s, the Kayapó became world famous for their opposition to the Belo Monte Dam and other hydroelectric megaprojects that Brazil planned to construct along the Xingu River. A coalition of environmental NGOs continued depicting Indigenous peoples as natural protectors of the rainforest (Fisher 1994, 229; Conklin and Graham 1995; Conklin 1997). Raoni, a Kayapó leader, toured the world with British rock star Sting. Paulino Payaka, another Kayapó representative, traveled to Washington, DC, with U.S. anthropologists Darell Posey and Janet Chernela to advance their political demands before the World Bank, the source of funding for Brazil's infrastructural projects (Rabben 2004, 14). Given that the Xingu residents had become part of the national imaginary, Indigenous rights activists and environmental groups were successful at attracting the media's attention and mobilized the Kayapó in 1987 and 1988 during Brazil's Constitutional Assembly. In 1991, after modifying the Indigenous land titling model, President Collor titled the Kayapó and Capoto/Jarina Indigenous lands (3.9 million hectares). Sting managed to raise over $1 million dollars to pay for the titling of Mekragnoti in 1993—the biggest Indigenous land in the Xingu Cluster region (4.9 million hectares). In 2003 and 2008, President Lula titled an additional 1.7 million hectares for the Kayapó.[33]

The Indigenous land titling in the Xingu Cluster region constitutes an exceptional case in which media attention works in favor of land claimants because of the particular history of the Xingu National Park. The global media has had its eyes on the Xingu region since the early 1950s; first as a result of the state-backed campaign to create the Xingu National Park and then in opposition to the construction of the Belo Monte Dam. But, again, the experience of the Kayapó is not representative of other cases in Brazil.

The Xingu Cluster region shows both the promise and the precariousness of relying on the NGO strategy. Even powerful international NGOs must carefully select which fights to fight and which fights to let go. In the exceptional case of Xingu, international NGOs chose an area that had already attracted substantial media attention and had gained important political significance. In fact, international NGOs targeted these cases because they held the promise of success. NGOs simply do not have the resources to monitor the titling of hundreds of Indigenous lands that are spread over the enormous Amazonian region. Moreover, the attention of the global media, indispensable for the "naming and shaming" strategy used by international NGOs, is sporadic. Maria Guadalupe Moog Rodrigues agrees when she writes, "international attention and support have been elusive and are driven by factors outside the control of Brazilian indigenous peoples. As a result, international mobilization constitutes, at best, a circumstantial advantage, rather than a dependable resource for indigenous peoples" (2002, 489). The tests in Appendix A show the Xingu Cluster as an outlier.

Conclusion

Indigenous land titling is highly uneven in Brazil. The chapter analyzed the variation in the approval of Indigenous land claims located in the Amazonian northern frontier zone—an unlikely case of high levels of titling from the perspective of economic structuralism and administrative theories. The frontier zone is mostly inaccessible and rich in coveted mineral resources (gold, diamonds, uranium, and niobium, for instance)—all factors often seen as impediments to titling. Notwithstanding these obstacles, state elites have focused on titling Indigenous lands in the northern frontier zone, above and beyond other localities in the Amazonian interior. What accounts for these patterns?

The chapter documents that external challenges to state power during the early 1990s played an important role. Nevertheless, external pressure was not enough to explain the observed outcomes. State interests are a condition that mediates external pressures and tell us how titling happens. Creating and approving Indigenous lands is an important strategy for securing military control over the otherwise stateless borderlands. State elites have subordinated Indigenous rights to national interests. State elites guaranteed military interests inside Indigenous lands before titling Indigenous lands. The revamped titling model strengthens military functions inside Indigenous lands.

Through a combination of subnational case studies, I show that state elites are more likely to title Indigenous lands in the northern frontier zone. The Indigenous land titling model implemented in Brazil deviates substantially from the demands of pro-indigenous groups. Activists have demanded full internal autonomy and Indigenous self-determination, including restraints on the power of the military to act inside Indigenous lands. I show that state elites have rejected the anti-military argument: they have titled in a way that allows the military to extend its reach in the borderlands. To be sure, external pressure did push state elites to allocate large Indigenous areas in the early 1990s. But external normative and economic pressure is not sufficient to subordinate military interests to indigenous rights.

Rather than limiting the power of the armed forces, state officials encourage the military to recruit soldiers from indigenous villages and implement military operations and defense policies in the frontier zone, where the titled Indigenous lands are located. In this way, Indigenous groups that are dispersed over an enormous, inaccessible area are absorbed into the modern state and subordinated to a wide range of federal policies. Through the process of identifying and designing Indigenous lands the state erects jurisdictional units and builds the administrative apparatus to govern and control Indigenous peoples who are in fact outside of the state. In short, titling helps to regulate the relationship between Indigenous peoples and federal agents, as well as providing state elites the means to manage territory.

To conclude, state officials have responded selectively to transnational activists' demands. State elites exercised considerable autonomy from transnational activists in upholding and reinforcing the primacy of military interests over Indigenous land and resource rights. Once the state's security interests are safe, Indigenous land titling serves to establish a governing system in strategically important areas. Federal officials reinforce state authority by recruiting local people to the military and creating a differentiated array of institutions to implement federal policies in remote localities. Over time, the state permeates social life and incorporates dispersed and diverse peoples into the modern state.

PART III
CONCLUSION

7
New Ethnic Communal Property Regimes

The Devil is in the Details: Legal Implementation, International Norms, and State-Building in the Americas

Central Findings

A large body of literature has documented the spread of multicultural constitutions in the Americas, which include formal institutions that recognize the right of Indigenous and other ethnic groups to land and natural resources. Major works have pointed out that transnational activism matters for the implementation of these formal institutions since beneficiaries are members of economically and socially marginalized groups that have little domestic political influence (Keck and Sikkink 1998; Brysk 2000; Stocks 2005). Nevertheless, analysts have yet to scrutinize exactly how, and to what extent, external pressure matters. In particular, scholars need to study the remarkable differences in the observed patterns of implementation.

In this book, I investigated in detail the variation in implementation outcomes within and between countries and arrived at a surprising finding: the implementation of Indigenous land and resource rights via Indigenous land titling is not always a response to external pressure. The quickest and most systematic instance of titling happened in moments of low external pressure, namely in Nicaragua in 2007. Also, Indigenous land titling can happen very slowly and unsystematically despite high levels of external concern, as in Brazil. Moreover, transnational pressure leads to outcomes that differ substantively from the expectations of activists. State elites align titling models to advance their own institutional objectives. Whereas transnational activists prefer titling to ensure internal Indigenous self-determination (a high degree of cultural and political autonomy), state elites install communal property regimes that restrict Indigenous self-government. After prolonged and heightened levels of external pressure, as in the case of Brazil from the mid-1980s to the early 1990s, state elites have managed to radically adjust the titling model to guarantee state interests. Even in Brazil, one of Latin America's most targeted states by international human rights and environmental activism, transnational activists have not been able to ensure their preferred outcome.

Although transnational activist networks have become denser and more visible over time, external pressure has not produced the desired substantive results. In fact, domestic factors have had a more positive effect. For instance, in Honduras and Nicaragua, countries where external pressure did not inspire titling, Indigenous and other people gained a higher—although still restricted—degree of local autonomy. For this study, the differences in concrete outcomes are extraordinarily important because they show that constructivism overestimates the importance of transnational activist networks.

In sum, there are clear and stark differences in the temporal and spatial patterns of Indigenous land titling: quick and systematic titling happened under low external pressure, and slow and selective titling coincided with high external pressure. In none of the cases under scrutiny did external pressure result in the substantive outcome advocated by transnational activists. This observed variation, as well as the way in which titling happens, is remarkable and makes it particularly difficult to assert that external pressure is the most important, and even necessary, factor that explains the phenomenon. At the same time, high levels of repression against grassroots organizations that advocate for Indigenous land and resource rights in Central America and non-Amazonian regions go against the expectations of social movement theories.

Titling vast, resource-rich regions to Indigenous peoples and ethnic groups contradicts widely held economic-structural accounts, which predict little, if any, titling in areas coveted by powerful and well-connected economic elites. As I documented in the empirical chapters, state elites go against the preferences of powerful economic groups and engage in Indigenous land titling in the face of perceived security threats. Finally, theories of administration, which expect little to no activity in weak states and peripheral regions, cannot explain the high performance of low-capability states, like Nicaragua and Honduras, and the underperformance of a relatively strong state like Brazil. From the perspective of theories of administration, the observed concentration of titled lands in remote regions of countries is particularly puzzling. Indeed, even in continent-sized countries like Brazil, titled Indigenous lands cluster in the most remote borderlands.

Because of the limitations of existing frameworks, I developed a new explanation for titling outcomes in Latin America that emphasizes the institutional motivations of high-ranking government officials to shape the implementation of Indigenous land and resource rights. Instead of social persuasion, economic influences, or administrative limitations being most important in explaining outcomes, the emphasis here has been on the fundamental institutional interests of state officials to preserve and reproduce the territorial power of the modern state. Top government officials design titling models in a way that advances their institutional interest in territorial control, border enforcement, and supervision of people and their movements. To guarantee state interests, government elites use titling as a device to extend the reach of the state over Indigenous peoples and their ancestral homeland. In particular, state elites engage in titling to intensify the role and the presence of the state in outlying areas. State officials cast a net of new institutions and governing arrangements that serve to secure and consolidate state control. Put differently, state elites build a differentiated institutional framework at the local level, which molds preexisting governing structures. Through a strengthened institutional regime that establishes a state presence, state elites can effectively control people in remote, resource-rich territories.

State elites title Indigenous lands when and where they perceive security challenges due to internal threats or external pressure and pay attention to Indigenous demands for secure property rights whenever internal threats or external pressures reach a critical threshold, with the potential to obstruct the state's ability to control people and territory in unguarded localities. They use Indigenous land titling to resolve conflicts about access, control, and governance of the territory. Importantly, the way in which state elites carry out the task is completely in line with fundamental state interests, rather than reflecting societal preferences and practices. In particular, in contexts of high internal threats—the greatest challenge—state elites act rapidly and systematically, titling Indigenous lands in the region where the threat originates. Under this condition, state elites are motivated to build institutional hierarchies that the central government can manipulate from the top down without facing local push-back. State elites also neutralize external pressure. Under high levels of external pressure—the lesser challenge—state elites first guarantee state interests and then act slowly and selectively where the state needs to intensify control. They design a titling model that ensures military power, which allows them to govern Indigenous areas from a few strategic outposts that the central government commands. Therefore, state interests mediate both internal threats and external pressure and radically shape substantive outcomes.

Specifically, state interests help explain the speed and scope of Indigenous land titling in Central America. As Chapter 4 showed with a wealth of primary and secondary evidence, state elites acted swiftly and systematically in the face of high internal threats. In Nicaragua, to prevent the recurrence of violent ethnic conflict over land rights, state elites designed and implemented a dense web of institutions that allow the central government to circumvent local political authority. As a result, state elites implemented a titling model that effectively imposed state rule and suppressed local political elites, without causing massive local resistance. To reiterate, the ethnic communal property regime put in place greatly diminishes the de facto autonomy of local communities because it is rooted in the preferences of state elites, not the preferences of Indigenous peoples nor other ethnic groups. Thus, instead of upholding preexisting customary structures, state elites superimposed an institutional apparatus that effectively reinforced state authority and greatly reduced Indigenous self-government. Because Indigenous land titling serves as a strategy to quell internal threats, rather than as a response to external pressure, state elites titled lands in the east, where there is a legacy of ethnic conflict, but ignored claims from the west, where there is none. State interests, then, explain the stark regional gap in outcomes that is plainly evident in Nicaragua. State interests provide the causal mechanisms that underlie a core feature of the new communal property regimes, namely, the transformation of existing informal institutions at the community level to achieve top-down control.

The imperative to maintain control over people and territory motivates Indigenous land titling. State elites deploy land titling programs to ensure the state's presence in localities where state power is threatened. An exponential increase in the territorial power of criminal organizations can cause security crises that trigger action. As Chapter 5 shows, when organized crime challenges state dominance of specific localities, state elites use titling as a strategy to regain control of the contested region. In Honduras, drug flows to the eastern territory caused a surge of homicides in the rest of the country. Because drug lords threatened the ability of the state to access and operate in the eastern territory, state elites quickly titled large Indigenous lands there. State elites completely ignored demands before organized crime jeopardized the state's power, as demonstrated in Chapter 5. Only after the country was engulfed in chaos caused by drug trafficking, did state elites begin to pay attention to the eastern territory, the entryway to U.S.-bound drugs. State elites used titling as a noncoercive way to penetrate local civil society and combat organized crime effectively. Through the implementation program, state elites created alliances with local Indigenous leaders and built a network of institutions to reinforce their power in the eastern territory. Importantly, the state does not title a single Indigenous homeland. On the contrary, state elites designed a small number of manageable jurisdictional units from a larger territory that Indigenous leaders claim as their ancestral homeland. In Honduras, the allocation of land based on ethnicity follows not Indigenous land demands or external pressure but rather the state's need to reinforce its power in remote and unguarded localities.

As explained in Chapter 3, external pressure can also challenge the institutional interests of state elites. This type of threat emerges when local civil society has little capacity to engage in effective collective action and must rely on the strategies of global activists to push for the implementation of rules on the books. Once a transnational coalition is formed, external activists demand implementation as a corrective to nation-building exercises and capitalist expansion; their goal is to hold state institutions at bay and insulate Indigenous communities from the pressures of modern society. In that sense, external pressure may threaten the state's ability to penetrate Indigenous areas.

As Chapter 6 amply documents, however, high levels of external pressure are insufficient to motivate state elites to adopt transnational activists' demands. In fact, state elites actively block these forces to guarantee fundamental state interests. In the process, state elites transform the implementation model that transnational activists advance by upholding the primacy of military interests inside Indigenous lands. Put differently, state elites turn Indigenous land titling models from a state-debilitating tool to a state-building mechanism. In this way, state elites use Indigenous land titling as an effective way to impose state rule in remote geographies where the military has complete jurisdiction. The state redesigns the institutional landscape by establishing jurisdictional boundaries that guide federal action, while disregarding customary governing arrangements. Through titling, state elites neutralize external pressure and extend the reach of the state in the borderlands. The case of Brazil demonstrates that state interests shape implementation in a significant way: state elites frustrate the aspiration of transnational activists and impose an institutional apparatus that reinforces state power in Indigenous areas. Even in Brazil, where transnational constructivism expects external pressure to be effective, state interests are fundamental to explain the distinctive patterns and substantive attributes of outcomes.

In sum, state interests help explain the spatial and temporal patterns, as well as the core features of titled Indigenous lands across two different subregions of the Americas. State elites, motivated by fundamental institutional concerns, have manipulated demands for implementation and produced a new titling model that ensures and reinforces the state's power over people and territory. Across the Americas, state elites have adopted titling models that frustrate local and transnational demands because they effectively limit de facto Indigenous autonomy. High-ranking government officials use the new titling models to ensure military and administrative control over stateless localities effectively. In short, although internal threats and external pressures prompt states to consider implementing formal Indigenous land and resource rights, state interests are the crucial mediating factor that radically shapes its character and the ultimate outcome.

Comparative Perspective

My main contribution is a new state-centric theory of Indigenous land titling in the Latin American context. High-ranking government officials title Indigenous lands to maintain and reinforce the presence and function of the state in remote regions. State interests mediate societal challenges and explain subnational patterns in three developing economies of Latin America since (re)democratization: Brazil, Honduras, and Nicaragua.

Can the state-centric theory proposed in this book explain titling patterns in other countries of the Global South outside Latin America? Can my theory account for within-country variation in non settler postcolonial nations where governments may resist Indigenous peoples' demands? My state-centric argument expects Indigenous land titling to co-vary with triggered state interests. In other words, state elites should title lands when and where they face significant security challenges. Thus, I will assess in the following analysis whether my theory has broader applicability beyond the countries examined in Chapters 4, 5, and 6.

I have concentrated on countries that meet two criteria: (1) they codify Indigenous land rights and, (2) they experienced especially high degrees of external pressure or internal threat. To meet the first requirement, I focused on the Americas. No other region in the world has higher levels of codification of communal property rights for Indigenous peoples and ethnic groups than Latin America, although some countries in Africa and Asia have adopted these formal institutions as well (RRI 2014; Hodgson 2011; Wily 2001). To meet the second condition, I concentrated on South America for external pressure and Central America for internal threat. Brazil, which is at the center of the empirical investigation in Chapter 6, scores especially high on external pressure because it holds the majority of the Amazon River Basin, a geographical region that has been a priority for transnational activists since the late 1980s (Moog Rodrigues 2003, Ch. 3). As regards internal threat, Chapters 4 and 5 demonstrate that Nicaragua and Honduras reached particularly high levels of internal threat in 2007 and 2012, respectively. Because the countries examined here rank high along either of these two dimensions, they allow for a clear illustration of different aspects of my account about Indigenous land titling.

In the following subsection, I consider the generalizability of my findings by conducting a preliminary examination of two different country cases: one from Africa and the other from Southeast Asia. I analyze titling patterns in Kenya and Indonesia, two nonsettler postcolonial countries that have adopted communal property rights based on indigeneity. I chose these countries, rather than explore cases from Western liberal welfare states like Canada or Australia where there is a growing body of research on Indigenous politics, to maintain the analytical focus in the developing economies of the Global South.

Variation in Indigenous Land Titling in Africa and Southeast Asia

Kenya, in Africa, and Indonesia, in Southeast Asia, are two particularly good cases for exploring the applicability of my approach because each has drawn much research, which makes a comparative assessment based on secondary literature feasible. Kenya scores high in internal threat; external pressures were especially high in Indonesia. In Kenya, my approach expects titling processes to unfold quickly and systematically. Since external pressure is the weaker stimulus, my approach expects slow and selective implementation in Indonesia. That is, we should expect low titling levels to occur, and only in localities where the state intends to increase its presence. My state-centric argument also suggests that state-backed titling models are likely to depart radically from models advocated by transnational activists: state elites will redesign communal land rights to install governing arrangements that contain local autonomy, rather than enhance it. If these patterns play out in countries with radically different historical and geographical features, then these empirical results would provide a strong corroboration of my state-centric approach.

Kenya: Titling for Internal Order

In Central America, Indigenous land titling varies in line with the causal factors highlighted in this book. Titling processes advanced quickly and systematically in eastern Nicaragua and Honduras when internal threat was high: the state was determined to maintain territorial power and safeguard internal political order; state elites titled lands rapidly and systematically in troubled areas. In Kenya, as in Central America, internal threats, rather than external pressure, triggered state interests. Rulers designed communal lands based on ethnicity to ensure internal political order under colonial regimes and postcolonial governments. Thus, the Kenyan experience shows that the path of internal threats triggering state interests for Indigenous land titling is not unique to Central America. Because titling in Kenya occurs as a result of internal threats, my theory predicts that the state will title large communal areas.

Similar to the Central American cases, state elites in Kenya have titled Indigenous lands to contain internal threats. There is one crucial difference between the Central American and East African experience: communal property regimes based on ethnicity were first installed by colonial rulers and were later reinforced by the postcolonial state (Hodgson 2011; Boone 2003, 6–9, 2014, Ch. 2). Colonial regimes organized communities into "tribes," designed new "tribal homelands" or "ethnic reserves," and introduced an array of institutional arrangements on land access and management to rule over the local population via chiefs and elders who acted as state agents (Young 1994, Ch. 4; Bøås and Dunn 2013, Ch. 4). In other words, communal property regimes in Kenya are the institutional remnants of colonial indirect rule that were maintained after independence in 1963 (Mamdani 1996, Ch. 5).

To be sure, transnational activism has pushed Kenya to recognize or reinforce Indigenous land and resource rights in contemporary times. Since the 1990s and early 2000s, advocates have framed communal land rights under the Indigenous rights banner on behalf of pastoralists and hunter-gatherer communities (Boone 2019; Hodgson 2011; Igoe 2006). Activists have linked themselves to the transnational indigenous rights movement to advocate for the recognition or reaffirmation of ancestral rights to land, to protect communities from land expropriation and expulsion and assert rights to cultural self-determination (Sing'Oei and Shepherd 2010; Boone 2019, 8–9). The Maasai are among the groups that demand reaffirmation of land rights established during colonial rule. The Ogiek exemplify groups that were not recognized by the colonial overlords but that demand recognition as Indigenous peoples entitled to territorial claims under contemporary laws (World Bank 2006; ILO 2009, 20). By joining the Indigenous rights movement, as well as reform agendas centered on decentralization and community-based natural resource management, activists have managed to increase their international visibility, as well as attract the support of multinational institutions like the United Nations, international NGOs like Cultural Survival, and bilateral and multilateral donors and funding agencies (Boone 2019, 390; Hodgson 2011, Ch. 2; UN 2007). For instance, the World Bank has stipulated that "some communities such as *Ogiek, Sengwer, Ilchamus, Boni and Waata, and some pastoral communities amongst the Maasai, Yaaku, and Samburu*" meet the Indigenous peoples criteria and should receive special consideration (emphasis in original, 2016, 9). In addition, activists have won important legal cases before the African Commission and the African Court on Human and Peoples' Rights (Lynch 2012). For example, the Court has ruled that Kenya must grant legal title to the Ogiek for lands located in the Mau Forest Complex in the Great Rift Valley province (*ACHPR v. Republic of Kenya*, May 26, 2017).[1]

Recent developments notwithstanding, the allocation of Indigenous land is a political strategy intended to secure internal order, with roots in colonial times. As Morten Bøås and Kevin Dunn, citing geographer Claire Médard, explain, "'In Kenya, the link made between land, territory, and ethnicity ... is, first and foremost, part of an administrative [colonial] tradition'" (2013, 58). After independence, the post-colonial state has continued to reinforce the institutionalized colonial practice of assigning specific areas of territory to state-recognized groups (Ribot 1999; Boone 2019, 386). For instance, in

1968 the government passed the Land (Group Representatives) Act, which granted collective land rights to pastoral and nomadic groups in arid and semiarid lands, which account for approximately 80 percent of Kenya's territorial landmass (ILO 2009, 36–37; Mwangi 2007, 4). In the 1970s, the state began demarcating "group ranches," the label given to land designated and legally allocated at the inter-village level to a tribe, clan, or other group (ILO 2009, 36). In many of the arid and semiarid areas of Kenya, land is still collectively held as group ranches (Mwangi 2007, 4). Estimates put communal lands and group ranches as covering more than 60 percent of Kenya's total land area (LandMark 2017). Since the transnational indigenous rights movement gained momentum in Kenya in the 1990s, clearly the instauration of communal property regimes could not have been the result of external pressure.

In Kenya, Indigenous land titling resulted from the interests of ruling elites to contain internal threats, namely an ever-present threat of violence, which were high before and after independence. As Mahmood Mamdani argues, colonial rulers designed tribal homelands, limited the growth of land markets, and imposed indirect rule because they feared that a dispossessed and landless peasantry would threaten colonial order (1996, Ch. 5). More importantly, the postcolonial state maintained these land tenure institutions for the same reason: attempts at modifying property rights entitlements over territorial ethnic units faced strong societal resistance and risked producing full-fledged ethnic conflicts (Bøås and Dunn 2013, Ch. 4; Boone 2019, 13–14). To avoid violent challenges to state power, the state maintained the colonial governing strategy that controlled the rural population with land tenure regimes, which determined not only the livelihoods but also the internal social stratification of agrarian societies (Mamdani 1996). In particular, postcolonial governments allocated land to groups along ethnic lines and vested county councils as trustees of communal lands. In these "Trust Lands," the state granted county councils ample discretion to allocate, manage, or regulate land relations (Wily 2015). In other words, the state renewed the power of local elites and bolstered the land prerogatives of established communities inside these subnational territorial units (Ribot 1999).

Since 2010, Kenya has reaffirmed Indigenous land rights in law. In particular, the state confirmed formal Indigenous land rights in Articles 61–63 of the 2010 Constitution, the 2012 Land Act, and the 2016 Communal Land Act. Importantly, the central government has maintained hierarchical structures to manipulate intermediaries and, indirectly, rule over the local population. The state has reinforced institutional mechanisms of control through four key provisions. First, communal land rights are subordinate to public interests or purpose (Constitution 2010, Art. 40; Land Act 2012, Sections 107–133). Second, the central government controls all public land, non registered communal land, and resettlement schemes. Third, communities must first form legal entities with registered (listed) members approved by the central government to secure land certification and registration as "communal lands" (Communal Land Act 2016). Finally, the constitution bars groups from obtaining legal title to a forest, wildlife, water, or other protected area of national or local importance (Constitution 2010, Art. 62). In other words, the institutional framework limits the rights of hunter-gatherer groups, who largely reside in government forest and wildlife reserves, to obtain title to their ancestral homelands (Wily 2015).

In sum, Indigenous land titling in Kenya shares similar characteristics to the process that unfolded in Central America, especially in Nicaragua, although in radically different contexts. The findings corroborate the argument that Indigenous land titling can be a proactive strategy utilized by state elites to ensure internal political order. That is, titling in Kenya is not a response to transnational indigenous rights activism but rather a mechanism to contain internal threats. Moreover, it seems that the state-centric approach substantiated here can explain the character of the titling model adopted there. The institutional structures that are created through titling programs enhance, rather than limit, the presence and power of the state at the local level. Finally, Kenya also confirms my assertion that external pressure, although present, does not alter the relationships between ethnic groups and the state. The current formal institutional framework does not conform to the models advanced by the United Nations and international NGOs. State elites continue to reinforce their dominance over peoples through the mechanisms of indirect rule.

Indonesia: Titling to Extend the State's Reach

The slow and highly selective way in which state officials title Indigenous lands in Indonesia offers further corroboration for my state-centric argument. In Indonesia, transnational activists have been insistently demanding Indigenous land titles for over two decades, since the early 1990s (Li 2001; Bourchier 2007, 122; Moniaga 2007, 281). In 1998, after the end of the repressive Suharto dictatorship (1966–1998), transnational activism intensified (Li 2000). Linked to a dense global network of environmentalists, Indigenous rights activists have argued that rights to land and resources are an essential feature of an environmental protection policy centered on natural resource management techniques employed by local communities drawing on local traditions (Li 2000, 155–57; Henley and Davidson 2007, 7–8; Li 2007, 343–54; Tyson 2010); this is especially true in Sulawesi, Kalimantan, Lampung, and Papua (Moniaga 2007, 280–83; Bourchier 2007, 123; Afiff and Lowe 2007). Yet, transnational activists have been unable to persuade state officials to prioritize Indigenous land and resource rights (Moniaga 2007, 285). For instance, despite strong opposition from indigenous and environmental NGOs, land and land-based and subsoil resources remain "under the powers of the State" according to the 1945 Constitution (Art. 33.3). Moreover, the 1960 Basic Agrarian Law establishes that customary laws apply to property relations as long as they are consistent with national or state interests (Art. 2(4), Arts. 3, 5, 11(2)). To be sure, Arts. 18B(2) and 28 of the Constitution recognized traditional customary rights, Art. 6 of the 1999 Human Rights Act established traditional rights to communal land, and a 2012 Constitutional Court decision held that indigenous communities (or *adat*) have property rights to forestlands. But all of these rights are subordinate to state interests.[2] Thus, in Indonesia, Indigenous land rights include the rights of access and use and some exclusion prerogatives, but exclude the right to own houses, cultivate crops, exploit forest products, and contravene the government's environmental directives (Fitzpatrick 2007, 141). In short, transnational activists have been unable to persuade state officials to recognize full property rights to Indigenous groups over areas they claim as ancestral homelands (Li 2001, 658).

Moreover, as in Brazil—and different from Nicaragua, Honduras, and Kenya—land titling has not been triggered by internal threats, but mostly by external pressure (Henley and Davidson 2007; Li 2001, 2007; Sangaji 2007; Peluso 2004, 231–33). The fact that transnational activism prompts titling is a particularly striking indication of the insularity of state elites; domestic social movements could not get their point across and had to rely on international normative and material support to advance their cause (Li 2001, 647–48). Hence, indigenous rights activists in Indonesia have linked themselves with global environmentalists and—with the economic and political support of international donors (including USAID and OXFAM)—have framed land claims as "ways of life linked to the specific ancestral territories of distinctive cultural groups" (Li 2001, 648). For instance, a network of NGOs called the Alliance of Indigenous Peoples of the Archipelago (or Aliansi Masyarakat Adat Nusantara, AMAN) asserts cultural distinctiveness as the grounds for securing rights to land and resources, as well as the right of indigenous communities ("masyarakat adat") that predate the creation of the modern state to "govern themselves and the resources on which they depend" (Li 2001, 647). Indigenous rights activists in Indonesia have learned from the strategies of their Brazilian counterparts whereby land politics are framed in terms of the intrinsic value of cultural difference useful for environmental conservation and even decolonization efforts (Henley and Davidson 2007, 28; Acciaioli 2007, 303–309).

As in Brazil, external pressure has had limited effects in Indonesia. To be sure, transnational activists have been successful in reframing land demands based on ancestry, rather than on economic or class terms. It is certainly impressive that these activists have managed to do so in Indonesia, a non settler postcolonial country where determining who is and isn't indigenous is a prickly issue (Li 2014, Ch. 1). However, I argue that these are partial successes. In addition to a strong persistence of military influence in most areas of political life since democratization (Henley and Davidson 2007, 18), land titling has occurred slowly and only in peripheral regions. Transnational activists have demanded titling in all of the islands that compose Indonesia, including in the province of Java, the economic and political center of the state. Yet, the state has mostly acknowledged land claims that originate from peripheral islands. In nearly two decades, state elites have titled only about 42 percent of the admitted claims, most of which are located in the frontier zone of forested areas with low population density in the provinces of West Kalimantan and South Sulawesi (LandMark 2017). The slow progress toward titling selected land claims suggests that state elites have enough autonomy to decide which claims to ignore, which to accept as legitimate, and which to title. According to Adam Tyson, a political scientist specializing in Indonesian ethnic politics, the reason for reclassifying rural communities and establishing borders in remote areas is to improve "the scope and reach of the state apparatus, including the ability to penetrate distant regions, expand resource extraction and limit or co-opt potential sources of resistance" (2010, 164).

Apart from shaping the spatial and temporal patterns of communal land titling, state elites also decisively design titling models in a way that extends the reach of the state in peripheral localities. In other words, transnational activists have been unable to persuade state elites to adopt titling models that further cultural self-determination by enhancing the autonomy of communities. On the contrary, titling has served state elites to revive and expand the governing mechanisms that were initially introduced under Dutch indirect rule (Li 2001, 2007, 2014; Biezeveld 2007, 218–19), whereby the central government manipulates state-backed traditional elites to govern ethnic collectivities (Henley and Davidson 2007, 2–5; Bourchier 2007, 123). As David Henley and Jamie S. Davidson (2007, 24) explain,

> Custom, in Dutch colonial discourse, was also associated with the reinforcement by the state of internal hierarchy within the "adat communities" themselves.... Client (or puppet) leaders were cast as *adathoofden* or "adat chiefs," whose right to rule—and judge according to adat law—rested neither on the state nor in a direct way on the popular will but rather on the authority of custom .... [Contemporary state elites justify the creation of new adat chiefs] in Kalimantan as "a government-initiated stimulation of ordered community according to principles known in custom (such as consultation, hierarchical representation."

In other words, state officials are aware that communal property regimes can be created and manipulated to expand the power of the central government. In fact, state elites can wield a high degree of freedom to engage in institutional engineering at the local level (Scott 2009, 258). Government officials have used land titling as a way to reinforce the prestige of traditional local elites, which in turn enforce the policies established by the central government (Bourchier 2007, 124). For instance, anthropologist Tania M. Li explains that in the province of Central Sulawesi, the central government is forming or strengthening customary (*adat*) councils at the sub-district level "to operate as tools or even as branches of government . . . to facilitate smooth government" (2007a, 363). To do so, the central government has given *adat* councils the power to manage communal land, wealth, and natural resources, which leaves council headmen prone to state manipulation (Li 2007a, 365). To put it succinctly, the Indonesian state has reconfigured Indigenous land titling models in a way that revives systems of indirect rule in contemporary times.

In conclusion, the Indigenous land titling patterns that exist in countries not examined closely in this book, namely Kenya and Indonesia, largely corroborate my state-centric argument. Where land titling progresses relatively quickly and in a widespread fashion in a targeted subnational region, the trigger was internal threat, not external pressure. Where external pressure triggers state interests, state elites take their time to cherry-pick which claims to resolve and where to install new communal property regimes. Moreover, the very character of communal property regimes differs radically from the titling model preferred by transnational activists. In practice, communal property regimes grant only carefully constrained autonomy to local elites, who are manipulated or co-opted by the central government. That is, in these communities, people themselves have no option but to manage conflicts and follow the directives of the political elites or leaders that the central government supports. The stark discrepancy between what transnational activists want and the state actually enacts further supports my point that ethnic communal property regimes are just a new way to extend the power of the state into remote, vulnerable, and de facto stateless localities. These regimes do not disturb, in any significant way, the state's clout and decision-making power. Thus, the theory delineated here seems to hold, especially in its insistence that state elites will modify core elements of ethnic communal property regimes to fit their security and governability needs.

Broader Theoretical Contributions

My empirical findings and theoretical conclusions speak to several broader debates about multiculturalism, including the limitations of a rights-based framework to further Indigenous self-determination, the power of the modern state in a globalized era, the politics regarding the implementation of formal institutions, and contemporary strategies of state building. In particular, my cross-national and longitudinal analysis of Indigenous land titling questions the extent to which transnational activism can be effective in changing state behavior. In addition, this work centers on how state elites adapt to the exigencies of the modern world to guarantee internal order and territorial control.

Although the substantive focus has been on Indigenous land rights, broad questions about the spread of multiculturalism and its post-liberal challenge motivate this study (Kymlicka 1995; Yashar 1999). This book speaks to the controversial debate about whether social movements rallying behind Indigenous peoples and their rights and norms regarding self-determination produce either meaningful progress toward creating democratic institutions at the grassroots level or unintended regressive and potentially authoritarian reversals. Does the implementation of Indigenous land and resource rights bolster the commitment to observe human rights and strengthen civil society as transnational activists expect? Or rather, does Indigenous land titling institutionalize a system that restricts Indigenous self-determination? On this issue, transnational constructivism arrives at an optimistic conclusion. To date, research on the diffusion of formal multicultural institutions has generally emphasized the power of transnational activists in shaping the interests and behavior of states. Scholars emphasize the remarkable success of the transnational Indigenous rights movements, which began in the countries that experienced settler colonialism in the Americas (Ramos 1998; Merlan 2005) and, with the help of international organizations like the United Nations, expanded their advocacy to other parts of the world, namely Africa and Southeast Asia (Hodgson 2011; Li 2000; Davidson and Henley 2007). Scholars highlight how the transnational Indigenous rights movement has persuaded state elites into accepting norms that ensure Indigenous self-determination and self-government, even when these norms initially encounter strong state opposition. Transnational constructivists see these norms as a corrective to the individualistic ethos of neoliberalism. Under this reading, Indigenous land and resource rights are crucial components of a progressive package of multicultural institutions that, once adopted and implemented by states, promise to correct historic injustices, ensure collective well-being, and even boost democracy at the local level.

The central finding of the present investigation, namely that state interests are a crucial mediating factor in the implementation of Indigenous land and resource rights, casts doubt on the optimistic expectations of transnational constructivists. As amply documented in the empirical chapters of this book, state elites shape the specific attributes of titling models based on the exigencies of territorial control and internal order. At the implementation stage, state elites simply block the realization of the international norms that transnational activists advocate. As a result, state elites obstruct their potentially emancipatory, progressive features. In fact, rather than changing state interests, these norms become challenges for state elites to overcome and manage. As the detailed study of communal property regimes in Central America and Brazil shows, top government officials refashion titling models into governing arrangements that are quite different from those advocated by transnational activists.

State elites enact titling programs without the essential features demanded by transnational activists. In particular, government officials configure titling models in a way that entrenches the state's capacity to dominate civil society, rather than devolve power to the grassroots level. The resulting institutional apparatus constraints, rather than promotes, Indigenous self-determination in order to strengthen state power. State elites consciously engineer institutional mechanisms that anoint selected local elites with the power to allocate, manage, and resolve land-related manners; these intermediaries then become vulnerable to political manipulation and co-optation. In other words, the state creates and reinforces hierarchies within newly designed territorial units in a way that gives the central government the upper hand vis-à-vis local elites and, by extension, the local population. Even when they stop short of instituting a micromanaging system to discipline Indigenous subjects (as in Brazil), state elites ensure state domination over territory through militarization. In short, the state supports Indigenous land claims because it allows state elites to justify their rule over Indigenous peoples or to establish the institutional apparatus needed for administrative discipline in the borderlands.

This study helps to contextualize narratives about the effectiveness of transnational activism in spreading multiculturalism in the developing world. It demonstrates that the power and interests of the modern state continue to be paramount in political decision-making, especially in the implementation of international norms. Even when coping with high levels of external pressure, state elites have enough room to maneuver and can substantially modify international policies to safeguard their security interests. State officials have not only the will but also the capacity to repurpose implementation models to maintain and even expand the state's reach and control over Indigenous territory and people. Hence, this study provides additional evidence in favor of arguments that point to the limitations of multiculturalism and to the dangers in relying too much on a rights-based approach, which has excluded alternative conceptions of Indigenous self-determination (Kuokkanen 2019), in articulating and advocating for Indigenous rights.

My work also underscores important sources of variation in the implementation of formal institutions. These findings speak to concerns about how institutions work and change, specifically the way in which selective implementation may produce substantial political changes without modifying formal law (Mahoney and Thelen 2010; Levitsky and Murillo 2005, 3–5, 270–79, 2009, 127–28). A contribution of my study is to show that state interests can make sense of the temporal and geographical patterns of implementation. Indigenous land titling serves to fashion new communal property regimes at the grassroots level, which allows the central government to impose state authority in peripheral regions. This insight provides leverage to understand this selective implementation as a tool that state elites have at their disposal to engage in state building. In other words, state elites choose to engage in titling programs that affect the character of the state and the nature of state-society relations.

Political scientists often view state building as the creation and maintenance of durable and effective institutions designed to manage societal relations directly and function according to a codified set of transparent criteria (Kurtz 2013). In this sense, state building is construed as the act of engineering the institutional apparatus throughout the national territory that would enable the reiterative practices of government (typically, provide public goods and services). My research has demonstrated that state builders in Latin America have a panoply of methods to engage in state building (that is, to manage state-society relations and to maintain state authority). As a first-order strategy, state elites may seek to create strong and durable institutions that penetrate civil society directly, which may lead to the unfiltered provision of public goods and services. But state elites may also need to resort to second-best options to reach their objectives: they can create a differentiated set of mechanisms to manage societal conflict and demands indirectly. I provided detailed evidence that in the Americas, state elites consider the installation of new ethnic communal property regimes as beneficial for two reasons. First, these institutions aid them in realizing their need to extend the reach of the state apparatus in the farthest reaches of the territory. Second, these land tenure regimes are an acceptable, if imperfect, solution to their broader, long-term problem of ensuring internal political order. In particular, I demonstrate that state elites title Indigenous lands to manage the threat of insurrection (Chapter 4), reinforce power in vulnerable, stateless regions (Chapter 5), and ensure the state's permanent presence in porous borderlands (Chapter 6). To ignore Indigenous land demands by installing a different type of property regimes would be too costly and risk a backlash. In other words, the evidence presented here supports the conclusion that state elites view Indigenous land titling as a tool to fulfill security functions. In this sense, this study confirms the proposition that the installation of ethnic communal property regimes is what others have described as an overarching strategy to reconstitute the state's hegemony (Postero 2007, 13–15).

Indigenous land titling offers a useful method to reinforce state power where direct imposition would most likely lead to unwanted outcomes.

Through the design and allocation of communal land, state elites restructure the institutional landscape and establish the lines of power that serve to control economic and political life in rural settings. The state engages in a process that installs a new, more simplified and legible property regime vis-à-vis the status quo that is amenable to manipulation from the center, as James Scott would put it (1998, 33–52). State-backed ethnic communal property regimes serve to tame the economic and political autonomy of local subjects, a useful feature that the central government can wield to minimize internal conflict and ultimately reproduce its power. Thus, my explanation goes beyond noting that there is a correlation between internal threat or external pressure and Indigenous land titling. I dig deeper and specify exactly how state interests shape the terms of the titling model and fundamentally transform its function. By carefully designing the core features of the titling model, the state enhances its ability to penetrate society and insert itself in local life through intermediaries. In the end, state elites distance themselves from directly managing the affairs of Indigenous peoples on property matters, delegating these managerial prerogatives to new hierarchical governing systems of land institutions.

This book advances theorizing about the contemporary tools of state building. Assuming that Indigenous land titling enhances local power and autonomy, scholars of Latin America have overlooked its use as a state-building tool. By contrast, my in-depth analysis of two different regions of the Americas shows that state elites selectively use Indigenous land titling as a strategy to reinforce state power. Under pressure, state elites adapt titling models to manage Indigenous peoples in a top-down fashion and reinforce their power over territory. State elites turn to the implementation of formal institutions to create an institutional nexus that furthers state domination, rather than restrict state power. State elites have found a remarkable adaptation to reinforce their power in contemporary times.

Further research needs to probe the direct and indirect effects of ethnic communal property regimes and how societal actors manage to contest and resist the indirect imposition of state domination. For instance, Indigenous peoples in Central America and Brazil create civil society organizations, make alliances with transnational advocacy groups, and resort to international legal systems.

In Nicaragua, the Alliance of Indigenous and Afro-descendant Peoples of Nicaragua (APIAN), an independent civil society organization created in 2015, has denounced the government-imposed structures that override customary authorities inside Indigenous lands before the Inter-American System of Human Rights and has advocated against the export of untraceable goods that might be sourced illegally from Indigenous lands as a way to resist the decisions of these captured local authorities (CEJIL 2021; Oakland Institute, 2020, 32–34, 46–50).

In Honduras, where Indigenous peoples face serious repression, civil society organizations work together with coordinated NGOs, such as the Defending Land and Environmental Defenders Coalition, to advocate for protection for land and environmental defenders (EarthRights International 2020, 7–8, 25–27).

In Brazil, advocates have resorted to the Inter-American Commission on Human Rights, which has granted protective measures in favor of the Guajajara and Awá peoples of the Araribóia Indigenous Land to guarantee their right to health, life, and personal integrity given the presence of unauthorized third parties in their territory (IACHR, Resolution No. 1/21, PM 754-20). In addition, Indigenous peoples' organization in Brazil, such as the Coordination of Indigenous Organizations of the Brazilian Amazon (COIAB) and the Japaú Indigenous Association of the Uru-eu-wau-wau Indigenous land, have been working with transnational NGOs like the World Wide Fund for Nature (WWF) to build the capacity of Indigenous peoples to negotiate better terms for communities when managing resources inside titled Indigenous lands and adopt new forest monitoring systems technology (USAID 2020; Pfeifer 2020). These are only a few examples of how Indigenous peoples continue to defend their rights and negotiate their relationship with the modern state in contemporary times. A systematic analysis of Indigenous peoples' strategies that takes a bottom-up approach can expand our understanding of the most feasible strategies that Indigenous peoples can employ to resist state co-optation and further local democratic practices in the developing economies of the Global South.

APPENDICES

APPENDICES

APPENDIX A

Quantitative Test, Indigenous Land Titling in Brazil

The statistical analysis that follows is based on the Brazil Database. It uses event history analysis to better understand the dynamics of Indigenous land titling as a longitudinal process in Brazil. The guiding questions are whether, and to what extent, news coverage about international NGO activism, location in the frontier zone, and value of the land claim affect the approval of titling proceedings.

The Dependent Variable

The dependent variable is Indigenous Land titling, defined as the presidential approval of administrative proceedings that allocate land to Indigenous groups. This binary variable$_i$ is based on information made available by FUNAI.[1] For the current study, titling proceedings with complete records pending approval since 1988, the year Brazil adopted its current Constitution, are included.[2] According to the above-mentioned criteria, the final sample has 636 land claims.

Explanatory Factors

To test my state-centric hypothesis, the database contains information about the location of Indigenous Lands, including overlap with the frontier zone (Furtado 2013, 55). The variable *Location* was coded as four binary (0/1) variables that represent Indigenous Lands that either overlap with the Northern Frontier Zone, those located in the Xingu Cluster, or those inside or outside Amazonia; Indigenous Lands inside of Amazonia served as the reference category for comparison. The geographical partition in *Location* is based on the identification of statistically significant (p-value < 0.10) spatial clusters (or hot spots) using the Getis-Ord Gi* statistic (a z-score).[3] The Getis-Ord Gi* statistic measures the difference in the expected titling rate of an Indigenous Land and its neighbors compared proportionally to the titling rate of all Indigenous Lands in the country. When that difference is too large to be the result of random chance, the Getis-Ord Gi* statistic is significant. In other words, *Location* accounts for spatial dependency (or spatial autocorrelation) in the data.

Additional indicators in the dataset are the following: environment; minerals & hydrocarbons; World Bank; INGO news. *Environment* measures the percentage of overlap between Indigenous Lands and environmental conservation units before titling. *Minerals & Hydrocarbons* is a binary variable coded 1 for the known existence of oil and gas deposits inside or within a radius of one mile from an Indigenous Land before titling and 0 otherwise. The variable also captures if there are known deposits of gold, diamonds, niobium, uranium, or other valuable minerals inside Indigenous Lands before titling.

World Bank is a binary variable coded 1 if the World Bank administered international financial loans for the titling of an Indigenous Land and 0 otherwise, based on the final evaluation report of an Indigenous land titling program by the World Bank.[4] *INGO news* is a geocoded count variable measuring the number of news reports of international NGO activity inside an Indigenous Land, scaled by the time interval between the moment FUNAI accepts the land claim until its titling. Specifically, this indicator reflects the amount of news coverage generated for an Indigenous Land by international NGOs, or local NGOs connected with international networks, that advocate for Indigenous land and resource rights.[5] The variable is based on a digital repository and a physical archive of daily newspapers with national and international circulation covering the period 1983–2016. The Instituto Socioambiental, a well organized and prominent Brazilian NGO with headquarters in São Paulo, keeps and updates the newspaper collection daily, which contains newspaper clippings of events that have made world and national headlines. For example, the mining activities in the Yanomami area from the early 1990s, which generated the highest number of news coverage worldwide, are included in the digital archive.

I use the following variables as controls: existence of multiple Indigenous groups, size of Indigenous Lands (area in hectares), Indigenous peoples in the state, and the agricultural potential of the land. Table A.1 shows the descriptive statistics for these variables.

Table A.1 Descriptive Statistics

Variable	Percentage			
No. observations	636			
Location:				
Northern Frontier Zone	8.6%			
Xingu Cluster	1.1%			
Amazonia (River Basin)	50.9%			
Other (Outside Amazonia)	39.4%			
Total	100%			
World Bank	25.3%			
Multiple Groups	14.2%			
Minerals & Hydrocarbons	17.4%			
Agricultural Potential	14.4%			
	Mean	Standard Deviation	Minimum	Maximum
Environment (overlap)	0.04	0.19	0	1
INGO news	5.37	21.31	0	376
Size (ha)	171,462	724,439	0	9,664,975
Indigenous Population	69,203.76	58,056.90	2,596	167,511

Table A.2 Factors Driving Indigenous Land Titling without Considering Duration and Spatial Dependence

Variable	Coefficient	Standard Error	P-value
Constant	0.55	0.02	0.000
World Bank	0.14***	0.04	0.001
INGO News	0.002***	0.00	0.006

*** Significant at the 0.01 level; ** Significant at the 0.05 level; * Significant at the 0.1 level (two-tailed significance tests).
N = 636; R-squared = 0.02

Table A.2 presents the results of a linear regression with two important variables that are widely understood to be the drivers of Indigenous land titling: *World Bank* and *INGO News*. My objective is to describe the relationship between these two variables and titling without accounting for duration and spatial dependence.

The results show that *World Bank* is statistically significant at the 0.01 level (p = 0.001). As generally expected, land claims with World Bank support have 0.14 higher titling rates than those that do not. The effect of INGO News is also positive and statistically significant at the 0.01 level (p = 0.001). For a 1 unit increase in INGO News, there is a 0.002 unit increase in titling. Thus, support from the World Bank and exposure through INGO-generated news are associated with higher titling. However, these results do not consider the duration of the titling process. For a more complete assessment, I turn to event history analysis (Box-Steffensmeier and Jones 1997).

Statistical Model

To understand the determinants of presidential approval of Indigenous Land proceedings, I use a single-spell piecewise constant exponential event history model. Event history models are appropriate to analyze events occurring in time because the model considers timing as well as the occurrence of an event (Box-Steffensmeier and Jones 1997, 2004; Lott, Gardner, and Power 2009, 252; Allison 1984). The piecewise constant exponential model is appropriate for the analysis of continuous-time data—when the exact timing of an event (or waiting-time) is known—because it allows for the constant rate of the model to vary *within time intervals*, rather than assume a constant rate over time (Powers 2013, 6, 18–42).[6] In essence, this model assumes a constant rate for Indigenous Lands that are titled within the time-intervals specified by the analyst and allows the rate to increase or decrease across periods. Also, the model converges into a nonparametric model as the number of episodes increases and handles cluster-level random effects, such as the spatial dependency present in the data.

Statistical Results

Table A.3 presents multivariable models to assess the importance of the various factors outlined above for Indigenous Land titling. For purposes of substantive interpretation,

Table A.3 Estimates from Single-Spell Piecewise Constant Exponential Models of Indigenous Land Titling in Brazil, 1988–2016.

	Model 1	Model 2	Model 3	Model 4
Location				
Amazonia (River Basin)^	1	1	1	1
Northern Frontier Zone (NFZ)	5.34*** (3.23)	4.24*** (2.57)	4.53*** (3.66)	2.97** (1.82)
Xingu Cluster	0.51* (0.20)	0.62 (0.24)	0.49* (0.20)	0.65 (0.26)
Other (Outside Amazonia)	0.07*** (0.00)	0.07*** (0.00)	0.10*** (0.01)	0.10*** (0.01)
World Bank	0.11*** (0.01)	0.11*** (0.01)	0.36*** (0.03)	0.36*** (0.03)
INGO News	0.95*** (0.00)	0.96*** (0.00)	0.99*** (0.00)	0.99*** (0.00)
Environment	0.14*** (0.05)	0.14*** (0.06)	0.14*** (0.05)	0.21*** (0.08)
Minerals & Hydrocarbons	0.26*** (0.03)	0.21*** (0.02)	0.26*** (0.03)	0.22*** (0.03)
NFZ x Minerals & Hydrocarbons		13.90*** (4.62)		4.33*** (1.46)
Multiple Groups	0.41*** (0.05)	0.38*** (0.05)	0.45*** (0.06)	0.51*** (0.07)
Size (ha)	0.99 (0.00)	0.99* (0.00)	1** (0.00)	1 (0.00)
Indigenous Population (State)			0.99*** (0.00)	0.99*** (0.00)
Agricultural Potential				0.38*** (0.05)
Log Likelihood	−1833.02	−1809.30	−1518.95	−1485.04
N (Indigenous Land-years)	1,305	1,305	1,305	1,305

*** Significant at the 0.01 level; ** Significant at the 0.05 level; * Significant at the 0.1 level (two-tailed significance tests). Standard Errors in parenthesis.

^ Denotes the reference category for comparison.

I rely on Model 1. Models 2–4 are robustness checks; the results are similar across models.[7] For further ease of interpretation, I will discuss the effects of predictors in terms of the percentage change (increase or decrease) in the rate of titling, or in terms of rate ratio, associated with a change in a predictor. Ratios greater than 1 are evidence of an increasing rate of titling associated with a change in that predictor, or for a particular category relative to a reference category. Conversely, ratios less than 1 indicate a lower rate associated with a change in that variable, or for a particular category relative to a reference category. Ratios that are statistically equal to 1 are evidence of "no effect" of that predictor.

Location: The Northern Frontier Zone

As mentioned earlier, the effects of *Location* are modeled using a set of binary variables representing four locations: Northern Frontier Zone, the Xingu Cluster, Amazonia interior, and Amazonia exterior. This categorization helps to gauge the importance of an overlap with the frontier zone, where the military has overarching jurisdiction. In other words, the coding does not treat location as a continuous variable.

I use *Amazonia (River Basin)* as the reference category because the majority of Indigenous Land claims originate from that region (60.68%). The statistical results in Model 1 show that Indigenous Land claims located in the Northern Frontier Zone are five times more likely to be approved in any year, compared to the reference category. In general, I find a lower rate of titling outside the Amazon region: those Indigenous Lands are 93 percent less likely to be titled in any time period than those located inside Amazonia. The model shows a statistically significant decrease in the titling of Indigenous Lands that originate from the Xingu Cluster region in any time period, compared to the reference category, but this significance is not consistent across models. These results are in line with the observation that the Xingu Cluster contains a small number of Indigenous Lands; these cases do not represent overall patterns in the country. The most important finding is that the statistical analysis confirms the argument that state elites are more likely to title Indigenous Lands in the Northern Frontier Zone, where the state has an interest in extending its administrative power.

World Bank and INGO News Exposure

The results of Model 1 show that the rate of titling in any period for Indigenous Lands that had titling funds dependent on the World Bank, while statistically significant, are 89 percent lower than other Indigenous Lands in any given period. In addition, I find that a unit increase in news coverage of INGO activism lowers the rate of titling by 5 percent. In fact, after taking into account the spatial and temporal dimensions of the titling process, the evidence seems to suggest that overall, news coverage of INGO activism and World Bank involvement hurts the chances of Indigenous Land titling. This counterintuitive finding may be explained in part by the fact that Indigenous Land claims that attract news coverage and World Bank support are particularly difficult to title. Therefore, *INGO News*, which measures media attention directly (not external pressure per se), and *World Bank* may be capturing processes that apply only to particularly difficult titling proceedings.

Economic and Environmental Value

Model 1 includes economic value as a predictor in addition to a variable tapping the percentage of overlap between Indigenous Lands and environmental conservation units. Specifically, the variable *Minerals & Hydrocarbons* indicates whether an Indigenous Land has known deposits of highly valuable minerals, gems, natural gas, and oil. I found that the rate of titling for Indigenous Lands that hold economic value are 74 percent lower than those without riches in any given period. In addition, a unit increase in overlap with environmental conservation units lowers the rate of titling by 86 percent at any given time. This finding suggests that Indigenous Lands with valuable mineral deposits are less likely to be titled at any given period. However, these effects are not uniform across Amazonia. Model 2 shows the results of a statistically significant interaction term that captures the effect of location in the Northern Frontier Zone and the existence of mineral deposits on the rate of titling. I found that Indigenous Lands with minerals that overlap with the Northern Frontier Zone are thirteen times more likely than other Indigenous Lands to be titled. Because the existence of mineral deposits does not deter titling activity in the Northern Frontier Zone, the result suggests that national security trumps economic potential in Indigenous Land titling. In this case, state elites forgo mineral exploitation and prefer to regularize Indigenous Lands to reinforce state power in the borderlands.

Controls

Results across models show that there is no evidence of a significant effect of size of Indigenous Land on the rate of titling. However, an Indigenous Land claim comprised of more than two Indigenous groups lowers the rate of titling by about 59 percent. The results of Model 3 show that there is no evidence that the size of the Indigenous population in the state has a positive effect on the rate of titling in any period. In fact, a unit increase in number of Indigenous peoples in the state decreases the rate of titling by 1 percent—a finding that is consistent with qualitative studies that stress the lack of a positive "demographic effect" on Brazilian indigenous politics (Ramos 2003; Stocks 2005). Finally, the results of Model 4 show that there is no evidence that the agricultural potential of the land subject to Indigenous Land proceedings affects the rate of titling for lands that overlap with the Northern Frontier Zone.

To sum up, the statistical results reported in this section have important implications for understanding the overall pattern of Indigenous Land titling. The results across models show a distinctive and significant increase in the rate of titling for Indigenous Lands that overlap with the Northern Frontier Zone in any time period, compared to the Indigenous Land claims that originate from the Amazonian interior. Another important finding is that news coverage of INGO activities for specific Indigenous Lands and World Bank involvement *lowers*, rather than increases, the rate of titling. Moreover, the results show that overlap with environmental conservation units does not significantly increase the rate of titling.

Taken together, these results would cast doubts on the argument that Indigenous Land titling occurs mainly as a direct reaction to international news coverage and in areas reserved for environmental protection. Finally, the statistical results also show the factors that moderate the effect of mineral deposits on titling. The statistical analysis shows that economic structuralism has a point because areas that hold mineral wealth have lower titling rates. Nevertheless, the existence of known valuable mineral deposits in the Northern Frontier Zone, *raises* the rate of titling in any time period, rather than lowering it.

Importantly, the findings corroborate my state-centric theory: Indigenous Lands that overlap with the Northern Frontier Zone are more likely to be titled than others inside the reference category. Hence, this strong correlation suggests that titling is more likely to occur in the borderlands, where the military has complete jurisdiction, as a way to extend the state's reach in otherwise uncontrolled areas.

APPENDIX B

Administrative Procedure to Title Indigenous Lands

The following contains a detailed description of the technical administrative proceeding for titling Indigenous lands in Nicaragua, Honduras, and Brazil. I specify the legislation that establishes the technical proceedings and the government agencies that make decisions throughout the process.

Nicaragua

Legislation: Law No. 445. Law of Communal Property Regime of the Indigenous Peoples and Ethnic Communities of the Autonomous Regions of the Atlantic Coast of Nicaragua and of the Bocay, Coco, Indio and Maiz Rivers (January 2003). I refer to this law as the Communal Property Regime Law (2003).

Deciding Government Agency: National Demarcation and Titling Commission (referred to as Titling Commission, CONADETI). The Communal Property Regime Law created the Titling Commission (CONADETI) to decide and resolve communal land claims in eastern Nicaragua (Communal Property Regime Law, Art. 41, 43).

Proceedings: Chapter VIII, Article 45 of the Communal Property Regime Law establishes a five-step process to title Indigenous lands: submission of the land claim, conflict resolution, measurement and demarcation of the land boundary, issuing the communal land title, and title clearing (see Figure B.1). The analysis of this book centers on titling (see Appendix C for my operationalization of the outcome).

Step 1: Claim Submission

The Communal Property Regime Law establishes the assembly of all community members as the highest authority of an Indigenous or ethnic community (Art. 5). Each community elects a communal government, which can join other nearby communities to form a Territorial Assembly and a Territorial Authority that must be approved by the central government (Art. 3). The representatives of the Territorial Authority submit the land claim on behalf of the communities to the corresponding Inter-Sectorial Demarcation and Titling Commission (henceforth the Inter-Sectorial Commission), which in turn coordinates the technical proceedings and prepares a diagnostic report about the regularization of the claimed land (Art. 44, 47). The Territorial Authority must prepare and submit reports with evidence of traditional occupancy of the lands. These reports must contain the following information:
  - Historical basis of the claim;
  - The communities' demographic, social, economic, and cultural characteristics;
  - Traditional land tenure modalities;

Figure B.1 Titling Proceedings, Nicaragua

- The name of the communities and of any other neighboring persons or entity;
- A list of potential conflicts with other communities or with third parties.

Step 2: Conflict Resolution

After the initial land claim, the corresponding Regional Council is responsible for solving any pending boundary dispute between Territorial Authorities that arise from overlapping land claims.

Step 3: Measurement and Demarcation

After the conflict resolution stage, the Titling Commission (CONADETI) must budget and plan for the Inter-Sectorial Commission to officially measure and mark the geographical boundaries of the lands (Art. 54-55).

Step 4: Issue of the Communal Title

The Titling Commission (CONADETI) issues the final communal land title. The title contains the name of the community or group of communities that are title holders; the land's territorial dimensions and geographic location; the communities' traditional tenure and natural resource management systems; and the collective character of the land. The Titling Commission is responsible for registering the communal land title in the corresponding land registry.

The communal land title defeats all other competing land titles; non-community members and corporations without lease agreements with the community must leave the land (Art. 37–38). There are two exceptions to the rule: (1) private property titles issued before 1987 for title holders that occupied the land before 1987; or, (2) private property titles of title holders that have occupied the land continuously since the issue of the title (Art. 35–36).

Step 5: Title Clearing

After obtaining the communal title, each community is responsible for requesting the technical and material resources from the government to clear the title and evict outsiders (Art. 59).

Honduras

Legislation: Decree No. 31-92 Agrarian Modernization and Development Law (1992) and Decree No. 82-2004 Property Law (2004).

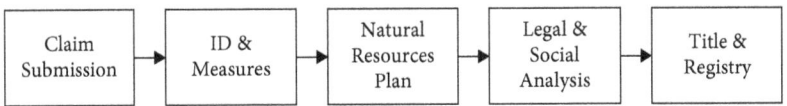

Figure B.2 Titling Proceedings, Honduras

Deciding Government Agency: Property Institute, National Agrarian Institute (INA), Institute for the Conservation of Forests (ICF), and Ministry of Natural Resources and Environment.

Proceedings: Chapter II of the Property Law Regulation (Resolution No. 003-2010) establishes a five-step process for titling Indigenous lands: submission, identification and measurement, natural resource management plan, legal and social analysis, titling and registration (see Figure B.2).

Step 1: Claim Submission

The Property Law Regulation formally establishes that an Indigenous or ethnic community, or group of communities, can directly begin the land regularization process and that the Property Institute can also start the process (Art. 259). A legal representative of a local political community organization that is approved by the central government must submit a land regularization request either to the INA or the IICF. The submission must be supported with an anthropological and historical study that identifies the territorial extension of the land and the relationship that the community or communities have with that land (Art. 261, 266.1).

Step 2: Identification and Measurement

After the initial request, INA or ICF is responsible for identifying the geographical boundaries and mapping the area to be designated as communal territory (Art. 261, 266.3).

Step 3: Natural Resource Management Plan

The Ministry of Natural Resources and Environment is responsible for elaborating a technical study that identifies the factors that are needed to preserve the habitats and biodiversity of the requested land (Art. 261, 266.3).

Step 4: Legal and Social Analysis

INA or ICF is responsible for conducting a legal and social analysis that identifies the restrictions of the property title (Art. 261, 266.4). The Property Law Regulation establishes a special communal property title for areas designated Eco-Ethnographic Reserves, where all human activities are prohibited except those that are strictly necessary for the conservation of ancestral ways of life (Art. 262–263).

Step 4: Titling and Registration

The Property Institute issues and registers the communal land title in the land registry (Art. 266.5).

The communal land title defeats all other competing tenure claims, including claims from title holders that voluntarily abandoned the land for more than ten years (Art. 265). The Property Law Regulation allows for the transformation of the communal land regime with a request of a community leader and three-fourths of able community members (Art. 267).

Brazil

Legislation: Law 6001 (1973) Indian Statute; Decree 1775 (1996) Indigenous Lands Law; and Regulation MJ No. 14 (1996).

Deciding Government Agency: Presidency of the Republic, Ministry of Justice, National Indigenous Agency (FUNAI).

Proceedings: The Indigenous Lands Law (Decree 1775, 1996) establishes a seven-step process for titling Indigenous lands: identification of the claimed land, acceptance of the identification study by the National Indigenous Agency (FUNAI), conflict resolution, identification of the geographical boundaries of the land, physical demarcation of the land boundaries, approval of FUNAI proceedings by the president of Brazil, and registry of the land (see Figure B.3).

Step 1: Land Identification Study

Based on a request submitted by an Indigenous community, FUNAI designates an anthropologist with thematic expertise to identify an Indigenous land. The anthropologist leads a land identification analysis conducted by a FUNAI working group. The FUNAI working group produces a technical report (called "Relatório Circunstanciado de Identificação e Delimitação") about the historical, sociological, legal, cartographic, and environmental factors, as well as a land survey, associated with the identified Indigenous land. According to Regulation MJ No. 14 (1996), the technical report must contain the following information:

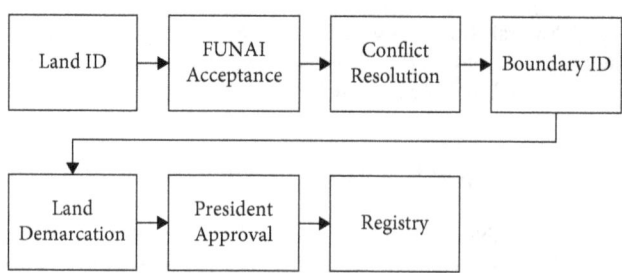

Figure B.3 Titling Proceedings, Brazil

- General information about the indigenous group or groups, including: details about their cultural and linguistic affiliation; migration patterns; demographic census; spatial distribution of the population and identification of factors that determine that distribution; land occupation history according to the group's collective memory; and identification of the group's eventual secession practices and its causal, temporal, and special factors.
- Permanent abodes: description of the distribution of villages with their population and location; an explanation of the criteria the group uses for the location, construction, and permanence of the villages; the area that the villages occupy; and the time the villages have remained in those locations. This information should be collected in collaboration with the respective group or groups.
- Productive activities: description of the productive activities of the group and identification, location, and dimensions of the areas used for these productive activities; description of the characteristics of the economy; identification of changes in the traditional economy after contact with the wider society and the way these changes occurred; and description of the social, economic, and cultural relationships with other Indigenous groups and wider society. This information should be collected in collaboration with the respective group or groups.
- Environment: identification and description of areas that are necessary for the preservation of the natural resources and economic and cultural well-being of the group and an explanation of the reasons these areas are necessary. This information should be collected in collaboration with the respective group or groups.
- Physical and cultural reproduction: data about the birth and mortality rates of the group in the last years, with an exposition of the causes, and hypothesis about the factors that affect these rates; a projection of population change of the group; a description of the cosmological aspects of the group, areas of ritual use, landmarks, sacred places, archeological sites, and other, explaining their relationship with the current situation of the group and providing detailed examples; and identification and description of the areas that are necessary for the physical and cultural reproduction of the group, explaining the reasons for their need. This information should be collected in collaboration with the respective group or groups.
- Land survey: identification and census of inhabitants that are non-Indigenous outsiders; description of the areas occupied by outsiders, with their corresponding dimensions, dates of occupation, and description of any improvements found; information about the nature of occupancy with an identification of the land titles that may exist, describing their quality and origin; for occupants with a title issued by a government body, there must be information about the methods and basis for issuing the document from the issuing government body.
- A proposal of the area to be marked as Indigenous Land that contains a map identifying the access routes by land, water, or air, as well as details about the group or groups.

Step 2: FUNAI Acceptance

The FUNAI president approves the technical report. FUNAI publishes a summary of the technical report in the Federal Official Gazette (Diário Oficial da União) and the Official Gazette of the corresponding state.

Step 3: Conflict Resolution

Any interested party, including states and municipalities, can dispute the technical report summary within ninety days of its publication in the Official Gazette. The interested party must submit the grievance with supporting evidence to FUNAI, which prepares a review file for the Ministry of Justice within sixty days of the complaint. The Ministry of Justice is responsible for resolving the complaint within thirty days.

Step 4: Boundary Identification

The Ministry of Justice is responsible for issuing a resolution that either identifies the boundaries of the area to be classified as Indigenous land or rejects the classification of the area as such.

Step 5: Land Demarcation

The National Indigenous Agency is responsible for marking the physical boundaries of the land. The National Institute of Colonization and Agrarian Reform (INCRA) is responsible for relocating non-Indigenous occupants inside the Indigenous land.

Step 6: Presidential Approval

The president of the Republic issues a decree that approves the administrative proceedings that demarcates the Indigenous land.

Step 7: Registry

The land is registered in the local land registry and in the Patrimony Secretariat of the Union (Secretaria de Patrimônio da União) within thirty days of the Presidential Decree approving the demarcation.

APPENDIX C

Coding and Operationalization of Indigenous Land Titling

I operationalized Indigenous land titling as a dichotomous variable. A value of 0 was assigned if the central government had technically accepted an Indigenous land claim but the administrative proceeding to regularize it was pending. A value of 1 was assigned if the central government officially approved the technical proceedings via formal property title or presidential decree. For Nicaragua and Honduras, I further specified if the formal land title was issued at the village level (listing one community) or at the inter-village level (listing two or more communities).

Country	Number of Observations	Sources of Information:
Nicaragua	23 communal land claims: all titled, all at the inter-village level	Attorney General's Office 2016; Alvarez 2016
Honduras	508 communal land claims: all titled, 13 at the inter-village level, and 495 at the village level.	IP 2016, ICF 2016, Anderson 2009; Forest Trends 2015
Brazil	730 Indigenous land claims: 256 pending titling and 474 titled.	FUNAI 2016

APPENDIX D

Survey on Indigenous Land Titling

I designed and implemented a face-to-face elite opinion survey of 20 national legislators in Nicaragua, 249 politicians (66 senators and 183 representatives) in Brazil, and 65 military officers in Honduras. The survey was administered by the research office of the National Assembly in Managua, Nicaragua, and a polling consultant in the National Congress in Brasília, Brazil. In Honduras, I administered the survey to military officers enrolled in post-graduate level courses at the Defense University. On average, the survey interview lasted 4 minutes.

Interviewers were experts in administering surveys to politicians. I trained the interviewers on the importance of respondent protection and privacy. On a separate sheet, interviewers recorded the phone number of each respondent's office for the purposes of later supervision. I conducted post-survey verification on a randomly selected 30 percent of the sample by telephone.

Among national legislators, the response rate for the survey was 21.97 percent for Nicaragua and 41.91 percent for Brazil. Among the military officers in Honduras, the response rate for the survey was 100 percent. The full translated questionnaire follows.

DEPARTMENT OF GOVERNMENT
THE UNIVERSITY OF TEXAS AT AUSTIN
158 W. 21st Street, Stop A1800, Austin, TX 78712-1704. 512-471-5121. Fax: 512-471-1061
www.utexas.edu/cola/depts/government

The Politics of Ethnic Land Titling
Academic Research by Giorleny Altamirano Rayo

Description of the Study

You are invited to participate in a research study entitled "The Politics of Ethnic Communal Property Rights" by Giorleny Altamirano Rayo, doctoral student at the University of Texas at Austin. The purpose of this project is to learn more about the causes of public support for redistributive land policies that benefit ethnic collectivities. You must be at least 18 years old to participate.

If you choose to take part in this study, I will ask you to answer a maximum of 10 questions. I expect that it will take about five minutes of your time to complete the questionnaire. You will not be compensated for participating in the study. The risks of participating in this project are no greater than everyday life. There are no costs for participating. You will not directly benefit from participating. Your name and contact information will only be kept during the data collection phase for supervision purposes only. **All identifying information will be stripped from the final dataset.**

Your participation in this project is completely voluntary. You may decide not to participate, choose not to answer any question, or stop participating at any time without any penalty. If you want to withdraw from the project, simply stop participating. If you have any questions, please contact Giorleny Altamirano Rayo via email at g.altamirano@utexas.edu or contact The University of Texas at Austin through mail at P.O. Box 7426, Austin, TX, USA 78713. This study was reviewed and approved by the University Institutional Review Board.

Questions about your rights as a research participant. If you have questions about your rights or are dissatisfied at any time with any part of this study, you can contact, anonymously if you wish, the University of Texas at Austin Institutional Review Board by phone at (512) 471-8871 or email at orsc@uts.cc.utexas.edu. If you agree to participate, please continue with the survey. By participating, you cede any copyrights or author's rights for your contribution.

Thank you.

1. Do you agree with the opinion that [country: Nicaragua, Honduras or Brazil] must follow the demand of the international community about regularizing all ethnic [if Brazil: Indigenous Lands] in the country?

   Strongly Agree   Agree   Somewhat Agree   No Opinion   Somewhat Disagree   Disagree   Strongly Disagree

2. Do you agree with the opinion that the government can install military bases inside ethnic lands [if Brazil: Indigenous Lands] without the authorization of local communities?

   Strongly Disagree   Disagree   Somewhat Disagree   No Opinion   Somewhat Agree   Agree   Strongly Agree

3. Do you agree with the opinion that the Armed Forces can act inside ethnic [if Brazil: indigenous] areas, in accordance to their functions, without consulting local communities?

   Strongly Agree   Agree   Somewhat Agree   No Opinion   Somewhat Disagree   Disagree   Strongly Disagree

4. Do you agree with the opinion that the regularization of ethnic lands [if Brazil: Indigenous Lands] in [subnational region: Autonomous Region of the North and South Atlantic, Gracias a Dios, or Amazonia] strengthens the control of the [country: Nicaragua, Honduras, or Brazil] in that region?

   Strongly Disagree   Disagree   Somewhat Disagree   No Opinion   Somewhat Agree   Agree   Strongly Agree

5. Do you support the titling of ethnic lands [if Brazil: Indigenous Lands] although it entails the eviction of non-ethnic rural farmers?

   Strongly Support   Support   Somewhat Support   Undecided   Somewhat Oppose   Oppose   Strongly Oppose

6. Would you support a law that allows for prospecting or exploring mineral resources inside ethnic lands [if Brazil: Indigenous Lands]?

   Strongly Support   Oppose   Somewhat Oppose   Undecided   Somewhat Support   Support   Strongly Support

7. Would you support a law that allows development projects inside ethnic lands [if Brazil: Indigenous Lands], such as the construction of hydroelectric dams, although that impacts negatively these communities?

   Strongly Support   Support   Somewhat Support   Undecided   Somewhat Oppose   Oppose   Strongly Oppose

8. Do you agree with the opinion that the ethnic [if Brazil: Indigenous] communities of [subnational region: Autonomous Region of the North and South Atlantic, Gracias a Dios, or Amazonia] have too much land for few people?

   Strongly Disagree   Disagree   Somewhat Disagree   No Opinion   Somewhat Agree   Agree   Strongly Agree

9. Do you think that in recent times international pressure to title all ethnic lands [if Brazil: Indigenous Lands] in [country: Nicaragua, Honduras, and Brazil]:

   Greatly Increased   Increased   Slightly Increased   No Change   Slightly Decreased   Decreased   Greatly Decreased

10. What do you think about the demand of ethnic [if Brazil: Indigenous] communities to land?

APPENDIX E

Sources of the Brazilian Indigenous Land Titling Database

The Brazilian Database contains geocoded information on all 730 federally designated Indigenous lands at different stages of the titling process. It also holds geocoded count data of international and national news reports regarding a particular land, since its inclusion in the to-do list of the National Indigenous Agency (FUNAI)—the agency in charge of implementing Brazil's indigenous policy—until its titling. Based on a digital repository and a physical archive of daily newspapers covering the period 1983–2016, the values reflect the amount of news exposure of NGO and international NGO activism in favor of a land claim from the moment the titling process began until its completion. The newspaper collection is kept and updated by the Instituto Socioambiental, a Brazilian nongovernmental organization with headquarters in São Paulo, Brazil. The collection contains newspaper clippings of events that have made world and national headlines, such as the mining activities in the Yanomami Indigenous Lands since the early 1990s. This indicator is intended to reflect the strength of transnational activists' strategic use of information to pressure states into compliance with formal institutions, an example of "information politics" (Keck and Sikkink 1998). I also reviewed the physical archives of the Instituto Socioambiental in São Paulo. The source of information for each of the variables of the database are specified in the table below.

Variable	Source of Information
Indigenous Land Titling	National Indigenous Agency (FUNAI), 2016
Proceedings start date	Instituto Socioambiental, Terras Indígenas, 2016; Imprensa Nacional, 2016
Proceedings approval date	Instituto Socioambiental, Terras Indígenas, 2016; Imprensa Nacional, 2016
Location	Brazilian Institute of Geography and Statistics (IBGE), 2016
World Bank	National Indigenous Agency (FUNAI) PPTAL 2005; World Bank, 2010
Multiple Groups	National Indigenous Institute, 2016
Minerals and Hydrocarbons	Brazilian Geological Service (CPRM), 2016
Agricultural Potential	Brazilian Portal of Geospatial Data (INDE), 2016
Environmental Overlap	Brazilian Portal of Geospatial Data (INDE), 2016
INGO News	Instituto Socioambiental, 2016
Size (ha)	National Indigenous Agency (FUNAI), 2016
Indigenous Population	Brazilian Institute of Geography and Statistics (IBGE), 2010

APPENDIX F

Interviews

Nicaragua

Alemán, Carlos. Representative, Regional Council North Caribbean Coast, August 10, 2015, Bilwi.
Campbell, Lumberto. Director, Secretariat for the Development of the Caribbean Coast, July 30, 2015, Managua.
Canales, Ramón. Executive director, Secretariat for the Development of the Caribbean Coast, July 21, 2015, Managua.
Hoppington, Marcos. Miskito leader, August 11, 2015, Bilwi.
McClean, Melba. Awas Tingni community leader, head of the former Central American University Research Unit at Bilwi, August 10, 2015, Bilwi.
Oquist Kelley, Paul. Private secretary for national policies, Presidency, August 6, 2015, Managua.
Rigby, Betty. Representative, Creole community, regional Titling Commission (2002–2004) and United Nations Development Program, August 10, 2015, Bilwi.
Rivera, Brooklyn. Miskito leader, August 11, 2015, Bilwi.
Rivera, Jesus Virgilio. United Nations Development Program, August 4, 2015, Managua.
Taylor, Evelyn. Miskito representative at the National Assembly, director of the Communal Titling Unit, Attorney General's Office (2007–2011), August 24, 2015, Managua.

Honduras

Amador Fúnez, Gustavo Adolfo. Colonel, Honduran Army, April 23, 2015, Tegucigalpa.
Caceres, Berta. Lenca leader, November 10, 2015, Austin, TX.
Chang Castillo, Rigoberto. Secretary of human rights, justice, government, and decentralization (2014–current), April 1, 2015, Tegucigalpa.
Espinoza Posadas, Rigoberto. Vice Admiral, deputy chief of the Armed Forces, May 25, 2015, Tegucigalpa.
Hernandez, Juan Orlando. President of Honduras (2014–current), May 31, 2015, Tela.
Lobo, Porfirio. President of Honduras (2010–2014), May 28, 2015, Tegucigalpa.
Osorio Canales, René. General, chief of the Armed Forces (2011–2014), June 30, 2015, Tegucigalpa.
Pacheco Tinoco, Julián. Minister of security (2014–current), June 19, 2015, Tegucigalpa.
Paz Escalante, Gustavo Adolfo. Infantry colonel, commander of FUSINA, June 18, 2015, Tegucigalpa.
Raudales, Julio. Minister of planning (2010–2014), June 1, 2015, Tegucigalpa
Reyes, Alfonso, Infantry colonel, director of the National Defense College, May 6, 2015, Tegucigalpa.

Rivera Amador, Ronald. General, director of the School for Commanders and Generals, May 13, 2015, Tegucigalpa.
Sivestri, Emilio. Minister of tourism (2014–current), May 29, 2015, Tegucigalpa.
Villanueva Reyes, Mario. General, Honduran Army, May 15, 2015, Tegucigalpa.
Wood Granwell, Maylo. Director, Indigenous and Afro-Honduran affairs (2014–2015), Gracias a Dios representative at the National Assembly (2009–2014), April 10, 2016, Tegucigalpa.

Brazil

Barros, Antonio Manoel de. General, commander of the San Gabriel de Cachoeira Army Base (Amazonas), October 29, 2015, San Gabriel de Cachoeira, AM.
Collor de Mello, Fernando. President of Brazil (1990–1992), February 23, 2015, Brasilia, DF.
Dantas, Roberto de Medeiros. Brigadier, director, Calha Norte Program, February 11, 2015, Brasília, DF.
Denys, Rubens Bayma. General, retired, secretary-general of the National Security Council (1985–1990), March 20, 2015, Rio de Janeiro, RJ.
Heleno, Augusto. General, head of the Amazon Military Command (2007–2009), March 16, 2015, Rio de Janeiro, RJ.
Lima, Cedemi. Adviser, Calha Norte Program, October 28, 2015, Tabatinga, AM.
Mansur, Carlos Alberto. General, commander of the 1st Infantry Brigade, October 30, 2015, Boa Vista, RR.
Mendes, Artur Nobre. President, National Indigenous Agency (FUNAI) (2002–2003), February 13, 2015, Brasilia, DF.
Menezes, Theresa. Professor of anthropology, March 27, 2015, Rio de Janeiro, RJ.
Poty, Ubiratan. Chief, Amazon Military Command (2015), October 26, 2015, Manaus, AM.
Prates, Rodrigo. Colonel, adviser, Ministry of Defense, February 27, 2015, Brasilia, DF.
Rego Barros, Otavio Santana do. General, chief of the army's Communication Office, December 13, 2014, Brasilia, DF.
Tempesta, Giovana Acacia. Office of Identification and Demarcation of Indigenous Lands, National Indigenous Agency (FUNAI), July 19, 2013, Brasilia, DF.
Zamith, Wagner Lopes de Moraes. Vice Admiral, commander of the 9th Naval District, October 26, 2015, Manaus, AM.

Notes

Chapter 1

1. In 2015, I observed this inspection during a week-long visit through Amazonia with the military, which included inspections of bases located along the border with Peru, Colombia, and Venezuela.
2. I thank Jonathan Bendor for this point.
3. UNDRIP is available online at https://undocs.org/A/RES/61/295.
4. In Brazil, autochthonous people represent a tiny fraction (~0.5%) of the county's population (IBGE 2011). In Nicaragua and Honduras, ethnic collectivities constitute 7–8 percent of the population, a number that is close to the Latin American average (INIDE 2005; INE 2013).
5. The problem of causation necessarily pushes me to use a variety of methods to generate, assess, and generalize explanatory propositions. Qualitative analysis is necessary to explain specific historical events. Quantitative analysis is essential to rigorously assess the plausibility of propositions beyond the case at hand. In addition, I achieve a more precise estimate of the causal relationship across cases by using qualitative research techniques after identifying a statistically significant pattern, than by employing a single methodological approach.
6. The Appendix D contains an English version of the survey and a more detailed description of the sources I used to compile the Brazilian Database.
7. I follow James Scott in *The Art of Not Being Governed* (2009, 209) in dividing formally recognized customary land regimes into "tight" or "loose" incorporation of non-state peoples into the modern state. Anthropologists and public policy practitioners call these two forms of Indigenous land titling "island demarcation" and "continuous demarcation" or "communal titling" and "inter-communal titling." See, for example, Herrera and Edouard 2013; Ramos 1998.
8. I do not use implementation as a synonym for "treaty implementation." Scholars of international relations define "treaty implementation" as the codification or enactment of domestic rules or regulations to facilitate compliance with international provisions (Simmons 1998, 77). I use the term implementation as more than the passing of formal rules but as the actual application of written rules to respond to practical demands at the local level.
9. The Mayangna community in Awas Tingni substantiated their land claims to AMASAU (Awas Tingni Mayangna Sauni Umani territory) on a court ruling by the Inter-American Court of Human Rights (IA-Court 2003).

Chapter 2

1. The absence of property rights is known as open access (Ostrom 2003, 249).
2. I thank Reviewer 2 for making this point.

Chapter 3

1. I thank Jonathan Bendor for this insight.
2. As of February 2015, there are thirty-four administrative proceedings ready for political approval in Brazil's Ministry of Justice. National Indigenous Agency (FUNAI), *Processos em Análise*, 2015.
3. Transparency International's Corruption Perception Index and the World Bank's Control of Corruption Indicator have consistently ranked Nicaragua and Honduras as among the most corrupt countries in Latin America. Their scores are similar to those of African countries like Mozambique and Cameroon. These rankings are good measures for estimating the amount of perceived corruption in senior political offices, or grand corruption (Ruhl 2011, 34).
4. Max Weber's interest was in understanding when the state claimed control over territory and people successfully, hence an emphasis on bureaucracy and technocracy. I highlight the action of claim*ing* control over territory and people as an ongoing process that is neither static nor has an end in sight. Political elites within state institutions must continuously seek ways to

maintain—and at times build—the organization of the state for their claim to be credible and for their political powers to hold.
5. I am indebted to Jonathan Bendor for pushing me to make this point clearly.
6. For a historical comparative analysis of Indian treaty-making policy as a strategy to incorporate Indigenous peoples into the state in Canada and the United States, see Jill St. Germain, *Indian Treaty-Making Policy in the United States and Canada, 1867–1877* (Lincoln: University of Nebraska Press, 2001).
7. With the exception of military force, external pressure combines "leverage" and "linkage" in the terminology of Levitsky and Way (2005, 21–25).
8. International campaigns pushing states to regularize customary land regimes do not always correspond with local mobilization or have local support. For instance, Agrawal and Ostrom analyze cases in Nepal where donor pressures to implement communal property rights have no matching in local groups (2001, 503–505).
9. Krupa makes a similar argument about bureaucratic practices as outreach devices when addressing land cadastral systems in general (2015, 99–125).
10. Boyer posits that the Brazilian state allocates Indigenous land as a "mode of governance . . . part of its administration of a national territorial space divided into closed and clearly identified subspaces" (2016, 156).

Chapter 4

1. A commander of the guerrilla movement that resisted the state in the 1980s, Rivera became the leader of YATAMA, an ethnic political party forged out of the war.
2. Interview, August 24, 2015, Managua, Nicaragua.
3. Interview, August 10, 2015, Bilwi, Nicaragua.
4. Decreto 782 (1981), available at http://www.asamblea.gob.ni/Informacion%20Legislativa/.
5. Acronym of Miskito, Sumo, Rama, Sandinista, and Asla Talanka (or Miskito, Sumo, Rama, and Sandinista United). MISURASATA is the predecessor of YATAMA, the current name of the Miskito political organization. See, Inter-American Commission on Human Rights (IACHR), *Report on the Situation of Human Rights of a Segment of the Nicaraguan Population of Miskito Origin*, OEA/Ser.L/V.II.62 doc. 10 rev. 3. November 29, 1983, Section D, available at http://www.cidh.org/countryrep/miskitoeng/toc.htm.
6. The first demand was for about 4.5 million hectares. By the end of the 1980s, that number dropped to roughly 3.2 million hectares (Ohland and Schneider 1983, 89–94, 163–77).
7. Interview, August 11, 2015, Bilwi, Nicaragua.
8. Interview, August 11, 2015, Bilwi, Nicaragua.
9. Interview, August 6, 2015, Managua, Nicaragua.
10. Interview, July 30, 2015, Managua, Nicaragua.
11. Canales, Ramón, SDCC executive director (2007–current), interview July 21, 2015, Managua, Nicaragua.
12. Acronym stands for Comisión Nacional de Demarcación y Titulación.
13. The Instituto Nicaragüense de Estudios Territoriales is the agency responsible for maintaining the national land cadaster.
14. Interview, August 24, 2015, Managua, Nicaragua.
15. Canales, Ramón, interview July 21, 2015, Managua, Nicaragua.
16. Interview, August 11, 2015, Bilwi, Nicaragua.
17. Interview, August 10, 2015, Bilwi, Nicaragua.
18. Rivera, Interview, August 11, 2015, Bilwi, Nicaragua.
19. Interview, August 6, 2015, Managua, Nicaragua.
20. Interview, August 10, 2015, Bilwi, Nicaragua.
21. Jesús Virgilio Rivera, UNDP Central Office, interview, August 4, 2015, Managua, Nicaragua.
22. Interview, August 10, 2015, Bilwi, Nicaragua.
23. Interview, August 10, 2015, Bilwi, Nicaragua.

Chapter 5

1. Article 346 of the Constitution (1982) declares, "it is the duty of the government to protect the rights and interests of existing indigenous communities in the country, especially with respect to land and forest where they are settled."
2. Honduras ratified ILO Convention No. 169 in 1995.

NOTES   221

3. Interview, Dr. Maylo Wood Granwell, director for Indigenous and Afro-Honduran affairs (2014–2015) and Miskito legislator for Gracias a Dios province (2009–2014), April 10, 2016, Tegucigalpa, Honduras. During this interview, Dr. Wood explained, "The Miskito wanted a single title for the entire La Mosquitia, but there was resistance due to fears of autonomy."
4. Infantry Colonel Alfonso Reyes remarked that state elites opposed titling a single Miskito territory "because one can infer that... they [the Miskito] want more than land but independence or autonomy." Interview, May 6, 2015, Tegucigalpa, Honduras.
5. Interview, Julio Raudales, minister of planning (2010–2014), June 1, 2015, Tegucigalpa, Honduras.
6. Interview, June 18, 2015, Tegucigalpa, Honduras.
7. Interview, General René Osorio Canales, former chief of the Armed Forces (2011–2014), June 30, 2015, Tegucigalpa, Honduras.
8. Interview, Juan Orlando Hernández, President of Honduras (2014–current), May 31, 2015, Tela, Honduras. Interview, Emilio Silvestri, political adviser and minister of tourism (2014–current), May 29, 2015, Tegucigalpa, Honduras. Interview, Julián Pacheco Tinoco, minister of security (2014–current), Tegucigalpa, Honduras.
9. Since 2010, the United States has supported Honduras's policy to combat transnational criminal organizations through the Central American Regional Security Initiative (CARSI).
10. Interview, Porfirio Lobo, president of Honduras (2010–2014), May 28, 2015, Tegucigalpa, Honduras.
11. Interview, Vice Admiral Rigoberto Espinoza Posadas, deputy chief of the Armed Forces, May 25, 2015, Tegucigalpa, Honduras.
12. Consejo de Comunicación y Ciudadanía (Nicaragua) 2012.
13. Press Interview cited in Honduras Weekly 2012.
14. Interview, May 25, 2015, Tegucigalpa, Honduras.
15. Interview, June 19, 2015, Tegucigalpa, Honduras. The emphasis is mine.
16. Interview, May 13, 2015, Tegucigalpa, Honduras. Between 2012 and 2013, General Rivera Amador was the commander of Fuerza de Tarea Paz-García, one of three military bases in Gracias a Dios province.
17. Interview, May 6, 2015, Tegucigalpa, Honduras.
18. Interview, Infantry Colonel Gustavo Adolfo Paz Escalante, June 18, 2018, Tegucigalpa, Honduras.
19. Interview, June 30, 2015, Tegucigalpa, Honduras.
20. Interview, June 30, 2015, Tegucigalpa, Honduras.
21. When comparing Lenca and Miskito political organizations, anthropologist Marc Anderson remarks that the latter lacked "the capacity to produce [mass] mobilizations" (2009, 147).
22. Interview, General Osorio Canales, June 30, 2015, Tegucigalpa, Honduras.
23. Interview, June 18, 2015, Tegucigalpa, Honduras.
24. Interview, May 25, 2015, Tegucigalpa, Honduras.
25. Interview, May 13, 2015, Tegucigalpa, Honduras.
26. Interview, April 23, 2015, Tegucigalpa, Honduras.
27. Interview, May 15, 2015, Tegucigalpa, Honduras.
28. Interview, April 1, 2015, Tegucigalpa, Honduras.
29. Interview, November 10, 2015, Austin, TX.

Chapter 6

1. Moran's I measures the average correlation of an observation with its neighbors. It allows for significance tests of the extent to which the observed levels of spatial clustering in a given sample, under the assumption of normality, differ from the null hypothesis of no spatial clustering. Moran's I takes on a range from -1 to $+1$ representing negative and positive spatial associations. Higher values of Moran's I indicate stronger positive geographical clustering. (Moran 1950; Ward and Gleditsch 2008, 23–27.)
2. Interview, Rio de Janeiro, Brazil, March 20, 2015. Denys insisted that "the issue is not whether to demarcate or not but *how much land* to reserve for the Indians."
3. Interview, Brasília, Brazil, February 23, 2015.
4. Interview, Brigadier Roberto de Medeiros Dantas, director, Calha Norte Program, Brasília, Brazil, February 11, 2015; Interview, Artur Nobre Mendes, president, National Indigenous Agency (FUNAI, 2002-2003), Brasília, Brazil, February 13, 2015.
5. Interview, Rio de Janeiro, Brazil, March 20, 2015.

6. Participant observation, presentation by Vice-Admiral Wagner Lopes de Moraes Zamith, commander of 9th Naval District, Manaus, Brazil, October 26, 2015.
7. Interview, Rio de Janeiro, Brazil, March 16, 2015.
8. Congressional Review Board FUNAI-INCRA, public hearing, 0:19 minute, Brasília, Brazil, March 30, 2016.
9. Interview, Artur Nobre Mendes, president, National Indigenous Agency (FUNAI 2002–2003), Brasília, Brazil, February 13, 2015.
10. Interview, Artur Nobre Mendes, February 13, 2015, Brasília, Brazil.
11. As explained earlier, this buffer zone is a bastion of the armed forces for national security reasons. It is a protected federal property per the Constitution and Law 6634 (1979).
12. Interview, Giovana Acacia Tempesta, Office of Identification and Demarcation of Indigenous Lands, National Indigenous Agency, (FUNAI) Brasilia, Brazil, July 19, 2013.
13. Ministry of Defense, Calha Norte Program, "Dossiê Sobre o CIMI," MSS, n.d., Ministry of Defense Archives (copy in the possession of the author).
14. Interview, Colonel Rodrigo Prates, adviser, Joint Command of the Armed Forces, Brasília, Brazil, February 27, 2015.
15. A video of this decision has been made available by the STF: (https://www.youtube.com/watch?v=1ICwz3ipY4s).
16. Ministry of Defense, March 3, 2015, Brazil.
17. Interview, February 27, 2015, Brasília, Brazil.
18. Interview, October 26, 2015, Manaus, Brazil.
19. Interview, October 30, 2015, Boa Vista, Brazil.
20. Interview, October 29, 2015, San Gabriel de Cachoeira, Brazil.
21. Interview, Brigadier Roberto de Medeiros Dantas, director, Calha Norte Program, February 11, 2015, Brasília, Brazil.
22. Interview, October 26, 2015, Manaus, Brazil.
23. Interview, General Otávio Santana do Rego Barros, chief of the Army's Communications Office, Brasília, Brazil, December 13, 2014.
24. Interview, General Ubiratan Poty, October 26, 2015, Manaus, Brazil.
25. Interview, Cedeli Lima, adviser, Calha Norte Program, October 28, 2015, Tabatinga, Brazil. See also, Centro de Comunicação Social do Exército 2006.
26. Over 90 percent of people that self-identify as indigenous have birth certificates (IBGE 2010).
27. Interview, October 26, 2015, Manaus, Brazil.
28. Interview, Thereza Menezes, professor of anthropology, March 27, 2015, Rio de Janeiro, Brazil.
29. Interview, October 26, 2015, Manaus, Brazil.
30. Interview, Colonel Rodrigo Prates, adviser, Joint Command of the Armed Forces, February 27, 2015, Brasília, Brazil.
31. Interview, Boa Vista, Brazil, October 30, 2015.
32. Interview, Brasília, Brazil, February 27, 2015.
33. The names of the Indigenous Lands are Badjonkore and Bau.

Chapter 7

1. The decision is published at https://www.youtube.com/user/africancourt/channels/live (accessed May 26, 2017).
2. In addition to these formal communal property rights, the Ministry of Agrarian Affairs passed a regulation that specifies the administrative mechanisms for recording and demarcating the boundaries of traditional communal lands (The State Minister of Agrarian Affairs/Head of the National Land Affairs Agency, Regulation No. 5, 1999).

Appendix A

1. I include only Indigenous land claims that FUNAI, the federal agency in charge of implementing Brazil's indigenous policy, has considered admissible to avoid biases associated with claims that the state has not accepted as legitimate from the outset. Hence, I do not use the number of Indigenous Lands reported by NGOs like the Instituto Socioambiental (ISA) and the Missionary Council for Indigenous Peoples (CIMI), who include in their list Indigenous land claims whether or not the state has admitted them.
2. The database contains geocoded information for all 730 land proceedings from 1903 through February 2016, with a total of 655 Indigenous Lands from January 1989 until February 2016.

There are only 19 cases, all from outside of Amazonia, for which I do not have the records of the onset of titling proceedings.
3. I used the Hot Spot Analysis tool in ArcGIS 10.3.1 to identify spatial clusters of statistically significant high or low values. Given a set of geo-referenced data points, such as the number of titled Indigenous Lands in Brazil, and operating under the expectation that data values are randomly distributed across the study area, this tool delineates clusters of blocks with higher than expected titling rates. These clusters are hot spots. The tool works by looking at each Indigenous Land within the context of its neighbors. For a statistically significant hot spot, an Indigenous Land will be titled and be surrounded by other Indigenous Lands that are titled.
4. The program is called the "Integrated Project to Protect the Populations and Indigenous Lands of the Amazônia Legal" (*Projeto Integrado de Proteção às Populações e Terras Indígenas da Amazônia Legal*, PPTAL). The PPTAL, a result of the 1992 UN's Earth Summit in Rio de Janeiro (Rio-92), is part of a larger US$428 million program called the Pilot Program to Conserve the Brazilian Rainforest (PPG7). The World Bank, KfW, and the German Agency for International Cooperation (GIZ) funded the PPTAL (GIZ invested Euros 16 million) (Valente 2010, Ch. 6; BenYishay, Heuser, Runfola, and Trichler 2016).
5. The issue-specific international NGOs are: Survival International, Conservation International, Greenpeace, World Wildlife Fund, Nature Conservancy, Amazon Watch, and Rainforest Foundation. The issue-specific Brazilian NGOs that are connected to a network of international activists are: Instituto Socioambiental (ISA), Missionary Council for Indigenous Peoples (Conselho Indigenista Missionário, CIMI), Brazilian Anthropological Association (ABA), Commission for the Creation of the Yanomami Park (Comissão pela Criação do Parque Yanomami, CCPY), National Indigenous Peoples Organization of Brazil (Articulação dos Povos Indígenas do Brasil, APIB), Coordination of the Indigenous Organizations of the Brazilian Amazon (Coordenação das Organizações Indígenas da Amazônia Brasileira, COIAB), and Federation of Indigenous Organizations from the Rio Negro (Federação das Organizações Indígenas do Rio Negro, FOIRN).
6. The Brazil Database contains information about the date the Indigenous Land titling proceedings began and were approved.
7. The only significant difference between Models 1 and 2, discussed in the text, is evidence of an interaction effect between *Northern Frontier Zone* and *Minerals & Hydrocarbons*.

Bibliography

Abers, Rebecca, and Margaret E. Keck. 2013. *Practical authority: Agency and institutional change in Brazilian water politics*. Oxford: Oxford University Press.
Acciaioli, Greg. 2007. "From Customary Law to Indigenous Sovereignty: Reconceptualizing the Scope and Significance of Masyarakat Adat in Contemporary Indonesia." In *The revival of tradition in Indonesian politics: The deployment of adat from colonialism to indigenism*, eds. Jamie S. Davidson and David Henley. London: Routledge, 295–318.
Acosta, María L. 2011. "Los retos del proceso de titulación y saneamiento como protección a la propiedad indígena." *Wani Revista del Caribe Nicaragüense* 60: 5–17.
Afiff, S., and C. Lowe. 2007. "Claiming Indigenous Community: Political Discourse and Natural Resource Rights in Indonesia." *Alternatives: Global, Local, Political* 32 (1): 73–97.
AGU (Advocacia-Geral da União) Brasil. 1995. *Parecer GQ-81. Demarcação de Terras Indígenas*. Brasília: Diário Oficial.
AGU (Advocacia-Geral da União) Brasil. 2012. *Portaria No. 303/201. Dispõe sobre as salvaguardas institucionais às terras indígenas conforme entendimento fixado pelo Supremo Tribunal Federal na Petição 3.388 RR*. Brasília: Diário Oficial.
Aguilar-Støen, Mariel, and Cecilie Hirsch. 2015. "Environmental Impact Assessments, Local Power and Self-Determination: The Case of Mining and Hydropower Development in Guatemala." *The Extractive Industries and Society* 2 (3): 472–79.
Agrawal, Arun, and Elinor Ostrom. 2001. "Collective Action, Property Rights, and Decentralization in Resource Use in India and Nepal." *Politics & Society* 29 (4): 485–514.
Åhrén, Mattias. 2016. *Indigenous peoples' status in the international legal system*. Oxford: Oxford University Press.
Alava, Holger. 2015. "FUSINA combate a las bandas hondureñas de la droga en la región de Costa de Mosquitos." Diálogo Revista Militar Digital. Foro de las Américas. dialogo-americas.com/es/articles/fusina-combate-las-bandas-hondurenas-de-la-droga-en-la-region-de-costa-de-mosquitos.
Albert, Bruce. 1992. "Indian Lands, Environmental Policy and Military Geopolitics in the Development of the Brazilian Amazon: The Case of the Yanomami." *Development and Change* 23 (1): 35–70.
Albertus, Michael. 2015. *Autocracy and redistribution: The politics of land reform*. New York: Cambridge University Press.
Allison, Paul D. 1984. *Event history analysis: Regression for longitudinal event data*. Beverly Hills, CA; London: Sage.
Almeida, Paul, and Allen Cordero, eds. 2015. *Handbook of social movements across Latin America. Handbooks of sociology and social research*. Dordrecht: Springer.
Altamirano-Jiménez, Isabel. 2013. *Indigenous encounters with neoliberalism: Place, women, and the environment in Canada and Mexico*. Vancouver; Toronto: UBC Press.
Álvarez, Rezaye. 2016. "Estado de Nicaragua cercena tierras creoles." *La Prensa*, April 9 www.laprensani.com/2016/04/09/nacionales/2015636-estado-de-nicaragua-cercena-tierras-creoles.
Amengual, Matthew. 2016. *Politicized enforcement in Argentina: Labor and environmental regulation*. Cambridge: Cambridge University Press.
Amnesty International. 2016. "Nicaraguan Canal and its Impact on Human Rights." www.amnesty.ca/node/72249.
Ampié, Mauro, and Gonzalo Carrión. 2017. "Hay una indiferencia criminal de las autoridades ante la violencia en el Caribe." *Envío* (420). www.envio.org.ni/articulo/5308.

Anaya, S. J. 2004. *Indigenous peoples in international law*. 2nd ed. Oxford; New York: Oxford University Press.
Anderson, Mark D. 2009. *Black and indigenous: Garifuna activism and consumer culture in Honduras*. Minneapolis: University of Minnesota Press.
Anderson, Perry. 1979. *Lineages of the absolutist state*. United Kingdom: Verso.
Andolina, Robert, Nina Laurie, and Sarah A. Radcliffe. 2009. *Indigenous development in the Andes: Culture, power, and transnationalism*. Durham, NC: Duke University Press.
Arce, Alberto. 2016. "Tres generales y un cartel: Violencia policial e impunidad en Honduras." *The New York Times*, April 15. www.nytimes.com/es/2016/04/15/tres-generales-y-un-car tel-violencia-policial-e-impunidad-en-honduras/.
Arnson, Cynthia J., and Eric L. Olson, eds. 2011. *Organized crime in Central America: The northern triangle*. Washington, DC: Woodrow Wilson International Center for Scholars.
Asher, Kiran. 2009. *Black and green: Afro-Colombians, development, and nature in the Pacific lowlands*. Durham, NC: Duke University Press.
Assies, Willem, Ton Salman, Salvador Martí i Puig, and Gemma van der Haar, eds. 2014. *Dignity for the voiceless: Willem Assies's anthropological work in context*. New York: Berghahn Books.
Assies, Willem. 2008. "Land Tenure and Tenure Regimes in Mexico: An Overview." *Journal of Agrarian Change* 8 (1): 33–63.
Attorney General's Office (Procuraduría General de la República) Nicaragua. 2009. *Informe Final: Plan de Participación de las Comunidades Indígenas del Norte y Centro Pacífico de Nicaragua, en el marco del Financiamiento Adicional del PRODEP*. documents1.worldbank. org/curated/es/371191468108869449/IPP3910SPANISH1igenous0Peoples0Plan.doc.
Attorney General's Office (Procuraduría General de la República) Nicaragua. 2013. *Proyecto de Ordenamiento de la Propiedad (PRODEP). Informe de Evaluación Final*. www.pgr.gob. ni/PDF/2014/prodep/Informe%20de%20Evaluacion%20Final%20PRODEP%20Revis ado%2006%20dic2013.pdf
Attorney General's Office (Procuraduría General de la República) Nicaragua. 2016. *Sistematización Titulación de Territorios del Régimen de Propiedad Comunal*. Document in the possession of the author.
Baird, Ian G. 2013. "Indigenous Peoples' and land: Comparing communal land titling and its implications in Cambodia and Laos." *Asia Pacific Viewpoint* 54 (3): 269–81.
Brands, Hal. 2012. *Latin America's Cold War*. Cambridge, MA: Harvard University Press.
Barahona, Marvin. 2005. "Del mestizaje a la diversidad étnica y cultural." In *Memorias del mestizaje: Cultura política en Centroamérica de 1920 al presente*, eds. Darío A. Euraque, Jeffrey L. Gould and Charles R. Hale. Guatemala: CIRMA, 215–51.
Barahona, Marvin, and Ramón D. Rivas. 2007, 1998. *Rompiendo el espejo: Visiones sobre los pueblos indígenas y Onegros en Honduras*. Tegucigalpa: Editorial Guaymuras.
Barbosa, Luiz C. 2015. *Guardians of the Brazilian Amazon rainforest: Environmental organizations and development*. London: Routledge.
Barelli, Mauro. 2016. *Seeking Justice in International Law: The Significance and Implications of the UN Declaration on the Rights of Indigenous Peoples*. London: Routledge.
Baron, Reuben M., and David A. Kenny. 1986. "The Moderator–Mediator Variable Distinction in Social Psychological Research: Conceptual, Strategic, and Statistical Considerations." *Journal of Personality and Social Psychology* 51 (6): 1173–82.
Bauer, Kelly. 2016. "Land Versus Territory: Evaluating Indigenous Land Policy for the Mapuche in Chile." *Journal of Agrarian Change* 16 (4): 627–45.
BBC (Latin American & Caribbean). 2016. "Honduras Indigenous Rights Activist Berta Caceres Killed." *BBC News*, March 3. www.bbc.com/news/world-latin-america-35719398.
Becher, Marie, and Jill Powis. 2016. "Leaving No One Behind: Land and Environmental Defenders at the Heart of Sustainable Development." *Reuters*, July 28. news.trust.org/item/20160728133450-5w2pg/.
Becker, Bertha K. [1990] 2001. *Amazônia*. São Paulo: Editora Atica.

Bengio, Ofra, ed. 2014. *Kurdish awakening: Nation building in a fragmented homeland*. Austin: University of Texas Press.
Bennett, W. L. 2005. "Social Movements beyond Borders: Understanding Two Eras of Transnational Activism." In *Transnational protest and global activism. People, passions and power*, eds. Donatella Della Porta and Sidney G. Tarrow. Lanham, MD: Rowman & Littlefield, 203–26.
BenYishay, Ariel, Silke Heuser, Daniel Runfola, and Rachel Trichler. 2016. *Geospatial Impact Evaluation of the Demarcation of Indian Territories Project (PPTAL) on Conflict and Deforestation*. Williamsburg, VA: AidData at William & Mary.
Biezeveld, Renske. 2007. "The Many Roles of Adat in West Sumatra." In *The revival of tradition in Indonesian politics: The deployment of adat from colonialism to indigenism*, eds. Jamie S. Davidson and David Henley. London: Routledge, 203–23.
Bitencourt, Luis. 2002. "The Importance of the Amazon Basin in Brazil's Evolving Security Agenda." In *Environment and security in the Amazon Basin*, eds. Joseph S. Tulchin and Heather A. Golding. Washington, DC: Woodrow Wilson International Center for Scholars, 53–74.
Bøås, Morten, and Kevin C. Dunn. 2013. *Politics of origin in Africa: Autochthony, citizenship and conflict*. London: Zed.
Boege Schmidt, Eckart. 2008. *El patrimonio biocultural de los pueblos indígenas de México*. México: Instituto Nacional de Antropología e Historia, Comisión Nacional para el Desarrollo de los Pueblos Indígenas.
Boone, Catherine. 2003. *Political topographies of the African State*. Cambridge: Cambridge University Press.
Boone, Catherine. 2014. *Property and political order in Africa*. New York: Cambridge University Press.
Boone, Catherine. 2019. "Legal Empowerment of the Poor through Property Rights Reform: Tensions and Trade-offs of Land Registration and Titling in sub-Saharan Africa." *The Journal of Development Studies* 55 (3): 384–400.
Börzel, Tanja A., and Thomas Risse. 2013. "Human Rights in Areas of Limited Statehood: The New Agenda." In *The persistent power of human rights: From commitment to compliance*, eds. Thomas Risse-Kappen, Stephen C. Ropp, and Kathryn Sikkink. Cambridge: Cambridge University Press, 63–84.
Bosworth, James. 2011. "Honduras: Organized Crime Gained amid Political Crisis." In *Organized crime in Central America: The northern triangle*, eds. Cynthia J. Arnson and Eric L. Olson. Washington, DC: Woodrow Wilson International Center for Scholars, 62–103.
Bourchier, David. 2007. "The Romance of Adat in the Indonesian Political Imagination and the Current Revival." In *The revival of tradition in Indonesian politics: The deployment of adat from colonialism to indigenism*, eds. Jamie S. Davidson and David Henley. London: Routledge, 113–29.
Box-Steffensmeier, Janet M., Henry E. Brady, David Collier, and Colin Elman, eds. 2009. *The Oxford Handbook of Political Methodology*. Vol. 1. Oxford: Oxford University Press.
Box-Steffensmeier, Janet M., and Bradford S. Jones. 1997. "Time is of the Essence: Event History Models in Political Science." *American Journal of Political Science* 41 (4): 1414.
Boyer, Véronique. 2016. "The Crisis of Multiculturalism in Latin America." In *The demand for recognition and access to citizenship: Ethnic labeling and territorial restructuring in Brazil*, ed. David Lehmann. New York: Palgrave Macmillan, 155–78.
Brady, Henry E., and David Collier. 2010. *Rethinking social inquiry: Diverse tools, shared standards*. 2nd ed. Lanham, MD.: Rowman & Littlefield Publishers.
Branch, Adam. 2011. *Displacing human rights: War and intervention in northern Uganda*. New York; Oxford: Oxford University Press.
Bratman, Eve. 2015. "Passive Revolution in the Green Economy: Activism and the Belo Monte Dam." *International Environmental Agreements: Politics, Law and Economics* 15 (1): 61–77.

Brehm, John, and Scott Gates. 1997. *Working, Shirking, and Sabotage*. Ann Arbor: University of Michigan Press.

Brinks, Daniel M. 2008. *The judicial response to police killings in Latin America: Inequality and the rule of law*. Cambridge: Cambridge University Press.

Brinks, Daniel M., and Sandra Botero. 2014. "Inequality and the Rule of Law: Ineffective Rights in Latin American Democracies." In *Reflections on uneven democracies: The legacy of Guillermo O'Donnell*, eds. Daniel M. Brinks, Marcelo Leiras, and Scott Mainwaring. Baltimore, MD: Johns Hopkins University Press, 214–39.

Brinks, Daniel M., Marcelo Leiras, and Scott Mainwaring, eds. 2014. *Reflections on uneven democracies: The legacy of Guillermo O'Donnell*. Baltimore, MD: Johns Hopkins University Press.

Brondo, Keri V. 2007. "Land Loss and Garifuna Women's Activism on Honduras' North Coast." *Journal of International Women's Studies* 9 (1): 99–116.

Brondo, Keri V. 2013. *Land grab*. Tucson: University of Arizona Press.

Brook, Mary M. 2005. "Re-scaling the Commons: Miskitu Indians, forest commodities, and transnational development networks." Dissertation, Doctor of Philosophy. University of Texas at Austin.

Brooke, James. 1989. "For an Amazon Indian Tribe, Civilization Brings Mostly Disease and Death." *The New York Times*, December 24. www.nytimes.com/1989/12/24/world/for-an-amazon-indian-tribe-civilization-brings-mostly-disease-and-death.html?pagewanted=all.

Bryan, Joe, and Denis Wood. 2015. *Weaponizing maps*. New York: The Guilford Press.

Brysk, Alison. 1996. "Turning Weakness into Strength." *Latin American Perspectives* 23 (2): 38–57.

Brysk, Alison. 2000. *From tribal village to global village: Indian rights and international relations in Latin America*. Stanford, CA: Stanford University Press.

Brysk, Alison. 2009. *Global good Samaritans: Human rights as foreign policy*. New York; Oxford: Oxford University Press.

Bull, Benedicte, and Mariel Aguilar-Støen. 2014. *Environmental politics in Latin America*. London: Routledge.

Bunck, Julie M., and Michael R. Fowler. 2012. *Bribes, Bullets, and Intimidation*. University Park: Pennsylvania State University Press.

Bunker, Stephen G. 1985. *Underdeveloping the Amazon*. Chicago, IL: University of Chicago Press.

Cajina, Roberto. 2014. "Remilitarización en Centroamérica: el retorno de los nunca se fueron." In *Documento de Opinión* No. 90. Madrid: Instituto Español de Asuntos Estratégicos. dialnet.unirioja.es/descarga/articulo/7651425.pdf

Capoccia, Giovanni. 2015. "Critical Junctures and Institutional Change." In *Advances in comparative-historical analysis*, eds. James Mahoney and Kathleen A. Thelen. New York: Cambridge University Press, 147–79.

Cardenas, Sonia. 2007. *Conflict and compliance*. Philadelphia: University of Pennsylvania Press.

Carey, John M. 2000. "Parchment, Equilibria, and Institutions." *Comparative Political Studies* 33 (6–7): 735–61.

Carrión, Luis. 1983. "The truth about the Atlantic Coast." In *National revolution and indigenous identity: The conflict between Sandinists and Miskito Indians on Nicaragua's Atlantic Coast*, eds. Klaudine Ohland and Robin Schneider. Copenhagen: IWGIA, 235–68.

Carruthers, David, and Patricia Rodriguez. 2009. "Mapuche Protest, Environmental Conflict and Social Movement Linkage in Chile." *Third World Quarterly* 30 (4): 743–60.

Carvalho, Georgia O. 2000. "The Politics of Indigenous Land Rights Brazil." *Bulletin of Latin American Research* 19 (4): 461–78.

Cassese, Antonio. 1996. *Self-determination of peoples: A legal reappraisal*. Cambridge: Cambridge University Press.

Castro, Celso, ed. 2006. *Amazonia: E defesa nacional*. Brasil: FGV Editora.

CEJIL (Center for Justice and International Law). 2015. "Organizations Denounce Human Rights Violations Caused by Construction of Interoceanic Canal in Nicaragua at the IACHR."

cejil.org/en/organizations-denounce-human-rights-violations-caused-construction-interoceanic-canal-nicaragua.
CEJIL (Center for Justice and International Law). 2021. "Inter-American Commission on Human Rights to Hold Public Hearing on Colonization of Indigenous Lands in Nicaragua." March 15. cejil.org/en/inter-american-commission-human-rights-hold-public-hearing-colonization-indigenous-lands-nicaragua.
Centeno, Miguel A., and Agustín Ferraro. 2013. *State and nation making in Latin America and Spain: Republics of the possible.* Cambridge: Cambridge University Press.
Centro de Comunicação Social do Exército (Brazil). 2006. "Amazônia—Pelotões Especiais de Fronteira." *Verde Oliva* 23 (189): 40–43. www.calameo.com/exercito-brasileiro/books/00123820643e6e0b8ee6a
Chapin, Mac, and Bill Threlkeld. 2001. *Indigenous landscapes: A study in ethnocartography.* Arlington, VA: Center for the Support of Native Lands.
Chiriboga Vega, Manuel. 2001. "El levantamiento indígena ecuatoriano de 2001: Una interpelación." *Íconos: revista de ciencias sociales* 10 (2): 28–33. hdl.handle.net/10469/1703.
CIMI (Assessoria de Comunicação). 2016. "União é responsabilizada por ação de militares em terra indígena na Operação Ágata 4." Conselho Indigenista Missionário. July 12. cimi.org.br.
Cizre, Umit. 2001. "The Truth and Fiction about (Turkey's) Human Rights Politics." *Human Rights Review* 3 (1): 55–77.
Colby, Jason M. 2013. *The Business of Empire: United Fruit, Race, and U.S. expansion in Central America. United States in the World.* Ithaca, NY: Cornell University Press.
Collier, David, and Colin Elman. 2009. "Qualitative and Multimethod Research: Organizations, Publication, and Reflections on Integration." In *The Oxford handbook of political methodology*, eds. Janet M. Box-Steffensmeier, Henry E. Brady, David Collier, and Colin Elman. Oxford: Oxford University Press, 779–95.
Conklin, Beth A. 1997. "Body Paint, Feathers, and VCRs: Aesthetics and Authenticity in Amazonian Activism." *American Ethnologist* 24 (4): 711–37.
Conklin, Beth A., and Laura R. Graham. 1995. "The Shifting Middle Ground: Amazonian Indians and Eco-Politics." *American Anthropologist* 97 (4): 695–710.
Consejo de Comunicación y Ciudadanía (Nicaragua). 2012. *Reunión de Daniel con Presidente Porfirio Lobo, Jefes de Seguridad de CA y empresarios centroamericanos.* www.el19digital.com/articulos/ver/titulo:7166-reunion-de-daniel-con-presidente-porfirio-lobo-jefes-de-seguridad-de-ca-y-empresarios-centroamericanos.
COPINH (Council of Indigenous and Popular Organizations of Honduras). 2016. "Urgent denunciation." copinhenglish.blogspot.com/2016/03/copinh-urgent-denunciation-march-6-2016.html.
Couso, Javier, Alexandra Huneeus, and Rachel Sieder, eds. 2010. *Cultures of legality: Judicialization and political activism in Latin America.* Cambridge: Cambridge University Press.
Cruz, Luisa, and FAO (Food and Agriculture Organization of the United Nations). 2010. *Una gobernanza responsable en la tenencia de la tierra: factor esencial para la realización del derecho a la alimentación documento de discusión.* Rome: FAO.
Cuéllar, Nelson, Andrew Davis, Fausto Luna, and Oscar Díaz. 2012. *Inversiones y Dinámicas Territoriales en Centroamérica: Implicaciones para la Gobernanza y la Construcción de Alternativas.* PRISMA. www.prisma.org.sv/uploads/media/Inversiones_dinamicas_terr itoriales_en_CA.pdf
Daley, Suzanne. 2016. "Lost in Nicaragua, a Chinese Tycoon's Canal Project." *The New York Times*, April 3. www.nytimes.com/2016/04/04/world/americas/nicaragua-canal-chinese-tycoon.html.
Danspeckgruber, Wolfgang F., and Arthur Watts, eds. 1997. *Self-determination and self-administration: A sourcebook.* Boulder, CO: L. Rienner.
Davidson, Jamie S., and David Henley, eds. 2007. *The revival of tradition in Indonesian politics: The deployment of adat from colonialism to indigenism.* London: Routledge.

Davis, Shelton H. 1980. "Mining projects endanger Amazon's Yanomamo tribe." *The Multinational Monitor*. February. www.multinationalmonitor.org/hyper/issues/1980/02/davis.html.

Deininger, Klaus W. 2003. *Land policies for growth and poverty reduction. A World Bank policy research report*. Washington, DC: World Bank.

Deininger, Klaus W., Clarissa Augustinus, Stig Enemark, and Paul Munro-Faure. 2010. *Innovations in land rights recognition, administration, and governance*. Washington, DC: World Bank.

Della Porta, Donatella, and Herbert Reiter. 2011. "State Power and the Control of Transnational Protests." In *Power and transnational activism*. Vol. 28. *Rethinking globalizations*, ed. Thomas Olesen. London: Routledge, 91–110.

Della Porta, Donatella, and Sidney G. Tarrow, eds. 2005. *Transnational protest and global activism. People, passions and power*. Lanham, MD: Rowman & Littlefield.

Dennis, Philip A., and Michael D. Olien. 1984. "Kingship among the Miskito." *American Ethnologist* 11 (4): 718–37.

Dezalay, Yves, and Bryant G. Garth, eds. 2002. *Global prescriptions: The production, exportation, and importation of a new legal orthodoxy*. Ann Arbor: University of Michigan Press.

Diacon, Todd. 2004. *Stringing together a nation: Cândido Mariano da Silva Rondon and the construction of a modern Brazil, 1906–1930*. Durham, NC: Duke University Press.

Dicklitch, Susan. 2001. "NGOs and Democratization in Transitional Societies: Lessons from Uganda." *International Politics* 38 (1): 27–46.

Doane, Molly. 2012. *Stealing shining rivers: Agrarian conflict, market logic, and conservation in a Mexican forest*. Tucson: University of Arizona Press.

Donnelly, Jack. 2013. *Universal human rights in theory and practice*. 3rd ed. Ithaca, NY: Cornell University Press.

EarthRights International. 2020. "Speak without Fear: The Case for a Stronger U.S. Policy on Human Rights Defenders." June. earthrights.org.

Eaton, Kent. 2003. "Can Politicians Control Bureaucrats? Applying Theories of Political Control to Argentina's Democracy." *Latin American Politics and Society* 45 (4): 33–62.

Edouard, Fabrice. 2010. *Gobernanza en la Tenencia de la Tierra y Recursos Naturales en América Central*. Rome: FAO.

Edwards, Michael, and John Gaventa, eds. 2001. *Global citizen action*. London: Earthscan.

Eisenstadt, Todd A. 2013. "Introduction: Reconciling Liberal Pluralism and Group Rights: A Comparative Perspective on Oaxaca, Mexico's Experiment in Multiculturalism." In *Latin America's multicultural movements: The struggle between communitarianism, autonomy, and human rights*, ed. Todd A. Eisenstadt. Trans. Michael S. Danielson, Moisés J. Bailón Corres, and Carlos Sorroza Polo. Oxford: Oxford University Press, 3–17.

Eisenstadt, Todd A., ed. 2013. *Latin America's multicultural movements: The struggle between communitarianism, autonomy, and human rights*. Trans. Michael S. Danielson, Moisés J. Bailón Corres and Carlos Sorroza Polo. Oxford: Oxford University Press.

EMBRAPA (Empresa Brasileira de Pesquisa Agropecuária). 2016. "Soja em números." www.embrapa.br/soja/cultivos/soja1/dados-economicos.

Engle, Karen. 2010. *The elusive promise of indigenous development: Rights, culture, strategy*. Durham, NC: Duke University Press.

Engerman, Stanley L., and Jacob Metzer. 2004. *Land rights, ethno-nationality, and sovereignty in history*. London: Routledge.

Environmental Resource Management (ERM). 2015. *Canal de Nicaragua: environmental and social impact assessment*. hknd-group.com/portal.php?mod=list&catid=45.

Escárcega, Sylvia. 2013. "The Global Indigenous Movement and Paradigm Wars: International Activism, Network Building, and Transformative Politics." In *Insurgent encounters: Transnational activism, ethnography, and the political*, eds. Jeffrey S. Juris and Alex Khasnabish. London; Durham, NC: Duke University Press, 129–49.

Euraque, Darío A., Jeffrey L. Gould, and Charles R. Hale, eds. 2005. *Memorias del mestizaje: Cultura política en Centroamérica de 1920 al presente*. Guatemala: CIRMA.

Evans, Peter. 1995. *Embedded autonomy: States and industrial transformation.* Princeton paperbacks. Princeton, NJ: Princeton University Press.
Evans, Peter. 2000. "Fighting Marginalization with Transnational Networks: Counter-Hegemonic Globalization." *Contemporary Sociology* 29 (1): 230–41.
Evans, Peter, Dietrich Rueschemeyer, and Theda Skocpol, eds. 1985. *Bringing the state back in.* Cambridge: Cambridge University Press.
Faundez, Julio. 2010. "Access to Justice and Indigenous Communities in Latin America." In *Marginalized communities and access to justice. Law, development and globalization,* eds. Yash P. Ghai and Jill Cottrell. Abingdon, UK; New York: Routledge, 83–109.
Fears, Darryl. 2016. "For Latin American Environmentalists, Death is a Constant Companion." *The Washington Post,* March 30. www.washingtonpost.com/national/health-science/for-latin-american-environmentalists-death-is-a-constant-companion/2016/03/25/85920f96-ec69-11e5-bc08-3e03a5b41910_story.html?utm_term=.3f3bbaea1308.
Finley-Brook, Mary, and Karl Offen. 2009. "Bounding the Commons: Land Demarcation in Northeastern Nicaragua." *Bulletin of Latin American Research* 28 (3): 343–63.
Finley-Brook, Mary. 2014. "Green Neoliberal Space: The Mesoamerican Biological Corridor." In *Indigenous peoples, national parks, and protected areas: A new paradigm linking conservation, culture, and rights,* eds. Stan Stevens. Tucson: University of Arizona Press, 172–96.
Finnemore, Martha, and Judith Goldstein, eds. 2013. *Back to basics: State power in a contemporary world.* New York: Oxford University Press.
Finnemore, Martha, and Kathryn Sikkink. 2001. "Taking Stock: The Constructivist Research Program in International Relations and Comparative Politics." *Annual Review of Political Science* 4 (1): 391–416.
Fisher, William. 1994. "Megadevelopment, Environmentalism, and Resistance: The Institutional Context of Kayapó Indigenous Politics in Central Brazil." *Human Organization* 53 (3): 220–32.
Fitzpatrick, Daniel. 2007. "Land, Custom, and the State in Post-Suharto Indonesia: A Foreign Lawyer's Perspective." In *The revival of tradition in Indonesian politics: The deployment of adat from colonialism to indigenism,* eds. Jamie S. Davidson and David Henley. London: Routledge, 116–35.
Folha de São Paulo. 1986. "Projeto para a Fronteira Norte opõe Militares e Igreja." *Folha de São Paulo,* November 1. acervo.folha.uol.com.br/fsp/1990/03/24/2//4088001.
Folha de São Paulo. 1990. "Presidente visita Calha Norte, FUNAI faz Críticas ao Projeto." *Folha de São Paulo,* March 24. acervo.folha.uol.com.br/fsp/1990/03/24/2/#.
Forest Trends. 2015. *Titling Ancestral Territories in the Honduran Muskitia: Exploring the Implications for the Country's Indigenous Peoples.* www.forest-trends.org/documents/files/doc_4974.pdf.
FUNAI (National Indigenous Agency) Brazil. 1984–2005. "Yanomami Land Demarcation Proceedings." Brasília. Document in the possession of the author.
FUNAI (National Indigenous Agency) Brazil. 2005. PPTAL: Projeto Integrado de Proteção às Populações e Terras Indígenas da Amazônia Legal. Brasília: PPTAL. acervo.socioambiental.org/sites/default/files/documents/F1D00148.pdf.
FUNAI (National Indigenous Agency) Brazil. 2016. *Terras Indígenas e Terras Indígenas em Estudo.* February. Document in the possession of the author.
Furtado, Renata. 2013. *Descobrindo a faixa de fronteira: A trajetória das elites organizacionais do executivo federal as estratégias, as negociações e o embate na constituinte.* Curitiba Brasil: Editora CRV.
Garfield, Seth. 2001. *Indigenous struggle at the heart of Brazil: State policy, frontier expansion, and the Xavante Indians, 1937–1988.* Durham, NC: Duke University Press.
Garfield, Seth. 2004. "A Nationalist Environment: Indians, Nature, and the Construction of the Xingu National Park in Brazil." *Luso-Brazilian Review* 41 (1): 139–67.
Garrard-Burnett, Virginia, Mark A. Lawrence, and Julio Moreno, eds. 2013. *Beyond the eagle's shadow: New histories of Latin America's cold war.* Albuquerque: University of New Mexico Press.

Gerring, John. 2007. *Case study research: Principles and practices*. Cambridge: Cambridge University Press.
Ghai, Yash P., and Jill Cottrell, eds. 2010. *Marginalized communities and access to justice. Law, development and globalization*. Abingdon, UK; New York: Routledge.
Ghanea-Hercock, Nazila, Alexandra Xanthaki, and Patrick Thornberry. 2005. *Minorities, peoples, and self-determination: Essays in honour of Patrick Thornberry*. Leiden; Boston: Martinus Nijhoff Publishers.
Gibbs, Stephen. 2009. "Nicaragua's Miskitos Seek Independence." *BBC*, August 3. news.bbc.co.uk/2/hi/8181209.stm.
Giddens, Anthony. [1981–1985] 2013. *The Nation-State and Violence*. Hoboken, NJ: Wiley.
Gilbert, Jérémie. 2006. *Indigenous peoples' land rights under international law: From victims to actors*. Ardsley, NY: Transnational.
GiZ. 2010. *Documento de trabajo: Pueblos Indigenas en Nicaragua*. Deutsche Gesellschaft für Internationale Zusammenarbeit GmbH. www.giz.de/fachexpertise/downloads/giz2010-eslaenderpapier-nicaragua.pdf.
Gleditsch, Kristian Skrede, Simon Hug, Livia Isabella Schubiger, and Julian Wucherpfennig. 2016. "International Conventions and Nonstate Actors: Selection, Signaling, and Reputation Effects." *Journal of Conflict Resolution* 62 (2): 346–80.
Global Witness. 2015. *Report*. www.globalwitness.org/annual-report-2015
Global Witness. 2017. "Honduras: The Deadliest Place to Defend the Planet." January. www.globalwitness.org/en/campaigns/environmental-activists/honduras-deadliest-country-world-environmental-activism/.
Global Witness. 2020. "Defending Tomorrow: The Climate Crisis and Threats against Land and Environmental Defenders." July. www.globalwitness.org/documents/19939/Defending_Tomorrow_EN_low_res_-_July_2020.pdf.
Goett, Jennifer. 2016. *Black autonomy: Race, gender, and Afro-Nicaraguan activism*. Redwood City: Stanford University Press.
Gómez Suárez, Águeda. 2004. *Patrones de movilización política de la acción indigena zapatista: Contextos, estrategias y discursos*. Vigo: Universidad de Vigo.
Gómez Isa, Felipe. 2016. "The Role of Soft Law in the Progressive Development of Indigenous Peoples' Rights." In *Tracing the roles of soft law in human rights*, eds. Stéphanie Lagoutte, Thomas Gammeltoft-Hansen, and John Cerone. Oxford: Oxford University Press, 185–212.
Gómez Meléndez, Agustin. 2014. *Atlas de los territorios indígenas de Costa Rica*. San José: Universidad de Costa Rica.
Goodale, Mark, and Nancy G. Postero, eds. 2013. *Neoliberalism, interrupted: Social change and contested governance in contemporary Latin America*. Stanford, CA: Stanford University Press.
Goodman, Ryan, and Derek Jinks. 2013. *Socializing states: Promoting human rights through international law*. Oxford: Oxford University Press.
Gordon, Edmundo T., Galio C. Gurdián, and Charles R. Hale. 2002. "Derechos, Recursos y Memoria Social de Lucha: Reflexiones Sobre un Estudio Acerca de los Derechos Territoriales de las Comunidades Indígenas y Negras en la Costa Caribe de Nicaragua." *Wani Revista del Caribe Nicaragüense* 29: 6–27. revistas.bicu.edu.ni/index.php/wani/issue/view/54/showToc.
Gordon, Edmund T., and Charles R. Hale. 2003. "Rights, Resources, and the Social Memory of Struggle: Reflections and Black Community Land Rights on Nicaragua's Atlantic Coast." *Human Organization* 62 (4): 369–81.
Graham, Laura R. 2003. "How Should an Indian Speak?: Amazonian Indians and the Symbolic Politics of Language in the Global Public Sphere." In *Indigenous movements, self-representation, and the state in Latin America*, eds. Kay B. Warren and Jean E. Jackson. Austin: University of Texas Press; Chesham: Combined Academic, 181–228.
Graubart, Jonathan. 2008. *Legalizing transnational activism: The struggle to gain social change from NAFTA's citizen petitions*. University Park: Pennsylvania State University Press.

Greenough, Paul R., and Anna L. Tsing. 2003. *Nature in the global south: Environmental projects in South and Southeast Asia*. Durham, NC: Duke University Press.

Griffiths, Thomas. 2004. "Indigenous Peoples, Land Tenure and Land Policy in Latin America." *Land Reform, Land Settlement and Cooperatives FAO* 1: 46–63.

Grugel, Jean. 2004. "State Power and Transnational Activism." In *Transnational activism in Asia: Problems of power and democracy*, eds. Nicola Piper and Anders Uhlin. London: Routledge, 26–42.

GSI (Gabinete de Segurança Institucional). 2004. *Seminário Faixa De Fronteira: Novos Paradigmas*. Brasília: Presidency. www.biblioteca.presidencia.gov.br/presidencia/dilma-vana-rousseff/publicacoes/orgao-essenciais/gabinete-de-seguranca-institucional/secretaria-de-acompanhamento-de-estudos-institucionais/seminario-faixa-de-fronteira-novos-paradigmas.

Gudmundson, Lowell, and Justin Wolfe, eds. 2010. *Blacks & blackness in Central America: Between race and place*. Durham, NC: Duke University Press.

Guyana Forestry Commission. 2015. Forest Carbon Partnership Facility (FCPF). Guyana's Submission: REDD+ Readiness Package (R-Package). forestry.gov.gy

Ha, Yong-Chool, and Myung-koo Kang. 2011. "Creating a Capable Bureaucracy with Loyalists: The Internal Dynamics of the South Korean Developmental State, 1948–1979." *Comparative Political Studies* 44 (1): 78–108.

Hafner-Burton, Emilie M., and Kiyoteru Tsutsui. 2005. "Human Rights in a Globalizing World: The Paradox of Empty Promises." *American Journal of Sociology* 110 (5): 1373–1411.

Hale, Charles R. 1994. *Resistance and contradiction: Miskitu Indians and the Nicaraguan State, 1894–1987*. Stanford, CA: Stanford University Press.

Hale, Charles R. 2011. "Resistencia para que? Territory, Autonomy and Neoliberal Entanglements in the 'Empty Spaces' of Central America." *Economy and Society* 40 (2): 184–210.

Hall, Derek, Philip Hirsch, and Tania Li, eds. 2011. *Powers of exclusion: Land dilemmas in Southeast Asia. Challenges of the agrarian transition in Southeast Asia (ChATSEA)*. Honolulu: University of Hawai'i Press.

Hall, Gillette, and Harry A. Patrinos. 2012. *Indigenous peoples, poverty, and development*. Cambridge: Cambridge University Press.

Hall, Peter A. 2006. "Systematic Process Analysis: When and How to Use It." *European Management Review* 3 (1): 24–31.

Hannum, Hurst. 1996. *Autonomy, sovereignty, and self-determination: The accommodation of conflicting rights*. Philadelphia: University of Pennsylvania Press.

Harper, Caroline. 2001. "Do the Facts Matter? NGOs, Research, and International Advocacy." In *Global citizen action*, eds. Michael Edwards and John Gaventa. London: Earthscan, 247–58.

Harris, Cole. 2002. *Making native space: Colonialism, resistance, and reserves in British Columbia*. Vancouver, BC: University of British Columbia Press.

Haughney, Diane. 2012. "Defending Territory, Demanding Participation: Mapuche Struggles in Chile." *Latin American Perspectives* 39 (4): 201–17.

Helms, Mary W. 1986. "Of Kings and Contexts: Ethnohistorical Interpretations of Miskito Political Structure and Function." *American Ethnologist* 13 (3): 506–23.

Henley, David, and Jamie S. Davidson. 2007. "Introduction: Radical Conservatism: The Protean Politics of Adat." In *The revival of tradition in Indonesian politics: The deployment of adat from colonialism to indigenism*, eds. Jamie S. Davidson and David Henley. London: Routledge.

Herrera, Adriana, and Fabrice Edouard. 2013. *Tenure of indigenous peoples territories and REDD+ as a forestry management incentive: The case of Mesoamerican countries*. Rome: FAO.

Hill, Daniel W. 2010. "Estimating the Effects of Human Rights Treaties on State Behavior." *The Journal of Politics* 72 (4): 1161–74.

Hochstetler, Kathryn, and Margaret E. Keck. 2007. *Greening Brazil: Environmental activism in state and society*. Durham, NC: Duke University Press.

Hodgson, Dorothy L. 2002. "Introduction: Comparative Perspectives on the Indigenous Rights Movement in Africa and the Americas." *American Anthropologist* 104 (4): 1037–49.

Hodgson, Dorothy L. 2011. *Being Maasai, becoming indigenous: Postcolonial politics in a neoliberal world*. Bloomington: Indiana University Press.

Hoekema, A. J., Gemma van der Haar, and Willem Assies. 2000. *The challenge of diversity: Indigenous peoples and reform of the State in Latin America*. Amsterdam: Thela Thesis.

Holland, Alisha C. 2015. "The Distributive Politics of Enforcement." *American Journal of Political Science* 59 (2): 357–71.

Honduras, República de. 2010. "Visión de País 2010–2038 y Plan de Nación 2010–2022 Presentados para consideración del Soberano Congreso Nacional." January. observatorioplanificacion.cepal.org/sites/default/files/plan/files/HondurasPlandeNacion20102022.pdf.

Honduras Weekly. 2012. *Lobo anti-drug trafficking strategy takes shape*. January 20. web.archive.org/web/20120126020839/http://hondurasweekly.com/lobo-anti-drug-trafficking-strategy-takes-shape-201201204759/.

Honey, Martha. 1994. *Hostile Acts: U.S. Policy in Costa Rica in the 1980s*. Gainesville: University Press of Florida.

Hooker, Juliet. 2010. "Race and the Space of Citizenship: The Mosquito Coast and the Place of Blackness and Indigeneity in Nicaragua." In *Blacks & blackness in Central America: Between race and place*, eds. Lowell Gudmundson and Justin Wolfe. Durham, NC: Duke University Press, 246–77.

House, Richard. 1990. "Brazil, in Reversal, Lets Miners Stay in Indian Area." *The Washington Post*, January 12.

Howe, James. 1998. *A people who would not kneel: Panama, the United States, and the San Blas Kuna*. Washington, DC: London: Smithsonian Institution Press.

Huber, John D., and Nolan Mccarty. 2004. "Bureaucratic Capacity, Delegation, and Political Reform." *American Political Science Review* 98 (03): 481–94.

Huneeus, Alexandra. 2011. "Courts Resisting Courts: Lessons from the Inter-American Court's Struggle to Enforce Human Rights." *Cornell International Law Journal* 44 (3): 493–533.

Hunter, Wendy. 1997. *Eroding military influence in Brazil: Politicians against soldiers*. Chapel Hill: University of North Carolina.

Huntington, Samuel P. 1968. *Political Order in Changing Societies*. New Haven, CT: Yale University Press.

IACHR (Inter-American Commission on Human Rights). 1970–2010. *Annual reports*. www.cidh.oas.org/annual.eng.htm.

IACHR (Inter-American Commission on Human Rights). 1983. *Report on the situation of human rights of a segment of the Nicaraguan population of Miskito origin*. cidh.oas.org/countryrep/Miskitoeng/toc.htm.

IACHR (Inter-American Commission on Human Rights). 1986. Annual Report 1985–1986. www.cidh.oas.org/annualrep/85.86eng/toc.htm.

IACHR (Inter-American Commission on Human Rights). 2009–2015. *Reports*. Washington, DC. www.oas.org/en/iachr/reports/country.asp.

IACHR (Inter-American Commission on Human Rights). 2013. "Resolution 12/2013, Precautionary Measure No. 416-13. Members of Movimiento Amplio por la Dignidad y la Justicia and their families." www.oas.org/en/iachr/decisions/pdf/Resolution12-13(MC-416-13).pdf.

IACHR (Inter-American Commission on Human Rights). 2015a. "Members of the Communities 'Esperanza, Santa Clara, Wisconsin y Francia Sirpi' in the Territory of the Miskitu Indigenous People." www.oas.org/en/iachr/decisions/precautionary.asp.

IACHR (Inter-American Commission on Human Rights). 2015b. "Hearing: Session: 154 Period of Sessions." www.oas.org/es/cidh/audiencias/TopicsList.aspx?Lang=en&Topic=27.

IACHR (Inter-American Commission on Human Rights). 2019. "Situación de los derechos humanos de los pueblos indígenas y tribales de la Panamazonía." www.oas.org/es/cidh/informes/pdfs/Panamazonia2019.pdf.

IACHR (Inter-American Commission on Human Rights). 2019. "Resolution 1/2021, Precautionary Measure No. 754-20. Members of the Guajajara and Awá Indigenous Peoples of the Araribóia Indigenous Land Regarding Brazil, January 4, 2020." www.oas.org/en/iachr/decisions/mc/2021/res_1-21_mc_754-20_br_en.pdf

IBC (Instituto del Bien Común). 2014. *Los Papeles de la Tierra: Superando los obstáculos a la titulación de las comunidades del Perú*. Lima: IBC.

IBGE (Instituto Brasileiro de Geografia e Estatística). 2011. *Censo Demográfico 2010*. Rio de Janeiro: IBGE.

IBGE (Instituto Brasileiro de Geografia e Estatística). 2012. *Os indígenas no Censo Demográfico 2010*. Rio de Janeiro: IBGE.

IBGE (Instituto Brasileiro de Geografia e Estatística). 2016. *Estrutura territorial*. Rio de Janeiro: IBGE. portaldemapas.ibge.gov.br.

ICF (Institute of Conservation and Forestry Development) Honduras. 2016. *Convenio Interinstitucional para la Regularización y Titulación de Tierras*. Document in the possession of the author.

ICJ (International Court of Justice). 1986. *Case concerning military and paramilitary activities in and against Nicaragua (Nicaragua v. United States of America): Merits*. The Hague: The Court.

Igoe, Jim. 2006. "Becoming Indigenous Peoples: Difference, Inequality, and the Globalization of East African Identity Politics." *African Affairs* 105 (420): 399–420.

ILO (International Labour Organization). 2009. *Indigenous & tribal peoples' rights in practice: A guide to ILO convention no. 169*. Geneva: ILO.

ILO (International Labour Organization). 2009. *Kenya: Constitutional, legislative and administrative provisions concerning indigenous peoples*. Trans. African Commission on Human & Peoples' Rights. Geneva: ILO.

ILO (International Labour Organization). 2013. *Understanding the Indigenous and Tribal People Convention, 1989 (No. 169): Handbook for ILO Tripartite Constituents*. Geneva: ILO.

INCSR (International Narcotics Control Strategy Reports). 2011. *International narcotics control strategy report*. Department of State, Bureau of International Narcotics Matters. 2009-2017.state.gov/j/inl/rls/nrcrpt/2011/index.htm.

INCSR (International Narcotics Control Strategy Reports). 2012. *International narcotics control strategy report*. Department of State, Bureau of International Narcotics Matters. 2009–2017.state.gov/j/inl/rls/nrcrpt/2012/index.htm.

Indian Law Resource Center. 1980. *Violations of the human rights of the Yanomami in Brazil: Communication to the Inter-American Commission on Human Rights*. Trans. American Anthropological Association. Indian Law Resource Center.

INE (Instituto Nacional de Estadística) Honduras. 2013. "Censo: XVII censo de población y VI de vivienda." Tegucigalpa. www.ine.gob.hn/index.php/25-publicaciones-ine/81-censo-de-xvii-poblacion-y-vi-vivienda.

INIDE (Instituto Nacional de Información de Desarrollo) Nicaragua. 2005. *Censo: VIII censo de población y IV de vivienda*. Managua: Instituto Nacional de Información de Desarrollo INIDE.

Instituto de Estudios del Ministerio Público (IEMP) Colombia. 2015. *Reflexiones sobre el Incoder y la institucionalidad agraria en Colombia*. Bogotá: Imprenta Nacional de Colombia.

Inter-American Court of Human Rights (IA-Court). 2003. *Caso de la comunidad Mayagna (Sumo) Awas Tingni vs. Nicaragua: Sentencia del 31 de agosto de 2001*. San José, Costa Rica: Secretaría de la Corte.

Inter-American Court of Human Rights (IA-Court). 2016. "Jurisprudence." www.corteidh.or.cr/cf/Jurisprudencia2/index.cfm?lang=es.

Inter-American Court of Human Rights (IA-Court). 2018. "Caso Pueblo Indígena Xucuru y sus miembros Vs. Brasil. Excepciones Preliminares, Fondo, Reparaciones y Costas. Sentencia de 5 de febrero de 2018. Serie C No. 346." www.corteidh.or.cr/docs/casos/articulos/seriec_346_esp.pdf

Inter-American Court of Human Rights (IA-Court). 2019. "Caso Comunidades Indígenas Miembros de la Asociación Lhaka Honhat (Nuestra Tierra) Vs. Argentina. Fondo, Reparaciones y Costas. Sentencia de 6 de febrero de 2020. Serie C No. 400." www.corteidh.or.cr/docs/casos/articulos/seriec_400_esp.pdf

International Criminal Court. 2015. *Situation in Honduras: Article 5 Report*. www.icc-cpi.int/iccdocs/otp/SAS-HON-Article_5_Report-Oct2015-ENG.PDF.

IP (Instituto de la Propiedad) Honduras. 2016. *Comunidades Tituladas Período 1993–2016*. geoportalouot.unah.edu.hn/documents/111/link.

Jarquín, Lilliam. 2014. "Ley que regula el Régimen de la Propiedad Comunal: Análisis comparativo del proyecto de ley del Ejecutivo y la propuesta de los Consejos Regionales Autónomos." *Wani Revista del Caribe Nicaragüense* 26: 6–20. revistas.bicu.edu.ni/index.php/wani/article/download/401/398.

Jenkins, James. 2013. "The Indian Wing: Nicaraguan Indians, Native American Activists, and U.S. Foreign Policy." In *Beyond the eagle's shadow: New histories of Latin America's cold war*, eds. Virginia Garrard-Burnett, Mark A. Lawrence, and Julio Moreno. Albuquerque: University of New Mexico Press, 1979–90.

Jetschke, Anja. 2011. *Human rights and state security: Indonesia and the Philippines*. Philadelphia: University of Pennsylvania Press.

Jetschke, Anja, and Andrea Liese. 2013. "The Power of Human Rights a Decade after: From Euphoria to Contestation?" In *The persistent power of human rights: From commitment to compliance*, eds. Thomas Risse-Kappen, Stephen C. Ropp, and Kathryn Sikkink. Cambridge: Cambridge University Press, 26–42.

Johnson, Dominic D., and Monica D. Toft. 2014. "Grounds for War: The Evolution of Territorial Conflict." *International Security* 38 (3): 7–38.

Jung, Courtney. 2008. *The moral force of Indigenous politics: Critical liberalism and the Zapatistas*. Cambridge: Cambridge University Press.

Juris, Jeffrey S. 2008. *Networking futures: The movements against corporate globalization*. Experimental futures. Durham, NC: Duke University Press.

Juris, Jeffrey S., and Alex Khasnabish, eds. 2013. *Insurgent encounters: Transnational activism, ethnography, and the political*. Durham, NC: Duke University Press.

Kaimowitz, David. 2016. Personal correspondence, May 14.

Kashwan, Prakash. 2017. *Democracy in the woods: Environmental conservation and social justice in India, Tanzania, and Mexico*. Oxford: Oxford University Press.

Kashwan, Prakash. 2002. "Amazônia in Environmental Politics." In *Environment and security in the Amazon Basin*, eds. Joseph S. Tulchin and Heather A. Golding. Washington: Woodrow Wilson International Center for Scholars, 31–52.

Keck, Margaret E., and Katherine Sikkink. 1998. *Activists beyond borders: Advocacy networks in international politics*. Ithaca, NY: Cornell University Press.

Khagram, Sanjeev, James V. Riker, and Kathryn Sikkink, eds. 2002. *Restructuring world politics: Transnational social movements, networks, and norms*. Minneapolis: University of Minnesota Press.

Kiser, Edgar, and Joachim Schneider. 1994. "Bureaucracy and Efficiency: An Analysis of Taxation in Early Modern Prussia." *American Sociological Review* 59 (2): 187.

Klinger, Julie M. 2015. "A Historical Geography of Rare Earth Elements: From Discovery to the Atomic Age." *The Extractive Industries and Society* 2 (3): 572–80.

Kohli, Atul. 1997. "The Bell Curve of Ethnic Politics: The Rise and Decline of Self-Determination Movements in India." In *Self-determination and self-administration: A sourcebook*, eds. Wolfgang F. Danspeckgruber and Arthur Watts. Boulder, CO; London: L. Rienner, 309–36.

Kröger, Markus, and Rickard Lalander. n.d. "Ethno-Territorial Rights and the Resource Extraction Boom in Latin America: Do Constitutions Matter?" *Third World Quarterly* 37 (4): 682–702.

Krupa, Christopher. 2015. "Cadastral Politics: Property Wars and State Realism in Highland Ecuador." In *State Theory and Andean Politics: New Approaches to the Study of Rule*, eds. Christopher Krupa and David Nugent. University of Pennsylvania Press, 99–125.

Krupa, Christopher, and David Nugent, eds. 2015. *State theory and Andean politics: New approaches to the study of rule*. Philadelphia: University of Pennsylvania Press.

Kuokkanen, Rauna J. 2019. *Restructuring relations: Indigenous self-determination, governance, and gender*. New York: Oxford University Press.

Kurtz, Marcus J. 2013. *Latin American state building in comparative perspective: Social foundations of institutional order*. Cambridge: Cambridge University Press.

Kymlicka, Will. 1995. *Multicultural citizenship: A liberal theory of minority rights*. Oxford, New York: Clarendon Press; Oxford University Press.

Kymlicka, Will, and Keith G. Banting, eds. 2006. *Multiculturalism and the welfare state: Recognition and redistribution in contemporary democracies*. Oxford: Oxford University Press.

La Noticia Honduras. 2016. "Miles de familias misquitas obtienen títulos de propiedad en La Mosquitia." April 8. lanoticia.hn/economia/miles-de-familias-misquitas-adquieren-titulos-de-propiedad-en-la-mosquitia/.

La Tribuna Honduras. 2016. "Histórica titulación de más de un millón de hectáreas." April 8. www.latribuna.hn/2016/04/08/historica-titulacion-mas-millon-hectareas/.

Lagoutte, Stéphanie, Thomas Gammeltoft-Hansen, and John Cerone, eds. 2016. *Tracing the roles of soft law in human rights*. Oxford: Oxford University Press.

Lakhani, Nina. 2019. "Berta Cáceres Murder: Seven Convicted Men Sentenced to up to 50 Years." *The Guardian*, December 2. www.theguardian.com/world/2019/dec/02/berta-caceres-murder-sentencing.

LandMark. 2017. "LandMark Map." www.landmarkmap.org/.

Leite, Ilka Boaventura. 2015. "The Brazilian Quilombo: 'Race,' Community and Land in Space and Time." *The Journal of Peasant Studies* 42 (6): 1225–40.

Levi, Margaret. 1989. *Of rule and revenue*. Berkeley: University of California Press.

Levitsky, Steven, and Maria Victoria Murillo. 2005. *Argentine democracy: The politics of institutional weakness*. University Park, PA: Pennsylvania State University Press.

Levitsky, Steven, and María V. Murillo. 2009. "Variation in Institutional Strength." *Annual Review of Political Science* 12 (1): 115–33.

Levitsky, Steven, and María V. Murillo. 2013. "Building Institutions on Weak Foundations." *Journal of Democracy* 24 (2): 93–107.

Levitsky, Steven, and María V. Murillo . 2014. "Building Institutions on Weak Foundations: Lessons from Latin America." In *Reflections on uneven democracies: The legacy of Guillermo O'Donnell*, eds. Daniel M. Brinks, Marcelo Leiras and Scott Mainwaring. Baltimore, MD: Johns Hopkins University Press, 189–213.

Levitsky, Steven, and Lucan Way. 2005. "International Linkage and Democratization." *Journal of Democracy* 16 (3): 20–34.

Levitsky, Steven, and Lucan Way. 2010. *Competitive Authoritarianism: Hybrid Regimes after the Cold War*. Cambridge: Cambridge University Press.

Li, Tania M. 2000. "Articulating Indigenous Identity in Indonesia: Resource Politics and the Tribal Slot." *Comparative Studies in Society and History* 42 (1): 149–79.

Li, Tania M. 2001. "Masyarakat Adat, Difference, and the Limits of Recognition in Indonesia's Forest Zone." *Modern Asian Studies* 35 (03): 645–76.

Li, Tania M. 2007a. "Adat in Central Sulawesi: Contemporary Deployments." In *The revival of tradition in Indonesian politics: The deployment of adat from colonialism to indigenism*, eds. Jamie S. Davidson and David Henley. London: Routledge, 337–70.

Li, Tania M. 2007b. *The will to improve: Governmentality, development, and the practice of politics*. Durham, NC; London: Duke University Press.

Li, Tania M. 2014. *Land's end: Capitalist relations on an indigenous frontier.* Durham, NC; London: Duke University Press.

Lieberman, Evan S. 2005. "Nested Analysis as a Mixed-Method Strategy for Comparative Research." *American Political Science Review* 99 (3): 435–52.

Lima, Antonio Carlos de Souza. 1995. *Um grande cerco de paz: Poder tutelar, intimidade e formação do estado no Brasil.* Petrópolis: Vozes.

Lima, Antonio Carlos de Souza. 2005. "Os povos indígenas na invenção do Brasil: Na luta pela construção do respeito à pluralidade." In *Enciclopédia da brasilidade: auto-estima em verde amarelo,* ed. Carlos Lessa. Rio de Janeiro: Casa da Palavra Produção Editorial, 218–31.

Lima, Antonio Carlos de Souza. 2009. *As órbitas do sítio: Subsídios ao estudo da política indigenista no Brasil, 1910-1967.* Rio de Janeiro RJ: Contra Capa; LACED.

Lima, Antonio Carlos de Souza. 2010. "Poder tutelar y formación del Estado en Brasil: Notas a partir de la creación del Servicio de Protección a los Indios y Localización de Trabajadores Nacionales." *Desacatos* 33: 53–66.

López, Luis E., and Francisco Sapón. 2011. *Recreando la educación intercultural bilingüe en América Latina: Trabajos presentados en el IX Congreso Latinoamericano de Educación Intercultural Bilingüe.* Guatemala, Guatemala: Ministerio de Educación Viceministerio de Educación Bilingüe Intercultural.

Lorío, Gema. 2014. *Saneamiento en territorios indígenas de Nicaragua: Un proceso en construcción dentro de la Autonomía Regional: el caso de Tuahka.* Vol. 50. *Cuaderno de investigación.* Managua: Nitlapan.

Lott, Joe L., Susan Gardner, and Daniel A. Powers. 2009. "Doctoral Student Attrition in the Stem Fields: An Exploratory Event History Analysis." *Journal of College Student Retention: Research, Theory & Practice* 11 (2): 247–66.

Lucero, José A. 2013. "Ambivalent Multiculturalism: Perversity, Futility, and Jeopardy in Latin America." In *Latin America's multicultural movements: The struggle between communitarianism, autonomy, and human rights,* eds. Todd A. Eisenstadt, Michael S. Danielson, Moisés Jaime Bailón Corres, and Carlos Sorroza Polo. Oxford: Oxford University Press, 18–39.

Lund, Christian, and Michael Eilenberg, eds. 2017. *Rule and rupture: State formation through the production of property and citizenship. Development and change book series.* Chichester, UK; Hoboken, NJ: John Wiley & Sons.

Lutz, Ellen L., and Kathryn Sikkink. 2000. "International Human Rights Law and Practice in Latin America." *International Organization* 54 (3): 633–59.

Lynch, Gabrielle. 2012. "Becoming Indigenous in the Pursuit of Justice: The African Commission on Human and Peoples' Rights and the Endorois." *African Affairs* 111 (442): 24–45.

Mahoney, James, and Kathleen A. Thelen. 2010. *Explaining institutional change: Ambiguity, agency, and power.* Cambridge: Cambridge University Press.

Mahoney, James, and Kathleen A. Thelen, eds. 2015. *Advances in comparative-historical analysis. Strategies for social inquiry.* New York: Cambridge University Press.

Majumder, Sarasij. 2010. "The Nano Controversy: Peasant Identities, the Land Question and Neoliberal Industrialization in Marxist West Bengal, India." *Journal of Emerging Knowledge on Emerging Markets* 2: 41–55.

Malkin, Elisabeth, and Alberto Arce. 2016. "Berta Cáceres, Indigenous Activist, Is Killed in Honduras." *The New York Times,* March 3. www.nytimes.com/2016/03/04/world/americas/berta-caceres-indigenous-activist-is-killed-in-honduras.html

Mamdani, Mahmood. 1996. *Citizen and subject: Contemporary Africa and the legacy of late colonialism.* Princeton, NJ; Chichester, UK: Princeton University Press.

Mann, Michael. 1986–2013. *The sources of social power.* Cambridge: Cambridge University Press.

Marques, Adriana Aparecida. 2007. "Amazônia pensamento e presença militar." Doutorado. Universidade de São Paulo.

Martí i Puig, Salvador. 2007. *Pueblos indígenas y política en América Latina: El reconocimiento de sus derechos y el impacto de sus demandas a inicios del siglo XXI.* Barcelona: Fundació CIDOB.

McSweeney, Kendra, and Z. Pearson. 2014. "Prying Native People from Native Lands: Narco Business in Honduras." *NACLA Report on the Americas* 46 (4): 7–12.
McSweeney, Kendra, Nielsen, E. A., Taylor, M. J., Wrathall, D. J., Pearson, Z., Wang, O., and Plumb, S. T. 2014. "Drug Policy as Conservation Policy: Narco-Deforestation." *Science* 343 (6170), 489–90. doi.org/10.1126/science.1244082.
Mechri Adler, Zohra. 2000. "Mouvement paysan, réforme agraire et politique agricoles au Nicaragua 1979–1990." Doctoral thesis. Paris: Université de la Sorbonne Nouvelle.
Meirelles Filho, João C. 2006. *O livro de ouro da Amazônia*. 5th ed. *Livro de ouro*. Rio de Janeiro: Ediouro.
Meinzen-Dick, Ruth. 2011. "Property Rights for Poverty Reduction." In Poor poverty: The impoverishment of analysis, measurement, and policy, eds. Jomo Kwame Sundaram and Anis Chowdhury. London: Bloomsbury Academic, 185–96.
Mejía, Thelma. 2010. "Honduras actúa para evitar convertirse en "narcoestado". *Inter Press Service (IPS) Agencia de Noticias*, October 22. www.ipsnoticias.net/2010/10/honduras-actua-para-evitar-convertirse-en-narcoestado/.
Mendoza, Jose E. 2014. "Encuentran en Honduras plano de submarino hecho por el cartel de Sinaloa." *La Prensa (Honduras)*, June 9. www.laprensa.hn/migrantes/hondurenosenestadosunidos/717390-98/encuentran-en-honduras-plano-de-sbmarino-hecho-por-el-cartel-de-sinaloa.
Mendoza, Rene, and Klaus Kuhnekath. 2005. "Conflictos en la costa: Expresión de la transnacionalización de conflictos sociales en Centroamérica." *Wani Revista del Caribe Nicaragüense* 41: 10–26.
Merlan, Francesca. 2005. "Indigenous Movements in Australia." *Annual Review of Anthropology* 34: 473–94.
Meyer, Peter J. 2010. *Honduran political crisis: June 2009–January 2010*. Congressional Research Service. fas.org/sgp/crs/row/R41064.pdf.
Meza, Laura E. 2009. "Mapuche Struggles for Land and the Role of Private Protected Areas in Chile." *Journal of Latin American Geography* 8 (1): 149–63.
Migdal, Joel S. 1988. *Strong societies and weak states: State-society relations and state capabilities in the Third World*. Princeton, NJ; Guildford: Princeton University Press.
Migdal, Joel S., Atul Kohli, and Vivienne Shue, eds. 1994. *State power and social forces: Domination and transformation in the Third World*. Cambridge: Cambridge University Press.
Ministério da Defesa (Brazil). Portaria No. 322-EME, "Aprova a Diretriz de Orientação aos Comandos Miliares de Área para o Emprego da Força Terrestre na Faixa de Fronteira." December 8. www.sgex.eb.mil.br/sg8/006_outras_publicacoes/01_diretrizes/04_estado-maior_do_exercito/port_n_322_eme_08dez2015.html.
Ministério da Defesa (Brazil). 2003. Portaria No. 983/DPE/SPEAI/MD, "Aprova a Diretriz para o relacionamento das Forças Armadas com as comunidades indígenas." October 17. www.gov.br/defesa/pt-br/arquivos/File/legislacao/emcfa/portarias/983a_2003.pdf.
Ministério da Defesa (Brazil). 2023. Portaria EME/C Ex No. 946, "Aprova a Diretriz para o relacionamento do Exército Brasileiro com as comunidades indígenas." static.poder360.com.br/2023/01/portaria-indigenas-31jan2023.pdf.
Miralda Bulnes, Danira. 2012. *Latwan Laka Danh Takisa: Los Pueblos Originarios y la Guerra de Baja Intensidad en el Territorio de La Moskitia, República de Honduras*. Tegucigalpa: Instituto Hondureño de Antropología e Historia.
Moyo, Sam. 2005. "The Land Question and the Peasantry in Southern Africa." In *Politics and Social Movements in a Hegemonic World: Lessons from Africa, Asia and Latin America*, eds. Luis Maira, Gladys Lechini de Alvarez, and Atilio Borón. Buenos Aires: CLACSO.
Newman, Lucia, 2018. "Nicaragua Unrest: Ruling Party Accused of Land Grabs." *Al-Jazeera*, August 2. www.aljazeera.com/news/2018/08/nicaragua-unrest-ruling-party-accused-land-grabs-180802094010735.html.
McCann. 1994. "Honduras: Indigenous Speak Out." *Envío* (158). www.revistaenvio.org/articulo/1800.

McCarthy, John. 2000. "The Changing Regime: Forest Property and Reformasi in Indonesia." *Development and Change* 31 (1): 91–129.

Milliken, William. 2006. "Conservation, Economics, Traditional Knowledge, and the Yanomami: Implications and Benefits for Whom?" In *Human impacts on Amazonia: The role of traditional ecological knowledge in conservation and development*, eds. Darrell A. Posey and Michael J. Balick. New York: Columbia University Press, 238–47.

Minerva Initiative (Minerva Initiative Grant for University-Led Research from U.S. Department of Defense). 2013. "Abstract: The Human Geography of Resilience and Change." minerva.dtic.mil.

Minerva Initiative (Minerva Initiative Grant for University-Led Research from U.S. Department of Defense). 2016. *Report: Policy Inputs to Honduran Government, Indigenous Federations, and NGOs.* Trans. University of Kansas. www.dtic.mil/dtic/tr/fulltext/u2/1010210.pdf.

Miranda Aburto, Wilfredo. 2016. "Corrupción y Muerte en Territorio Miskito." *Confidencial*, June 6. www.confidencial.com.ni/corrupcion-muerte-territorio-miskito.

Miranda, Wando D. 2012. "Defesa E Exército Na Amazônia Brasileira: Um estudo sobre a constituição dos Pelotões Especiais de Fronteira." Universidade Federal do Para.

Miroff, Nick. 2016. "A Killing in Honduras Shows That It May Be the World's Deadliest Country for Environmentalists." *The Washington Post*, March 3. www.washingtonpost.com/news/worldviews/wp/2016/03/03/prize-winning-environmentalist-berta-caceres-killed-in-honduras/?utm_term=.3c92adb4f035.

Mollett, Sharlene. 2013. "Mapping deception: The politics of mapping Miskito and Garifuna space in Honduras." *Annals of the Association of American Geographers* 103 (5): 1227–41.

Moloney, Anastasia. 2016. "Violent 2015 Sees Three Environmental Activists Killed Each Week." *Reuters*, June 19. www.reuters.com/article/us-global-landrights-violence-idUSKCN0Z601U.

Monachon, David, and Noémi Gonda. 2011. *Liberalization of ownership versus indigenous territories in the North of Nicaragua: The case of the Chorotegas.* Rome: International Land Coalition.

Moniaga, Sandra. 2007. "From Bumiputera to Masyarakat Adat: A Long and Confusing Journey." In *The revival of tradition in Indonesian politics: The deployment of adat from colonialism to indigenism*, eds. Jamie S. Davidson and David Henley. London: Routledge, 275–94.

Montez Rugama, Hatzel. 2015. "Acusan y destituyen a diputado misquito." *El Nuevo Diario*, September 22. www.elnuevodiario.com.ni/nacionales/371232-diputado-rivera-pierde-inmunidad

Moog Rodrigues, Maria G. 2003. *Global environmentalism and local politics: Transnational advocacy networks in Brazil, Ecuador, and India.* SUNY series in global environmental policy. Albany, NY: State University of New York Press.

Moran, PAP. "Notes on Continuous Stochastic Phenomena." *Biometrika* 37 (1/2): 17–23.

Morgan, R. 2004. "Advancing Indigenous Rights at the United Nations: Strategic Framing and Its Impact on the Normative Development of International Law." *Social & Legal Studies* 13 (4): 481–500.

Murtazshvili, Jennifer, and Ilia Murtazashvili. 2017. "Land, the State, and War: Property Institutions and Political Order in Afghanistan." Manuscript in the possession of the author.

Mwangi, Esther. 2007. *Socioeconomic change and land use in Africa: The transformation of property rights in Maasailand.* Basingstoke, UK: Palgrave Macmillan.

Nasasra, Mansour. 2017. *The Naqab bedouins: A century of politics and resistance.* New York: Columbia University Press.

Nascimento, Durbens M. 2006. "Projeto Calha Norte: A Amazônia segundo a política de defesa nacional." In *Amazonia: E defesa nacional*, ed. Celso Castro. Brasil: FGV Editora, 98–118.

Naseemullah, Adnan, and Paul Staniland. 2016. "Indirect Rule and Varieties of Governance." *Governance* 29 (1): 13–30.

Nietschmann, Bernard. 1995. "Conservación, Autodeterminación y el área Protegida Costa Miskita, Nicaragua." *Mesoamérica* 16 (29): 1–55.
North, Douglass C. 1990. *Institutions, institutional change and economic performance. Political economy of institutions and decisions.* Cambridge: Cambridge University Press.
North, Douglass C., and Robert Paul Thomas. 1976. *The rise of the western world: A new economic history.* United States: Cambridge University Press.
North, Douglass C., John J. Wallis, and Barry R. Weingast. 2009. *Violence and social orders: A conceptual framework for interpreting recorded human history.* Cambridge; New York: Cambridge University Press.
Nugent, Paul. 2010. "States and Social Contracts in Africa." *New Left Review* 63: 35–68.
Nuwer, Rachel. 2016. "The Rising Murder Count of Environmental Activists." *The New York Times*, June 20. www.nytimes.com/2016/06/21/science/berta-caceres-environmental-activists-murders.html.
Oakland Institute, The. 2020. *Nicaragua's Failed Revolution: The Indigenous Struggle for Saneamiento.* www.oaklandinstitute.org/nicaragua-failed-revolution-indigenous-struggle-saneamiento
O'Brien, Robert. 2000. *Contesting global governance: Multilateral economic institutions and global social movements.* Cambridge: Cambridge University Press.
O'Donnell, Guillermo. 1993. "On the State, Democratization and Some Conceptual Problems: A Latin American View with Glances at Some Postcommunist Countries." *World Development* 21 (8): 1355–69.
O'Donnell, Guillermo, Juan E. Méndez, and Paulo S. d. M. S. Pinheiro, eds., 1999. *The (un) rule of law and the underprivileged in Latin America.* Notre Dame, IN: University of Notre Dame Press.
OECD (Organisation for Economic Co-operation and Development), and World Bank. 2012. *Integrating human rights into development: Donor approaches, experiences and challenges.* Washington, D.C.: World Bank.
Offen, Karl H. 2003. "Narrating Place and Identity, or Mapping Miskitu Land Claims in Northeastern Nicaragua." *Human Organization* 62 (4): 382–92.
Ohland, Klaudine, and Robin Schneider, eds. 1983. *National revolution and indigenous identity: The conflict between Sandinists and Mískito Indians on Nicaragua's Atlantic Coast.* Copenhagen: IWGIA.
Olesen, Thomas, ed. 2011. *Power and transnational activism.* London: Routledge.
Olguín Martínez, Gabriela, and ILO (International Labour Organization). 2006. *Estudio base sobre las condiciones de vida de los pueblos indígenas del Pacífico, centro y norte de Nicaragua.* San José: OIT.
Ondetti, Gabriel. 2008. *Land, Protest, and Politics: The landless movement and the struggle for agrarian reform in Brazil.* University Park: Pennsylvania State University Press.
Orellana, Xiomara. 2014. "El poder de narcos 15 comunidades de La Mosquitia de Honduras." *La Prensa (Honduras)*, March 10. www.laprensa.hn/honduras/apertura/562509-98/en-poder-de-narcos-15-comunidades-de-la-mosquitia-de-honduras.
Ortega Hegg, Manuel, Malene Nissen Daza, and Marcelina Castillo Venerio. 2006. *Diversidad, identidades y relaciones interétnicas en Nicaragua la Costa Caribe y el pacífico: Conocimientos y percepciones interregionales.* Managua: Universidad Centroamericana. repositorio.cnu.edu.ni/Record/RepoUCA91/Details.
Ostrom, Elinor. 1990. *Governing the commons: The evolution of institutions for collective action. The political economy of institutions and decisions.* Cambridge, New York: Cambridge University Press.
Ostrom, Elinor. 2003. "How Types of Goods and Property Rights Jointly Affect Collective Action." *Journal of Theoretical Politics* 15 (3): 239–70.
Ostrom, Elinor. 2005. *Understanding institutional diversity.* Princeton paperbacks. Princeton, NJ; Woodstock: Princeton University Press.

Ostrom, Elinor, and Charlotte Hess. 2007. "Private and Common Property Rights." Research Paper No. 2008-11-01. Indiana University, Bloomington: School of Public & Environmental Affairs, SSRN: dx.doi.org/10.2139/ssrn.1936062

Pacheco, Diego. 2009. "Problems Undermining the Titling and Tenure Security of Common Property Lands: The Case of Indigenous People of Bolivia's Lowlands." In *Legalising land rights: Local practices, state responses and tenure security in Africa, Asia and Latin America*. Law, governance, and development, eds. Janine M. Ubink, A. J. Hoekema, and Willem Assies. Leiden: Leiden University Press, 325–54.

Palencia, Gustavo, and Enrique Pretel. 2016. "Environmental and Indigenous Rights Leader Murdered in Honduras." *Reuters*, March 3. www.reuters.com/article/us-honduras-crime-idUSKCN0W521R.

Pelcastre, Julieta. 2015. "Cooperation between Honduras and the U.S. Proves Positive." Diálogo Revista Militar Digital. Forum of the Americas. dialogo-americas.com/en/articles/cooperation-between-honduras-and-us-proves-positive.

Peluso, Nancy L. 2004. "Weapons of the Wild: Strategic Deployment of Violence and Wildness in Borneo Rainforests of Indonesia." In *In search of the rainforest. New ecologies for the twenty-first century*, eds. Candace Slater, Arturo Escobar, Dianne Rocheleau, and Suzana Sawyer. Durham, NC: Duke University Press, 204–45.

Pfeifer, Hazel. 2020. "Amazon Tribes Are Using Drones to Track Deforestation in the Brazilian Rainforest." *CNN*, September 1. www.cnn.com/2020/09/01/americas/amazon-drones-brazil-deforestation-cte-spc-intl

Pineda, Baron L. 2006. *Shipwrecked identities: Navigating race on Nicaragua's Mosquito Coast*. New Brunswick, NJ; London: Rutgers University Press.

Piper, Nicola, and Anders Uhlin, eds. 2004. *Transnational activism in Asia: Problems of power and democracy*. London: Routledge.

Plant, Roger and Soren Hvalkof. 2001. *Land Titling and Indigenous Peoples*. Sustainable Development Department Technical Papers Series IND-109 Washington, D.C.: Inter-American Development Bank.

Ponte Iglesias, Maria Teresa. 2013. "Derechos Humanos y Pueblos Indígenas de Venezuela." *Dereito* 22: 499–531.

Posey, Darrell A., and Michael J. Balick, eds. 2006. *Human impacts on Amazonia: The role of traditional ecological knowledge in conservation and development*. New York: Columbia University Press.

Posner, Eric A. 2014. *The twilight of human rights law*. Oxford; New York: Oxford University Press.

Postero, Nancy G. 2007. *Now we are citizens: Indigenous politics in postmulticultural Bolivia*. Stanford, CA: Stanford University Press.

Postero, Nancy G. 2013. "Bolivia's Challenge to 'Colonial Neoliberalism.'" In *Neoliberalism, interrupted: Social change and contested governance in contemporary Latin America*, eds. Mark Goodale and Nancy G. Postero. Stanford, CA: Stanford University Press, 25–52.

Powers, Daniel A. 2013. *Event history analysis: University of Michigan-Peking University*. University of Texas at Austin. n.p.

Presidency (Brazil). 1989. "Decreto No. 97.526, de 16 de Fevereiro de 1989. Homologa a demarcação administrativa da Terra Indígena YANOMAMI, que menciona, no Estado do Amazonas." www2.camara.leg.br/legin/fed/decret/1989/decreto-97526-16-fevereiro-1989-448498-publicacaooriginal-1-pe.html.

Presidency (Guatemala). 2015. *Informe Tercer Año de Gobierno 2014-2015*. Ciudad de Guatemala: Gobierno de Guatemala Presidencia.

Presidency (Honduras). 2016. *Otorgadas por Gobierno del presidente Hernández: Más de 17,500 familias de La Mosquitia beneficiadas con titulación de un millón de hectáreas de tierra*. Tegucigalpa. www.elinformativo.hn/archivos/39266.

Proceso Digital. 2016. "Presidente Hernández entrega títulos de más de un millón de hectáreas en La Mosquitia." April 8. proceso.hn/presidente-hernandez-entrega-titulos-de-mas-de-un-millon-de-hectareas-en-la-mosquitia/.

Puentes Riaño, Astrid, and AIDA. 2016. "Losing Berta Cáceres: the Breaking Point in the Struggle against Impunity." AIDA. www.aida-americas.org/blog/losing-berta-caceres-breaking-point-struggle-against-impunity.
Rabben, Linda. 2004. *Brazil's Indians and the onslaught of civilization: The Yanomami and the Kayapo*. Seattle: University of Washington Press.
Ramírez, William. 1982. "The Imperialist Threat and the Indigenous Problem in Nicaragua." In *National revolution and indigenous identity: The conflict between Sandinists and Miskito Indians on Nicaragua's Atlantic Coast*, eds. Klaudine Ohland and Robin Schneider. Copenhagen: IWGIA, 235–68.
Ramos, Alcida R. 1978. *The Yanoama in Brazil 1979: Yanomami Indian Park, proposal and justification*. Copenhagen: IWGIA.
Ramos, Alcida R. 1998. *Indigenism: Ethnic politics in Brazil*. Madison; London: University of Wisconsin Press.
Ramos, Alcida R. 2003. "Comments on Adam Kuper, 'The Return of the Native.'" *Current Anthropology* 44 (3): 397–98.
Ramos, Alcida Rita. 2008. "O Paraíso Ameaçado: Sabedoria Yanomami versus Insensatez Predatória." *Antípoda: Revista de Antropología y Arqueología* 7: 101–17.
Rauch, James E., and Peter B. Evans. 2000. "Bureaucratic Structure and Bureaucratic Performance in Less Developed Countries." *Journal of Public Economics* 75 (1): 49–71.
Registro de Información Catastral (RIC) Guatemala. 2011. *Memoria de Labores*. Guatemala.
Reyes-García, Victoria, Jaime Paneque-Gálvez, Patrick Bottazzi, Ana C Luz, Maximilien Gueze, Manuel J Macía, Martí Orta-Martínez, and Pablo Pacheco. 2014. "Indigenous Land Reconfiguration and Fragmented Institutions: A Historical Political Ecology of Tsimane' Lands (Bolivian Amazon)." *Journal of Rural Studies* 34: 282–91.
Riascos de la Peña, Juan Carlos. 2008. "Caracterización de las áreas indígenas y comunitarias para la conservación en Bolivia, Ecuador y Colombia." Informe Presentado para el Proyecto: Understanding and Promoting Community Conserved Areas (CCAS) for Conservation of Biodiversity and Sustainable Use of Natural Resources in Andean Region. IUCN.
Ribeiro, Darcy. 1970. *Os Índios e a civilização: A integração das populações indígenas no Brasil moderno*. Rio de Janeiro: Civilização Brasileira.
Ribot, Jesse C. 1999. "Decentralisation, Participation, and Accountability in Sahelian Forestry: Legal Instruments of Political-Administrative Control." *Africa* 69 (01): 23–65.
Ricardo, Carlos A. 1981–2016. *Povos Indígenas no Brasil*. Instituto Socioambiental and Centro Ecumênico de Documentação e Informação. www.socioambiental.org.
Rice, Roberta. 2012. *The new politics of protest: Indigenous mobilization in Latin America's neoliberal era*. Tucson: University of Arizona Press.
Riker, James V. 2002. "NGOs, Transnational Networks, International Donor Agencies, and the Prospects for Democratic Governance in Indonesia." In *Restructuring world politics: Transnational social movements, networks, and norms*, eds. Sanjeev Khagram, James V. Riker, and Kathryn Sikkink. Minneapolis: University of Minnesota Press, 181–205.
Risse-Kappen, Thomas. 2011. *Governance without a state? Policies and politics in areas of limited statehood*. New York: Columbia University Press.
Risse-Kappen, Thomas, Steve C. Ropp, and Kathryn Sikkink, eds. 1999. *The power of human rights: International norms and domestic change*. Cambridge: Cambridge University Press.
Risse-Kappen, Thomas, Steve C. Ropp, and Kathryn Sikkink, eds. 2013. *The persistent power of human rights: From commitment to compliance*. Cambridge: Cambridge University Press.
Rivero, María I. 2016. *Press Release No. 024/2016: IACHR condemns the killing of Berta Cáceres in Honduras*. Inter-American Commission of Human Rights: Media Center. www.oas.org/en/iachr/media_center/preleases/2016/024.asp.
Rodríguez-Garavito, César A., and Luis C. Arenas. 2005. "Indigenous Rights, Transnational Activism, and Legal Mobilization: The Struggle of the U'Wa People in Colombia." In *Law and globalization from below: Towards a cosmopolitan legality*, eds. Boaventura d. S. Santos and César A. Rodríguez Garavito. Cambridge: Cambridge University Press, 241–66.

Rodríguez-Piñero, Luis. 2005. *Indigenous peoples, postcolonialism, and international law: The ILO regime (1919-1989)*. Oxford; New York: Oxford University Press.
Rohter, Larry. 2002. "A New Intrusion of Soldiers, Threatens an Amazon Tribe." *The New York Times*, October 1. www.nytimes.com/2002/10/01/world/a-new-intrusion-of-soldiers-threat ens-an-amazon-tribe.html.
Roldán Ortega, Roque. 2000. *Legalidad y derechos étnicos en la Costa Atlántica de Nicaragua*. Nicaragua: Programa de Apoyo Institucional a los Consejos Regionales y las Administraciones Regionales de la Costa Atlántica RAAN-ASDI-RAAS.
Roldán Ortega, Roque. 2002. "La Demarcación de Tierras de la Costa en el Contexto Latinoamericano." *Wani Revista del Caribe Nicaragüense* 28: 6-15. revistas.bicu.edu.ni/ index.php/wani/issue/view/53/showToc.
Romero, Simon. 2012. "Brazil Sending More Troops to Guard Amazon borders." *The New York Times*, May 3. www.nytimes.com/2012/05/04/world/americas/brazil-sending-more-tro ops-to-guard-amazon-borders.html
RRI (Rights and Resources Initiative). 2014. "Tenure Data Tool." 2014. rightsandresources. org/en/work-impact/tenure-data-tool/#.WTbKUWjyvIU.
Rueda-Saiz, Pablo. 2017. "Indigenous Autonomy in Colombia: State-Building Processes and Multiculturalism." *Global Constitutionalism* 6 (2): 265-97.
Ruhl, J. M. 2011. "Political Corruption in Central America: Assessment and Explanation." *Latin American Politics and Society* 53 (1): 33-58.
SAE (Secretaria de Assuntos Estratégicos). 2012. *Seminário de Segurança da Amazônia (2011: Manaus)*. Brasília: Presidency.
Sandbrook, Richard. 2014. *Reinventing the left in the global South: The politics of the possible*. Cambridge, UK: Cambridge University Press.
Sangaji, Arianto. 2007. "The Masyarakat Adat Movement in Indonesia: A Critical Insider's View." In *The revival of tradition in Indonesian politics: The deployment of adat from colonialism to indigenism*, eds. Jamie S. Davidson and David Henley. London: Routledge, 319-36.
Santos, Boaventura d. S., and César A. Rodríguez Garavito, eds. 2005. *Law and globalization from below: Towards a cosmopolitan legality*. Cambridge: Cambridge University Press.
Sartori, Giovanni. 1970. "Concept Misformation in Comparative Politics." *American Political Science Review* 64 (4): 1033-53.
Sarukhán, José, and Jorge Larson. 2001. "When the Commons become Less Tragic: Land Tenure, Social Organization, and Fair Trade in Mexico." In *Protecting the commons: A framework for resource management in the Americas*," eds. Joanna Burger, Elinor Ostrom, Richard Norgaard, David Policansky, and Bernard Goldstein. Washington: Island Press, 45-69.
Sawyer, Suzana, and Edmund T. Gomez. 2014. *The politics of resource extraction: Indigenous peoples, multinational corporations and the state*. Basingstoke: Palgrave Macmillan.
Serva, Leão. 1989. "Sarney destina a mesma terra a Exército e índios." Folha de São Paulo, September 27. documentacao.socioambiental.org/noticias/anexo_noticia/50265_20190904_ 100924.PDF.
Sieder, Rachel. 2002. *Multiculturalism in Latin America: Indigenous rights, diversity and democracy*. Basingstoke: Palgrave Macmillan.
Sieder, Rachel. 2010. "Legal Cultures in the (Un)Rule of Law: Indigenous Rights and Juridification in Post-conflict Guatemala." In *Cultures of legality: Judicialization and political activism in Latin America*, eds. Javier Couso, Alexandra Huneeus, and Rachel Sieder. Cambridge: Cambridge University Press, 161-81.
Sikkink, Kathryn. 2002. "Transnational Advocacy Networks and the Social Construction of Legal Rules." In *Global prescriptions: The production, exportation, and importation of a new legal orthodoxy*, eds. Yves Dezalay and Bryant G. Garth. Ann Arbor: University of Michigan Press, 37-64.
Sikkink, Kathryn. 2005. "Patterns of Dynamic Multilevel Governance and the Insider-Outsider Coalition." In *Transnational protest and global activism. People, passions and power*, eds. Donatella Della Porta and Sidney G. Tarrow. Lanham, MD; Oxford: Rowman & Littlefield, 151-73.

Sikkink, Kathryn. 2011. *The justice cascade: How human rights prosecutions are changing world politics*. New York; London: W.W. Norton.
Silva, Eduardo. 2009. *Challenging neoliberalism in Latin America*. Cambridge studies in contentious politics. Cambridge: Cambridge University Press.
Silva, Eduardo. 2015. "Indigenous Peoples' Movements, Developments, and Politics in Ecuador and Bolivia." In *Handbook of social movements across Latin America*. Handbooks of sociology and social research, eds. Paul Almeida and Allen Cordero. Dordrecht: Springer, 131–44.
Silva, Gutemberg de Vilhena. 2008. "A Fronteira Política: Alguns apontamentos sobre este tema clássico." *Revista ACTA Geográfica* 2 (4): 7–15.
Simmons, Beth A. 1998. "Compliance with International Agreements." *Annual Review of Political Science* 1 (1): 75–93.
Simmons, Beth A. 2009. *Mobilizing for human rights: International law in domestic politics*. New York; Cambridge: Cambridge University Press.
SCGG (Secretaría de Coordinación General de Gobierno). 2015. *Consolidado de Propuestas de Proyectos del Gobierno Central para el Departamento de Gracias a Dios*. Document in the possession of the author.
Schmidt, Blake, and Marc Lacey. 2009. "An Independence Claim in Nicaragua." *The New York Times*, June 9. www.nytimes.com/2009/06/10/world/americas/10nicaragua.html.
Schwarz, Rolf. 2002. "Human Rights Discourse and Practice as Crisis Management: Insights from the Algerian case." *The Journal of North African Studies* 7 (2): 57–85.
Schwarz, Rolf. 2004. "The Paradox of Sovereignty, Regime Type and Human Rights Compliance." *The International Journal of Human Rights* 8 (2): 199–215.
Scott, James C. 1998. *Seeing like a state: How certain schemes to improve the human condition have failed*. New Haven, CT: Yale University Press.
Scott, James C. 2009. *The art of not being governed: An anarchist history of upland Southeast Asia*. New Haven, CT: Yale University Press.
Serrano Alfonso, Alex Garcia, and Al Jazeera America. 2015. "Titanic Canal Project Divides Nicaragua: Critics Say World's Largest-Ever Engineering Endeavor Marks New Era of Colonization." April 6. www.projects.aljazeera.com/2015/04/nicaragua-canal.
SGB/CPRM (Serviço Geológico do Brasil/Companhia de Pesquisa de Recursos Minerais). 2016. GeoSGB. geoportal.sgb.gov.br/geosgb/.
Shoichet, Catherine E., James Griffiths, and Dakota Flournoy. 2016. "Berta Cáceres, Honduran Activist, Killed." *CNN*, March 4. www.cnn.com/2016/03/03/americas/honduras-activist-berta-caceres-killed/index.html.
Sing' Oei, Korir A., and Jared Shepherd. 2010. "'In Land We Trust': The Endorois' Communication and the Quest for Indigenous Peoples' Rights in Africa." *Buffalo Human Rights Law Review* 16: 57.
Skocpol, Theda. 1979. *States and social revolutions: A comparative analysis of France, Russia and China*. Cambridge: Cambridge University Press.
Slack, Keith. 2009. "Digging Out from Neoliberalism: Responses to Environmental (Mis)governance of the Mining Sector in Latin America." In Beyond neoliberalism in Latin America? Societies and politics at the crossroads, eds. John Burdick, Philip Oxhorn, and Kenneth M. Roberts. New York: Palgrave Macmillan, 117–34.
Slater, Candace, Arturo Escobar, Dianne Rocheleau, and Suzana Sawyer, eds. 2004. *In search of the rain forest*. North Carolina: Duke University Press.
Slater, Dan. 2010. *Ordering power: Contentious politics and authoritarian leviathans in Southeast Asia*. Cambridge University Press.
Slater, Dan, and Diana Kim. 2015. "Standoffish States: Nonliterate Leviathans in Southeast Asia." *TRaNS: Trans-Regional and -National Studies of Southeast Asia* 3 (1): 25–44.
Smith, Jackie G., Charles Chatfield, and Ron Pagnucco, eds. 1997. *Transnational social movements and global politics: Solidarity beyond the state*. Syracuse, NY: Syracuse University Press.
Snyder, Richard. 2001. "Scaling Down: The Subnational Comparative Method." *Studies in Comparative International Development* 36 (1): 93–110.

St Germain, Jill. 2001. *Indian treaty-making policy in the United States and Canada, 1867–1877*. Lincoln: University of Nebraska Press.

Stahler-Sholk, Richard, Harry E Vanden, and Marc Becker. 2008. *Rethinking Latin American social movements: Radical action from below*. Lanham: Rowman and Littlefield.

Staniland, Paul. 2012. "States, Insurgents, and Wartime Political Orders." *Perspectives on Politics* 10 (02): 243–64.

Stavenhagen, Rodolfo. 2013. *The Emergence of Indigenous Peoples*. Berlin: Springer.

Stocks, Anthony. 2005. "Too Much for too Few: Problems of Indigenous Land Rights in Latin America." *Annual Review of Anthropology* 34: 85–104

Sullivan, LaShandra. 2013. "Identity, Territory and Land Conflict in Brazil." *Development and Change* 44 (2): 451–71.

Survival International. 1991. *Yanomami: Survival Campaign*. London: Survival for Tribal Peoples.

Survival International. 2000. *Action*. London: Survival.

Summers, James. 2013. *Peoples and international law*. Leiden: Brill.

Tarrow, Sidney G. 2005. *The new transnational activism. Cambridge studies in contentious politics*. Cambridge: Cambridge University Press.

Tarrow, Sidney G. 2011. *Power in movement: Social movements and contentious Politics* (3rd ed). New York: Cambridge University Press.

Tarrow, Sidney G., and Doug McAdam. 2005. "Scale Shift in Transnational Contention." In *Transnational protest and global activism. People, passions and power*, eds. Donatella Della Porta and Sidney G. Tarrow. Lanham, MD: Rowman & Littlefield, 121–50.

The Economist. 2017. "Enemies Wanted: The Brazilian Army is Turning into a de facto Police Force." July 6. www.economist.com/news/americas/21724839-its-plodding-infantry-are-ill-suited-repel-threats-natural-resources-brazilian-army.

The Guardian. 2016. "UN Envoy Warns of Environmental Activist Murder 'Epidemic.'" *The Guardian*, March 18. www.theguardian.com/environment/2016/mar/18/un-envoy-warns-of-environmental-activist-epidemic.

Thornberry, Patrick. 2005. *Indigenous peoples and human rights*. Manchester: Manchester University Press.

Tilly, Charles. 1985. "War Making and State Making in Organized Crime." In *Bringing the state back in*, eds. Peter B. Evans, Dietrich Rueschemeyer, and Theda Skocpol. Cambridge: Cambridge University Press, 169–86.

Transparency International. 1995–2016. "Corruption Perception Index." www.transparency.org/research/cpi/overview.

Trejo, Guillermo. 2012. *Popular movements in autocracies: Religion, repression, and indigenous collective action in Mexico*. New York: Cambridge University Press.

Tulchin, Joseph S., and Heather A. Golding, eds. 2002. *Environment and security in the Amazon Basin*. Washington, DC: Woodrow Wilson International Center for Scholars.

Tyson, Adam D. 2010. *Decentralization and adat revivalism in Indonesia: The politics of becoming indigenous*. London: Routledge.

Ubink, Janine M., A. J. Hoekema, and Willem Assies, eds. 2009. *Legalising land rights: Local practices, state responses and tenure security in Africa, Asia and Latin America*. Law, governance, and development. Leiden: Leiden University Press.

UN (United Nations). 2007. *Declaration on the Rights of Indigenous Peoples*. www.un.org/development/desa/indigenouspeoples/wp-content/uploads/sites/19/2019/01/UNDRIP_E_web.pdf.

UN (United Nations). 2010. *Report of the United Nations High Commissioner for Human Rights on the violations of human rights in Honduras since the coup d'état on 28 June 2009*. Human Rights Council. www2.ohchr.org/english/bodies/hrcouncil/docs/13session/A-HRC-13-66.pdf.

UNDP (United Nations Development Program). 2005. *Informe de desarrollo humano: Las regiones autónomas de la Costa Caribe ¿Nicaragua asume su diversidad?* Managua: PNUD.

UNDP (United Nations Development Program). 2011. *Informe PNUD Nicaragua 2010.* Managua: PNUD.
Unidad Técnica de MASTA. 2013. *Estudio Antropológico de los Concejos [sic] Territoriales de Wamakklisinasta, Truktsinasta, Lainasta, Watiasta y Bamiasta.* Miskitu Asla Takanka. Document in the possession of the author.
UNODC (United Nations Office on Drugs and Crime). 2004–2013. *World drug report.* New York: United Nations. www.unodc.org/wdr2014/en/previous-reports.html.
UNODC (United Nations Office on Drugs and Crime). 2004–2013. *World drug report.* New York: United Nations. www.unodc.org/documents/wdr/WDR_2010/World_Drug_Report_2010_lo-res.pdf.
UNODC (United Nations Office on Drugs and Crime). 2012. *Transnational organized crime in Central America and the Caribbean.* New York: United Nations. doi.org/10.18356/7594176a-en.
UNODC (United Nations Office on Drugs and Crime). DATAUNODC. "Victims of Intentional Homicide, 1990–2018." dataunodc.un.org/content/data/homicide/homicide-rate.
USAID (United States Agency for International Development). 2020. "Amazon Indigenous Rights and Resource Activity (AIRR): Safeguarding Indigenous People's Rights and Resources while Preserving Biodiversity and Cultural Knowledge." August. www.usaid.gov/documents/fact-sheet-amazon-idigenous-rights-and-resources-activity-airr.
US Congress. 1987–1988. *Iran-Contra investigation: Joint hearings before the Senate Select Committee on Secret Military Assistance to Iran and the Nicaraguan Opposition and the House Select Committee to Investigate Covert.* Washington DC: U.S. G.P.O.
Valente, Renata C. *A GTZ no Brasil: uma etnografia da cooperação alemã para o desenvolvimento.* Rio de Janeiro: E-papers, 2010. www.e-papers.com.br/apresenta.asp?codigo_produto=2784.
van Cott, Donna L. 2000. *The friendly liquidation of the past: The politics of diversity in Latin America.* Pittsburgh: University of Pittsburgh Press.
van Cott, Donna L. 2006. "Multiculturalism versus neoliberalism in Latin America." In *Multiculturalism and the welfare state: Recognition and redistribution in contemporary democracies,* eds. Will Kymlicka and Keith G. Banting. Oxford: Oxford University Press, 272–96.
van Cott, Donna L. 2010. "Indigenous Peoples' Politics in Latin America." *Annual Review of Political Science* 13 (1): 385–405.
van Evera, Stephen. 1997. *Guide to methods for students of political science.* Ithaca, NY; London: Cornell University Press.
Victor, David G., Kal Raustiala, and Eugene B. Skolnikoff. 1998. *The implementation and effectiveness of international environmental commitments: Theory and practice.* Laxenburg, Austria: International Institute for Applied Systems Analysis.
Warren, Kay B., and Jean E. Jackson, eds. 2003. *Indigenous movements, self-representation, and the state in Latin America.* Austin: University of Texas Press.
Watts, Jonathan. 2016. "Berta Cáceres, Honduran Human Rights and Environment Activist, Murdered." *The Guardian,* March 4. www.theguardian.com/world/2016/mar/03/honduras-berta-caceres-murder-enivronment-activist-human-rights.
Weaver, Jace. 2014. *The Red Atlantic: American Indigenes and the Making of the Modern World, 1000–1927.* Chapel Hill: University of North Carolina Press.
Weaver, Thomas, James B. Greenberg, William L. Alexander, and Anne Browning-Aiken. 2012. *Neoliberalism and Commodity Production in Mexico.* Boulder, CO: University Press of Colorado.
Weir, Margaret, and Theda Skocpol. 1985. "State Structures and the Possibilities for 'Keynesian' Responses to the Great Depression in Sweden, Britain and the United States." In *Bringing the State Back In,* eds. Peter B. Evans, Dietrich Rueschemeyer, and Theda Skocpol. Cambridge: Cambridge University Press, 107–52.

Weber, Max. 1978. *Economy and society*. Edited by Guenther Roth and Claus Wittich. Berkeley: University of California Press.
Weyland, Kurt G. 2006. *Bounded rationality and policy diffusion: Social sector reform in Latin America*. Princeton, NJ; Oxford: Princeton University Press.
Weyland, Kurt G. 2009. "Institutional Change in Latin America: External Models and Their Unintended Consequences." *Journal of Politics in Latin America* 1 (1): 37–66.
Weyland, Kurt G. 2014. *Making waves: Democratic contention in Europe and Latin America since the revolutions of 1848*. Cambridge: Cambridge University Press.
Wheatley, Steven. 2005. *Democracy, minorities and international law. Cambridge studies in international and comparative law*. Cambridge: Cambridge University Press.
Wily, Liz. 2001. "Reconstructing the African Commons." *Africa Today* 48 (1): 77–99.
Wily, Liz. 2015. "The Global Platform of Indigenous and Community Lands." LandMark. www.landmarkmap.org.
Wiggins, Armstrong. 2002. "El caso Awas Tingni o el Futuro de los Derechos Territoriales de los Pueblos Indígenas del Caribe Nicaragüense." *Wani Revista del Caribe Nicaragüense* 30. revistas.bicu.edu.ni/index.php/wani/issue/view/55/showToc.
Williamson Cuthbert, Dennis. 2003. "Tipología de conflictos sobre la propiedad comunal en el municipio de Puerto Cabezas." *Wani Revista del Caribe Nicaragüense* 35: 43–52.
Wilson, Ceferino. 2012. "La demarcación y titulación de tierras casi concluye, la etapa de saneamiento nos exige mucha madurez." *Envío* (362). www.envio.org.ni/articulo/4519.
World Bank WGI. 1996–2015. "World Wide Governance Indicators: Control of Corruption." info.worldbank.org/governance/WGI/#home.
World Bank. 2006. *Kenya—Agricultural productivity and sustainable management project: Indigenous peoples plan (Ilchamus, Ogiek and Sengwer)*. documents.worldbank.org/curated/en/281821468271845479/Indigenous-peoples-plan-Ilchamus-Ogiek-and-Sengwer
World Bank. 2016. *Kenya—Climate Smart Agricultural Project: Vulnerable and Marginalized Groups Framework*. Ministry of Agriculture, Livestock and Fisheries Development. documents.worldbank.org/curated/en/161821479207793853/pdf/SFG2646-IPP-P154784-Box396327B-PUBLIC-Disclosed-11-14-2016.pdf.
Wortham, Erica C. 2013. *Indigenous media in Mexico: Culture, community, and the state*. Durham, NC: Duke University Press.
Xanthaki, Alexandra. 2007. *Indigenous rights and United Nations standards: Self-determination, culture and land*. Cambridge: Cambridge University Press.
Yashar, Deborah J. 1999. "Democracy, Indigenous Movements, and the Postliberal Challenge in Latin America." *World Politics* 52 (1): 76–104.
Yashar, Deborah J. 2005. *Contesting citizenship in Latin America: The rise of indigenous movements and the postliberal challenge. Cambridge studies in contentious politics*. Cambridge: Cambridge University Press.
Young, Crawford. 1994. *The African colonial state in comparative perspective*. New Haven, CT: Yale University Press.
Zacher, Mark W. 2001. "The Territorial Integrity Norm: International Boundaries and the Use of Force." *International Organization* 55 (2): 215–50.
Zhouri, Andréa, ed. 2002. *O fantasma da internacionalização da Amazônia revisitado: Ambientalismo, direitos humanos e indígenas na perspectiva de militares e políticos brasileiros*. Document in the possession of the author.

Filho, João Café, 168–69
Forest Conservation Institute, Honduras, 111–12
FUNAI, 3, 29, 149–50

Global South, 19–20, 33, 180, 181, 194
Global Witness, 110–11
Gonzales, Arístides, 117–18

Heart of Amazonia, Brazil, 156–58, 167–68
Heleno, Augusto, 154
Hernández, Juan Orlando, 104–5, 113–15, 119, 124, 127
Honduras
 Colón, 29–30, 113–14
 Gracias a Dios, 22–23, 29–30, 52, 60–61, 113–14
 Intibucá, 22–23, 122, 127–28
 La Paz, 22–23, 122, 127–28
 Lempira, 22–23, 122, 127–28
 Olancho, 26, 29–30, 113–14
Honduras, Congress of, 119
Honduras, laws of
 Agrarian Modernization Law, 35
 Constitution, 35
 Property Law, 35, 111
Hoppington, Marcos, 80, 91

ILO Convention No. 169. *See* International Labour Organization Convention No. 169 on Indigenous and Tribal Peoples
Independent Liberal Party, Nicaragua, 89–90
indirect rule, 59, 65–66, 182, 184, 187–88
Indonesia, 181, 185–88
Indonesia, Constitutional Court of, 185–86
Indonesia, laws of
 Basic Agrarian Law, 185–86
 Constitution, 185–86
 Human Rights Act, 185–86
institutions, origin and evolution of, 15
Inter-American Commission on Human Rights, 81, 110–11, 194
Inter-American Court of Human Rights, 62–63, 75
Inter-American Development Bank, 19–20, 62
Inter-American System of Human Rights, 193–94
Internal threats, degrees of, 60
International Labour Organization Convention No. 169 on Indigenous and Tribal Peoples, 6–8, 18, 20, 21, 27, 94, 105, 113–14, 122
International Land Coalition, 100

Japaú Indigenous Association, 194

Kenya, 181, 182–85
Kenya, laws of
 Communal Land Act, 184–85
 Constitution, 184–85
 Land (Group Representatives) Act, 183–84

Lobo, Porfirio, 104–5, 109–10, 113–15, 118, 120, 124
Lula da Silva, Luíz Inácio, 163

Mansur, Carlos Alberto, 133, 164–65
McClean, Melba, 92, 98–99
Mesoamerican Biological Corridor, 18–19
Miskito Council of Elders, 87
Missionary Council for Indigenous Peoples (CIMI), 150
MISURASATA, 80–82
Mother Earth Program, Nicaragua, 75–76, 91

National Agrarian Institute, Honduras, 111–12, 129
National Defense University, Honduras, 119–20
National Indigenous Agency. *See* FUNAI
Nicaragua, 6
 Autonomous Region of the North Caribbean, 22
 Bosawás Biosphere Reserve, 18–19
 Madriz, 22, 94–95, 99–100
 North Caribbean, 94–97
 Rio Coco, 82
Nicaragua, laws of
 Autonomy Law, 35, 77–78, 82–84
 Communal Property Regime Law, 35, 76–77, 98–99
 Constitution, 6–8, 35, 71–72, 77–78, 82–84, 94–95
 Harrison-Altamirano Treaty, 79–80
 Treaty of Managua, 79–80
Nicaragua, National Assembly of, 89–90
North Caribbean Autonomous Region. *See* Nicaragua: North Caribbean

Oquist Kelley, Paul, 37, 71, 86, 97–98
Organization for Ethnic Communal Development (ODECO), 46–47
Ortega, Daniel, 71, 72–79, 90, 93, 102, 103, 114–15, 118
Osorio Canales, René, 119–21, 124
Ostrom, Elinor, 18–19, 34

Pacheco Rogedo, Isa, 151
Pacheco Tinoco, Julián, 104, 119–20

Index

For the benefit of digital users, indexed terms that span two pages (e.g., 52–53) may, on occasion, appear on only one of those pages

Administrative theory, 10, 13, 21–22, 37, 39, 40, 49–52, 57, 67, 77, 101–2, 129–31, 135–36, 137, 147–48, 171
African Commission, 183
African Court on Human and Peoples' Rights, 183
Agrarian Reform Law, Nicaragua, 79, 80, 81, 82–83
Alberto Mansur, Carlos, 162
Alcântara Gomes, Airton, 151
Alemán, Arnoldo, 85
Alemán, Carlos, 98–99
Alliance of Indigenous and Afro-descendant Peoples of Nicaragua, 193–94
Alliance of Indigenous Peoples of the Archipelago, 186–87
Amador Fúnez, Gustavo Adolfo, 125
Amazônia Legal, Brazil, 133–34
Attorney General Office, Nicaragua, 75–76, 90–91

Barrios de Chamorro, Violeta, 85
Barros, Antonio Manoel de, 162–63
Bayma Denys, Rubens, 133, 149–50, 152
Bolaños, Enrique, 85
Brazil
  Alto Rio Negro, 12, 48, 143–44, 145–47, 167
  Mato Grosso do Sul, 46–47
  Vale do Javari, 12, 48
Brazil, Congress of Brazil
  Amazon caucus, 150–51
  Rural caucus, 168
Brazil, laws of
  Constitution, 35, 149, 160
  Decree 4412, 162
  Indian Statute, Brazil, 35, 151, 152
  Law 97, 162
Brazil-Colombia-Venezuela (BCV) Frontier Zone, Brazil, 156–68

Broad Movement for Dignity and Justice (MADJ), Honduras, 110–11

Cabeça do Cachorro, Brazil, 138–39
Cáceres, Berta, 110–11, 128
Calha Norte Program, Brazil, 3, 149–50, 151, 163, 164
Campbell, Lumberto, 71, 86, 90–91
Cardoso, Fernando Henrique, 163
Carrión, Luis, 82
Central American University, Nicaragua, 88
Chang Castillo, Rigoberto, 125
Chile, 46–47
Collor de Mello, Fernando, 149, 150–52, 154, 155, 169–70
Colombia, 6, 51
colonial title, 9–10, 29–30, 94, 100
Coordination of Indigenous Organizations of the Brazilian Amazon, 194
Costa Rica, 6
Council of Popular and Indigenous Organizations of Honduras (COPINH), 110–11, 127–28
Cultural Survival, 183

Dantas, Roberto de Medeiros, 3, 164
Defending Land and Environmental Defender Coalition, 194
Denys, Rubens Bayma, 3, 133, 149–50, 152, 153
Dixon, Loria Raquel, 96–97

Economic structuralist theory, 10, 21–22, 37, 38–39, 40, 47–49, 75–77, 85, 101–2, 111, 135, 137, 145–47
El Salvador, 71–72
Espinoza Posadas, Rigoberto, 119, 125
Espinoza, Rigoberto, 104
External pressures, degrees of, 63

Panama, 60
Passarinho, Jarbas, 152, 153
Payaka, Paulino, 169–70
Paz Escalante, Gustavo Adolfo, 104, 114, 124
Poty, Ubiratan, 133, 162, 164
Prates, Rodrigo, 161–62, 165–66
private property, disregard of, 19–20
Property Institute, Honduras, 111–12
property rights
  concepts of, 27
  bundle of, 34–35
  communal, classification of, 28
  communal, implementation of, 27
  communal, implementation operationalization and measurement of, 30
  communal, subjects of, 35–36

Rabben, Linda, 143–44, 159–60
Ramírez, William, 81–82
Raoni, 169–70
Rebelo, Aldo, 154
Reyes, Alfonso, 119–20
Ribeiro, Darcy, 169
Rigby, Betty, 77, 99
Río Plátano Biosphere Reserve, Nicaragua, 18–19
Río San Juan Biosphere Reserve, Nicaragua, 18–19
Rivera Amador, Ronald, 120, 125
Rivera, Brooklyn, 72–74, 80, 90, 91, 96–97

Sarney, José, 149–50
Scott, James, 65–66, 192–93

Social movement theory, 10, 11–12, 21–22, 37–38, 45–47, 67, 110–11, 129–31, 137, 176
Southeast Asia, 181

Tauli-Corpuz, Victoria, 110–11
Taylor, Evelyn, 90–91, 96–97
Torres, Heloisa, 169
Transnational constructivist theory, 10–12, 37–38, 40–45, 57, 67, 109–10, 129–31, 135–36, 137–49

UNDRIP. *See* United Nations Declaration on the Rights of Indigenous Peoples
United Nations Declaration on the Rights of Indigenous Peoples, 16–17, 18, 20, 21, 27
United Nations Special Rapporteur for Indigenous Rights, 110–11
University of Defense, Honduras, 109

Vargas, Getúlio, 168–69
Villanueva Reyes, Mario, 125

Wagner, Jaques, 161–62
Weber, Max, 54
World Bank, 19–20, 62, 75, 90–91, 169–70, 183
World Wide Fund for Nature, 194

Xingu Cluster, Brazil, 136, 138–39, 156–59, 168–70

YATAMA, 86, 92

Zamith, Wagner Lopes de Moraes, 163
Zelaya, Manuel, 109–10, 115, 129–31

www.ingramcontent.com/pod-product-compliance
Lightning Source LLC
Chambersburg PA
CBHW021507O10525
26043CB00014B/147/J